Recovering Judaism

Recovering Judaism

The Universal Dimension of Jewish Religion

Jacob Neusner

Fortress Press / Minneapolis

RECOVERING JUDAISM
The Universal Dimension of Jewish Religion

Library of Congress Cataloging-in-Publication Data

Neusner, Jacob
    Recovering Judaism : the universal dimension of Jewish religion / Jacob Neusner.
        p. cm.
    Includes bibliographical references and index.
    ISBN 0-8006-3268-0 (alk. paper)
        1. Judaism—Essence, genius, nature. 2. Rabbinical literature. 3. Rabbinical literature—History and criticism. I. Title.

BM565 .N4835 2000
296.3—dc21   00-029358

Manufactured in the U.S.A.   AF 1-3268
04   03   02   01   00   1   2   3   4   5   6   7   8   9   10

Contents

Preface   ix

1. The Universalistic Message of Judaic Monotheism   1

The Universalism of Judaism   1
Dunn's Representation of Judaism as Particularistic   2
A Different Way of Addressing All of Humanity   4
Demonstrating the Universalistic Character of Judaism   5
The Starting Point   7
Israel as Counterpart to Humanity   7
The Monotheist Theology of the Torah: Four Principles   10
The Universalistic Character of Judaic Monotheism   11
"Israel" as Ethnic, as Supernatural: The Issue Joined   13

2. The Legal Medium:
From the Particular Case to the Governing Rule   15

Norms of Behavior, Norms of Belief   15
How Does the Halakah Speak to Humanity at Large?   16
The Particular as the Medium for the General   17
Rational Analysis of Data: Classes of Things   19
Natural History in Mishnaic Analysis   24
Where Does God Abide in Reasoned Analysis?   25
Science: The Universal Knowledge   26
Rules of Natural History: Aristotle and the Sages   27
Where the Sages Part Company with Aristotle   30
Where Material Things Become Means of Revelation   32

3. The Legal Message:
Restoring Eden through Israel   35

God's Unity and Dominion   35
Between Israel and God: *Shebi'it*   36
Israel's Social Order:
    Sanhedrin-Makkot and the Death Penalty   43
Inside the Israelite Household: *Shabbat-'Erubin*   50
What These Cases Tell Us   60

4. The Narrative-Exegetical Medium:
Paradigmatic Thinking   63

Scripture's Narratives and Laws:
    Governing Principles of the Social Order   63
Judaism Rejects Historical Thinking   64
The Modes of Paradigmatic Thinking   65
How to Find Paradigms   67
How Paradigms Replace Historical Time   69
Past and Present   70
Philosophy Replaces History   73
The Universalization of the Patriarchs and Matriarchs   75
"Israel" as the Paradigm   76
Paradigms Discerned through Particular Cases   77
Particular Historical Narrative
    to Exemplary Social Generalization   82
The Four Principal Models for Organizing Events   84
Supernatural Israel Transcending the Tides of Time   88
The Purpose of Paradigmatic Thinking   91
From Scripture to Torah   93
The Character of the Torah's Paradigms   94

5. The Narrative-Exegetical Message:
Restoring Adam to Eden, Israel to the Land   97

Restoring Israel to the Land, Humanity to Eden   97
The Resurrection of the Dead and Judgment   99
Standing under God's Judgment   107
The Restoration of Humanity to Eden   109
Exile and Return   111
Redemption from Egypt, for the World to Come   114
Creation the Model of Redemption   119
Humanity at Large in the Eschatology of Judaism   122

Who and What Then Is Israel? 123
From Concrete Event to Evocative Symbol 125
Life in the World to Come 127
Idolaters = Gentiles and the World to Come 129

6. Rational Israel: God's Justice, Humanity's Reason 137

Humanity Explains the Reason Why 137
Everyone Has the Power to Understand 138
God's Justice: The Reason 140
Scripture: God Obeys the Rules of Justice 142
The Reason Why Not 144
When Israel ("Those Who Know God") Sins 152
Measure for Measure 156
Predestination and Free Will 160
Suffering Is Reasonable Too 163
Anomalies in the Just Order 166
Beyond Reason, the Human Condition 169

Epilogue: Recovering Judaism 173

Notes 185

Glossary 191

Index of Ancient Sources 195

Index of Subjects and Authors 199

Preface

This book aims to prove that, in its normative writings, Judaism is a universalistic religion, speaking a language common to all humanity and offering a place in God's kingdom to everyone. That proof is required because Judaism is commonly portrayed by both the faithful and the competing religions as ethnic and particularistic, exclusive and unwelcoming. Two forces today aim at the ethnicization of Judaism into a mere culture, Christianity and Jews themselves.

From New Testament times, Christianity has represented Judaism as insufficient because it excludes the gentiles from that "Israel" of which Scripture speaks, the Israel that knows and worships the one and only God of all humanity. But on its own, Christianity cannot stifle the vitality of Judaism within the community of the faithful.

The Jewish community defines itself in ethnic and political terms, and even rabbis function more often than not as ethnic cheerleaders. Jews, so people maintain, have attitudes and feelings and opinions acquired through birth and upbringing and not accessible to other people, as do all other ethnic or racial groups. By *Judaism,* then, people mean, the Jews' ethnic culture. Then in an age of ethnic celebration, a time in which people emphasize difference and not commonality, Judaism finds itself represented as an ethnic religion, which is not a religion at all. It is the sum of Jews' experience: the culture, the history, the sentiment, and consciousness of the Jewish people. So difference and particularity rule, and Judaism, a religion that I shall show from its origins means to address all humanity from beginning to end, from creation to redemption at the end of days, loses all hearing.

To state matters simply: the Jews used to be a people with one religion, Judaism. Now, Judaism is becoming merely the religion of one people, an ethnic religion, thus, in the monotheist framework of a universal God of all humanity, deprived of its religiosity altogether.

The argument of this book, with its stress on the universalistic character of the thought and argument of Judaism in its normative canon, means to reestablish the claim of Judaism to constitute a universal religious tradition, addressing the entirety of humanity exactly as do Christianity and Islam, competing with the other two monotheisms on an even playing field for the attention and affirmation of all who maintain that the one and only God who made heaven and earth has made himself known to humanity. All three monotheisms concur that there is only one God, and the naked logic of that concurrence requires that all three are speaking of one and the same God. Then the claim that one of the three monotheisms affords access to the one and only God to only one sector of humanity, a sector sustained principally through ethnic or racial ties, and that that one and only God is inaccessible to everybody else—that absurd claim laid against Judaism caricatures Judaism and violates the generative logic of monotheism, whether in its Islamic or Christian or Judaic formulation.

Each of the monotheist religions—Judaism, Islam, and Christianity—chooses its own medium to convey one universal message to all humanity concerning the one and only and unique God. All encompass in the story that they tell humanity the one God's self-manifestation to Abraham, then in the Torah given by God to Moses at Sinai, and, more generally, in the Hebrew Scriptures of ancient Israel. All concur on a further stage in revelation: God in Christ; God to the prophet, Muhammad; God in the Oral Torah, for Christianity, Islam, and Judaism, respectively. Judaism represents one of the three possibilities that inhere within the dialectics of monotheism. But while Christianity and Islam set forth a message of universal significance and appeal, Judaism finds itself represented as a backwater, not part of the mainstream of monotheism.

What I mean to demonstrate in these pages is that in its normative writings, Scripture as conveyed in the Mishnah, talmudic amplifications of the Mishnah, and midrash (terms defined in the Glossary), Judaism addresses all of humanity and appeals to everyone to accept the yoke of God's kingdom as set forth in the Torah of Moses. In this account of the method and message of the Judaic monotheism defined in the classical and normative documents of Judaism in their formative age, coinciding with the formation of Christianity and concluding at the eve of the advent of Islam, I show the universal character and appeal of Judaic monotheism in the mainstream of humanity.

It is, I demonstrate, a monotheism for all, not just for an "us." Appealing to the revelation of Sinai, oral and written, Judaism frames a shared, accessible logic that forms of the Torah a universally applicable and compelling system of salvation. Judaic monotheism aims to persuade the world to accept the one and only God's dominion and to identify, in the world, the marks of God's rule. So addressing all of humanity Judaism appeals to a reasoned reading of revelation. As there is no ethnic physics or mathematics, so in the framework of monotheism, Judaism, like Christianity and Islam, claims there is no ethnic theology, only a universal claim on the intellect of every person in the world resting on the authority of God's revealed will recorded at the Torah—the instruction—of Sinai.

Specifically, Judaism transforms the specificities of the Torah into generalizations that encompass the story of all humanity, beginning, middle, and end. That story begins with Adam and Eve and their fall from Eden and the advent of death and ends with the restoration of humanity to eternal life. How do the sages of the Judaic documents of ancient times turn the particular story of Adam and Israel into the universal account of humanity at large? What transforms Scripture as portrayed by Judaic monotheism into a universal statement is its appeal to the shared intellectual qualities of the human mind. Common rules of thought and analysis, Judaism maintains, transform the Torah's particularities into universally accessible and rationally compelling truth.[1] We deal with a universality of intellectual medium, not only of message—a transcendence over particularities made possible by appeal to self-evidence: to the shared modes of thought and analysis that all reasonable persons find compelling. Judaism appeals above all to logic, reason, and rationality in the reading of the revealed Scripture common to the three monotheist religions.

Judaism's one God is portrayed by the sages' Torah as above all bound by the same reason and rationality that humanity in common shares; it is a universal monotheism based on shared intellect, not on the imposition of revelation from on high to the prophet, not on the formation of a universal message around a particular man, risen from the dead, as in the cases of Islam and Christianity. In Judaism resurrection marks common humanity, and prophecy takes the form of reasoned rules. But among the monotheist religions, all aiming to speak to all humanity, what choice did, and does, Judaism have but to rely upon the intangible force of a shared reasoning about common premises? Few in numbers, always subordinate in practical power, Judaism in its formative age and normative statement, in the first six centuries of the Common Era, chose the way of the weak, the road of rationality. Lacking all force but the power of reason, to make its case Judaism offered only argument based on irrefutable facts and compelling reason.

Denied access to politics, through which Christianity made its way in the West, speaking within a polity lacking all military prowess, through which Islam spread the word, Judaism took the third way, besides the political and the military ones. It was the way of re-presenting revelation through reason. The sages of the Torah, written and oral, therefore exercised the compulsion of rational argument, following the model not of Moses before Amalek and Moab but Abraham confronting God at Sodom: "Will not the Judge of all the world do justice?" That is why the particular statement of monotheism represented by Judaism insists upon the well-constructed, rational argument when it speaks of both revealed facts and ordinary matters. Judaism speaks of sanctification in terms of the here and now and of salvation and justice in the framework of practicalities pertinent to the generality of the human condition. Therein I find the universalistic character of Judaic monotheism, and that is what in detail, through the native categories of Judaism, halakah or norms of behavior, haggadah or norms of belief, I demonstrate in these pages.

This book forms part of a long-term effort on my part to translate the results of literary and historical scholarship into accounts accessible to a wider reading public. To construct this history-of-religions interpretation of Judaism as a universalistic, and universalizing, mainstream-monotheism, I call in part upon and rework completed research of mine into theology and haggadah, philosophy and halakah. That is with special reference to three works, two for theology and haggadah: *The Presence of the Past, the Pastness of the Present. History, Time, and Paradigm in Rabbinic Judaism*[2] and *The Theology of the Oral Torah. Revealing the Justice of God*[3]; and one for philosophy and halakah, *The Halakhah. An Encyclopaedia of the Law of Judaism.*[4]

The translations of Rabbinic texts throughout are my own. For biblical texts, I ordinarily cite the Revised Standard Version (New York: Thomas Nelson & Sons, 1952), and acknowledge with thanks the right to use that fine translation. Occasionally, the context in Rabbinic literature requires some alterations, but these are uncommon. Since the sources for normative Judaism are not widely accessible, I reproduce them in detail; I have invented a reference system for the entire formative canon of Judaism but for the present volume have omitted it, since I conduct no analytical inquiry in these pages. The Glossary defines the various documents that are cited.

My thanks go, as always, to my academic homes, the University of South Florida (through the academic year) and Bard College for annual research grants of considerable value. This material support for my work both encourages and, in concrete ways, sustains everything I do. I am grateful to the deans, provosts, and presidents who make it possible.

I don't remember when I began to publish books with Fortress, and I don't know how many there have been. But I remember all the editors with whom I have dealt, every one of them a professional and a source of encouragement and joy. To all of them I express thanks, now to the last but not the least, Michael West. Fortress has made itself an important medium for scholarship on Judaism in the context of the academic study of religion, and I have been a beneficiary. Thanks for much.

1. The Universalistic Message of Judaic Monotheism

The Universalism of Judaism

The Torah—that is to say, the religion the world calls Judaism—embodies the universal within the particular and so delivers a message of salvation to all humanity. Specifically, the Torah as set forth by the Judaic sages of late antiquity, the first six centuries of the Common Era (also known as A.D.), turns Scripture's story of Adam, then Israel, into a statement of the human condition, which is embodied by Adam, then Israel. It is the genius of the singular version of monotheism set forth by Judaism to speak of humble things but thereby to refer to exalted ones, to find in homely commonplaces transcendent messages of eternity, and to do so within a logic that is both particular in its expression and universal in its range and extension. It follows that, like its counterpart-monotheisms, Christianity and Islam, Judaism addresses undifferentiated humanity with a message of universal application. It is a religion that speaks of one God for all the world.

But that is not how the other monotheisms regard and represent Judaism. They see it as ethnic and particular, not as universal—and therefore as not really monotheism. The representation of Judaism as particularistic, narrow, and ethnic characterizes Christian accounts of Judaism, whether explicitly apologetic or merely insidiously so. Indeed, Christian scholarship on Christian origins invents a grotesque ethnocentric, tribal religion of automatons, then assigns to that caricature traits that violate the very logic of monotheism. In the form of historical scholarship, theology based on the Gospels and Paul's letters invariably contrasts Christian universalism with Judaic particularism, and, these days, that is all given the authoritative form of historical fact.

Christian theology in times past and contemporary scholarship of a historical character as well take as their starting point the position that "Israel" in the Judaism of that time is ethnic and that consequently Judaism, while affirming one God, kept God to itself. Then, the Christian theological apologetic goes on, the gospel improved upon Judaism's monotheism by bringing to all the peoples of the world what had originally been kept for only one people alone. So for Judaism "Israel" refers to the ethnic group, a particular people, defined in quite this-worldly terms. And the contrast between the ethnic and particularistic Judaism and the universalistic Christianity follows.

But Judaic monotheism builds upon what the sages conceive to constitute the shared traits of intellect of all humanity, reading Scripture in the manner of natural history, as any reasonable person might do. So here, by contrast to the prevailing caricature, we shall see that Judaism reaches into the common, rational mind of humanity for its reading of the one and only God's self-revelation to Israel in the Torah of Sinai. Accordingly, I show in detail, Judaism sets forth a universalistic message of monotheisms. This it does in two steps. First, the sages of Judaism appeal for knowledge of God to precisely the revelation invoked by Christianity and Islam, that is to say, the Hebrew Scriptures of ancient Israel. Second, by appeal to modes of thought and analysis common to all rational persons, they set forth out of revealed Scripture—they would say, out of the Torah, written and oral—an account of the human situation that pertains, without ethnic distinction, to everybody who has ever lived.

Dunn's Representation of Judaism as Particularistic

Lest readers suppose I exaggerate the Christian representation of Judaic monotheism, let me point to a single, current, and representative statement of the ethnic reading of Judaic monotheism. It derives from James D. G. Dunn's *The Partings of the Ways between Christianity and Judaism and Their Significance for the Character of Christianity.*[1] Dunn takes as his question the explanation of "how within the diversity of first-century Judaism, the major strand which was to become Christianity pulled apart on a sequence of key issues from the major strand which was to become Rabbinic Judaism." The parting of the ways "began with Jesus, but without Easter and the broadening out of the gospel to the Gentiles"; the break may not have taken place at all. How, then, does Dunn explain the parting of the ways? He appeals to the particularity and ethnicity of Judaism, as against the meta-ethnic, universalizing power of Christianity to reach out beyond the ghetto walls of an ethnic Israel. Here is his language (including his italics):

> For the Judaism which focussed its identity most fully in the Torah, and which found itself unable to separate ethnic identity from religious identity, Paul and the Gentile mission involved an irreparable breach.[2]
>
> *Christianity began as a movement of renewal breaking through the boundaries first within and then round the Judaism of the first century.* At its historic heart Christianity is a protest against any and every attempt to claim that God is our God and not yours, God of our way of life and not yours, God of our "civilization" and not yours . . . against any and every attempt to mark off some of God's people as more holy than others, as exclusive channels of divine grace.[3]

Dunn's premise is that "Israel" found definition in both an "ethnic" and a religious identity. Certainly for our own day his view prevails, since a broad consensus maintains that Judaism is "the religion of the Jews," a conglomerate of Jews' public opinion, whatever that may be, and that the Jews form an ethnic group, with the religious part also constituting a religious community. So by *Judaism* people mean an ethnic ideology bearing religious pretensions.

But as a matter of fact, distinguishing the "ethnic" from the religious aspect of "Israel" for the documents of the dual Torah simply defies the evidence in hand, that is to say, the formative writings of normative Judaism that came to closure in the first six centuries C.E., from the Mishnah through the Talmud of Babylonia. Dunn reads Judaism through the figure of Paul. But in the Torah, the written as conveyed through the oral, there is no ethnic Israel that is distinct from a supernatural Israel at all. Such a distinction does not take place in the sources that attest to the Judaism of which Dunn speaks.[4] So what I find in Dunn's formulation of matters is the explicit claim that Judaism in its normative sources takes second place in the hierarchy of religions because it is ethnic, while Christianity overspreads the bounds of ethnic identification.

As we shall see in these pages, Judaism sets forth a statement of monotheism no less universal than Christianity's or Islam's. But it finds its own way to address all of humanity. Specifically, while Christianity formulates a categorical monotheism ("no Greek nor Jew in Christ Jesus"), Judaism appeals for its universality to a shared rationality governing all of humanity. Christianity imposes, Judaism invokes. It identifies and utilizes for its medium and its message an applied reason and a practical logic that transcend time, space, and ethnic boundaries. It is, specifically, the monotheism of a reasoned, generalizing reading of Scripture, stated solely on the premise that the Hebrew Scriptures reveal God, a premise that Christianity and Islam share. If the Old Testament can give good service to the New, the written Torah can with equal pertinence to Greek and Jew alike take shape through the oral Torah.

A Different Way of Addressing All of Humanity

To state the matter bluntly: Judaism as defined by the sages of the Mishnah, midrash, and Talmuds is what emerges from the Hebrew Scriptures read rationally for all humanity. If, as Brevard Childs states, "The evangelists read from the New [Testament] backward to the Old,"[5] we may say very simply that the sages read forward from the Old. And, concretely, they read the written Torah as philosophers read nature and society. Through the medium of philosophical modes of thought, those, specifically, of an ahistorical, but teleological natural history, the sages produced the oral Torah. Accordingly it is through a rigorous, universal, public logic, accessible to anyone anywhere that the two together—written via oral—make their statement, about the one and only God self-manifest at Sinai. And those traits of mind, I contend, mark Judaism as a fully realized monotheism: the religion that proclaims to all humanity the will and dominion of the one and only God.

How does Judaism accomplish its universalistic aspiration? In its world-encompassing conception, Judaism tells the story of God and humanity, specifically, of God's failure and hopes for ultimate success in making humanity. The story takes shape in stories of beginnings, specifically accounts of Eden and the fall from grace to death, then Israel and its fall from the land to exile. But Judaism carries the story forward to Israel's ultimate return, guided by the Torah, to the Eden of the land of Israel. Then the Torah, within the tale of Judaism, comprises God's self-manifestation to Moses at Mount Sinai, God's will for humanity set forth to Israel in oral and written form. Adam's fall from Eden, embodied in death that comes to everyone, finds its counterpart in Israel's exile from the land of Israel, but then the counterpart, Israel's return to the land at the end of time, inaugurates the final chapter in resurrection, judgment, and entry into life eternal in "the world to come." Israel then stands for humanity, fallen into death, risen into eternal life.

Now "Israel" within the same story encompasses all those who know the one and only God: the saving remnant of humanity in the aftermath of Adam and Eve, this time destined to life eternal. The simplest possible statement of the matter is as follows: "All Israelites have a share in the world to come, as it is said, 'your people also shall be all righteous, they shall inherit the land forever; the branch of my planting, the work of my hands, that I may be glorified'" (Isa. 60:21; *m. Sanh.* 11:1). To state matters in general terms by turning the predicate into the subject: "all those who have a share in the world to come are Israel[ites]," and, within the framework of the Torah, its monotheism and prophecy, that will ultimately include nearly the whole of humanity. Nor do I speak only of an ancient and superseded universalism. For that same restoration of humanity to God, praying Israel beseeches God three times a day even now: this very morning, noon, and night.

Defined in this way, as is done in Judaic doctrine and liturgy alike, "Israel" no more forms an ethnic group or a mere nation in a this-worldly sense than the church is a mere *imperium* or the abode of Islam a mere this-worldly political entity—or the Israel of Moses compares with the Moab of Balak, who hired Balaam. Stated in this manner, Judaism is no more an ethnic religion than Christianity is a bearer of culture alone or than Islam is nothing more than a means of social amelioration. And that is despite Judaism's resort to the language of peoplehood, Christianity's power to define the paramount world civilization, that of the West, and Islam's manifest, commendable devotion to the poor and needy. But while everyone recognizes the universality of Christianity and Islam in their statement of monotheism, Judaism finds itself represented as particularistic and ethnic, and not only by its competition within monotheism.[6] So far as that representation appeals to religious and theological, not merely political facts, it vastly misses the mark, as Dunn's christological apologetics shows.

Demonstrating the Universalistic Character of Judaism

How do I show the universalistic character of Judaic monotheism? It is, specifically, by setting forth in the reading of revealed Scripture a rationality common to all humanity. I tell the story of how the Judaic statement of a universalistic-intellectual monotheism is realized in the normative laws, or halakah, and in the normative reading of Scripture, or haggadah. I do so by tracing the flow from the eddies of a local, ethnic religion-culture embodied by Scripture to the mainstream vision of a universal fate and faith for all humanity. For both behavior and belief

I show the formulation of a method of universal accessibility in the formation of the sages' message of universal relevance.

That is a story that has long awaited telling. Everyone knows how Christianity in the first six centuries of the Common Era framed Christian monotheism with the same universal conception extending to all humanity, beginning in Scripture's details of a local culture and ending in a vision, both political and theological, of world-salvation. Eloquent writing has narrated the story through the ages. No one doubts that Christianity frames the monotheist theology in a universal idiom, the figure of Christ finding plausible portrayal in all skin tones and all cultural media. And the power of Islam to set forth in every clime and culture the message that there is no God but God gains reinforcement in the universal voice of the prophet, Muhammad, as Christianity does in the timeless words of Jesus Christ. But the equally universalistic character of Judaism's realization of the inner logic of monotheism in a conception of all humanity subject to the will and grace of the one and only God is only imperfectly grasped, if it is understood at all.

If Judaism has found itself absorbed within the Islamic system or declared old and obsolescent by the Christian one, the Jews too have contributed to obscuring the universalistic and transcendent character of Judaic monotheism. For those who embodied the Torah and represented its sanctity in the disciplines of ordinary life and thought have failed as well. That is in two ways. First, though worshiping the one and only God of all flesh, articulately addressing God as Lord of all souls, they have ceased to aspire to speak to all humanity in competition with Islam and Christianity. So by their conduct they failed to give public signals of a message bearing upon the fate of all humanity. Second, the faithful have faced inward, commonly missing the public and compelling character of the reasoned reading of the Torah that the sages accomplished. The continuators mastered the details but lacked perspicacity as to what the details embody and represent. So they lost sight of the remarkable power of intellect to think about Scripture philosophically and then speak theologically, to think within a universal logic but to speak in a particular idiom, about religious matters. From the myriad cases of sanctification of the here and now, the faithful have tended not to move onward toward the general truths of sanctification embodied and conveyed through the details. The one whole Torah, oral and written, speaks of particulars but conveys universal truths. But that mode of monotheist discourse that the sages uniquely framed as the medium for the Torah's message lost purchase upon the inner life of Judaism, and the other monotheisms never acknowledged it to begin with.

The Starting Po...

Our starting point then is de C... ...e theology of Judaism sets forth a monotheist system along lines entirely familiar from the Christian one and entirely congruent with the Islamic one. All three monotheisms speak of creation and Adam, sin and atonement, mercy and forgiveness, justice and the last judgment and the world to come or paradise or Eden regained. As we shall presently see, the main lines of that theology that the sages put forth tell the tale of the fall of Adam from Eden to death and the restoration of humanity through Israel from death to eternal life. At stake in Judaism, therefore, is the resurrection of humanity from the state of death in which, by reason of the fall from grace, humanity finds itself in this age. That retelling of Israel's story in dialogue with humanity's treats Israel as counterpart of Adam, embodying a fate for all humanity that corresponds to, but is the alternative of, Adam's. The narrative then treats Israel as the microcosm of humanity, its experience of land, exile, and ultimate return, as the embodiment in the particulars of the here and now of that of all humanity lived out through Adam. The mode of thought to which I just referred, the realization of great truths in small cases, then embodies the grand vision of humanity writ small in Israel that constitutes the monotheism that Judaism sets forth.

So let me specify what I claim marks as universalistic the monotheist message of Judaism. When in the dual Torah, written and oral, that took shape in the writings from the Mishnah through the Talmud of Babylonia, Judaism made its normative statement, it addressed all of humanity with the message of the one and only God's self-revelation in the Torah. It told its story from creation to judgment, resurrection, and eternal life. That is what marks Judaism as a mainstream, universal religion, not merely the inner-facing ideology—cast in theological terms—of an ethnic group bearing gross and implausible pretensions of election for anything other than responsibility and culpability, as the prophets of Israel always insisted. The God self-manifest to Israel in the Torah set forth, in writing and in oral tradition, at Sinai made the world and rules all space and time.

Israel as Counterpart to Humanity

The story told in the Torah as Judaism records the tale of God's loving search for humanity's freely given love, God's failure in the original creation of Adam and Eve, God's faltering attempt to try again through the supernatural community of the faithful, Israel, the children of Abraham and Sarah and their descendants via Isaac and Rebecca, Jacob and Leah and Rachel. These God met at Sinai, according to Israel in the Torah, God's own self-revelation, written and oral. In the Torah God taught the teachings that would frame the community, Israel, capable of restoring humanity to the condition of Eden. So Judaism tells the tale of humanity's beginning in Eden and fall therefrom, then moving on to the painful story of God's quest for an Adam and Eve worthy of restoration to Eden, life beyond time, life eternal.

How, precisely, does this conception that Adam and Israel correspond come to expression in the very center of Scripture? What we are going to see is how the ancient sages found bases for the comparison of Adam and Israel in Scripture. Both, we shall see, were granted an abode in Eden, Israel entering the land being compared to Adam and Eve entering Eden. Both failed to respond to God's love with the loving exercise of free will; both rebelled; both lost Eden. God mourns for both. To understand the way in which the sages read Genesis, we have to keep in mind that to them (as to us today) Scripture sets forth facts awaiting reflection and systematization. And the rest follows.

That story that Judaism told therefore speaks of Adam and encompasses the whole of humanity in Adam's fall, Adam's counterpart, Israel, in the restoration to Eden. That message then marks Judaism as a universal in vision and in aspiration. Portrayed in its normative statement, Judaism teaches that God's encounter with humanity takes place in two phases, the first with Adam, the last with Israel, in this language, comparing Adam and Israel, the fall from Eden to the fall from the land of Israel with the destruction of Jerusalem and its holy temple. My comments are given in square brackets.

> A. R. Abbahu in the name of R. Yosé bar Haninah: "It is written, 'But they are like a man [Adam], they have transgressed the covenant' (Hos. 6:7).
>
> B. "'They are like a man,' specifically, like the first man. [We shall now compare the story of the first man in Eden with the story of Israel in its land.]
>
> C. "'In the case of the first man, I brought him into the garden of Eden, I commanded him, he violated my commandment, I judged him to be sent away and driven out, but I mourned for him, saying "How . . ."' [which begins the book of Lamentations, hence stands for a lament, but which, as we just saw, also is written with the consonants that also yield, 'Where are you'].

D. "'I brought him into the garden of Eden,' as it is written, 'And the Lord GOD took the man and put him into the garden of Eden' (Gen. 2:15).

E. "'I commanded him,' as it is written, 'And the Lord GOD commanded' (Gen. 2:16).

F. "'And he violated my commandment,' as it is written, 'Did you eat from the tree concerning which I commanded you?' (Gen. 3:11).

G. "'I judged him to be sent away,' as it is written, 'And the Lord GOD sent him from the garden of Eden' (Gen. 3:23).

H. "'And I judged him to be driven out.' 'And he drove out the man' (Gen. 3:24).

I. "'But I mourned for him, saying, "How? . . .".' 'And he said to him, "Where are you?"' (Gen. 3:9), and the word for 'where are you?' is written, 'How? . . .'

J. "'So too in the case of his descendants, [God continues to speak,] I brought them into the Land of Israel, I commanded them, they violated my commandment, I judged them to be sent out and driven away but I mourned for them, saying, "How? . . ."'

K. "'I brought them into the Land of Israel.' 'And I brought you into the land of Carmel' (Jer. 2:7).

L. "'I commanded them.' 'And you, command the children of Israel' (Exod. 27:20). 'Command the children of Israel ' (Lev. 24:2).

M. "'They violated my commandment.' 'And all Israel have violated your Torah' (Dan. 9:11).

N. "'I judged them to be sent out.' 'Send them away, out of my sight and let them go forth' (Jer. 15:1).

O. "'. . . and driven away.' 'From my house I shall drive them' (Hos. 9:15).

P. "'But I mourned for them, saying, "How? . . ."' 'How has the city sat solitary, that was full of people?' (Lam. 1:1)." (*Genesis Rabbah* XIX:IX.2)

Implicit in the comparison of Adam and Israel, the story of humanity gets told twice in succession, Adam, through whom God failed to accomplish the plan for creation, and Israel, in whom God has found disappointments, but through whom, at the end of days, all the living will return to Eden, embodied in Israel's return to the land of Israel, there to return to life through resurrection, stand in judgment, and enter upon eternal life, which is how God to begin with planned things. At stake in Judaism is death and life eternal, the universal fate of humanity, the hope that has sustained many, though not all, through recorded time.

The Monotheist Theology of the Torah: Four Principles

Let me set forth a somewhat more elaborate synopsis of the same story in these propositions, by which I mean to define the principles of the monotheist theology of the Torah in the sages' representation:

1. God formed creation in accord with a plan, which the Torah reveals. World order can be shown by the facts of nature and society set forth in that plan to conform to a pattern of reason based upon justice. Those who possess the Torah—Israel—know God, and those who do not—the gentiles—reject him in favor of idols. To be Israel then means to know God, and to be gentile means not to know God. What happens to each of the two sectors of humanity responds to their relationship with God. Israel in the present age is subordinate to the nations because God has designated the gentiles as the medium for penalizing Israel's rebellion, meaning through Israel's subordination and exile to provoke Israel to repent. Private life as much as the public order conforms to the principle that God rules justly in a creation of perfection and stasis.

2. The perfection of creation, realized in the rule of exact justice, is signified by the timelessness of the world of human affairs, their conformity to a few enduring paradigms that transcend change (theology of history). No present, past, or future marks time, but only the recapitulation of those patterns. Perfection is further embodied in the unchanging relationships of the social commonwealth (theology of political economy), which assure that scarce resources, once allocated, remain in stasis. A further indication of perfection lies in the complementarity of the components of creation, on the one side, and, finally, the correspondence between God and humanity, in God's image (theological anthropology), on the other.

3. Israel's condition, public and personal, marks flaws in creation. What disrupts perfection is the sole power capable of standing on its own against God's power, and that is the human will. What humanity controls and God cannot coerce is the human capacity to form intention and therefore choose either arrogantly to defy, or humbly to love, God. Because humanity defies God, the sin that results from the human rebellion flaws creation and disrupts world order (theological theodicy). The paradigm of the rebellion of Adam in Eden governs, the act of arrogant rebellion leading to exile from Eden thus accounting for the condition of humanity. But, as in the original transaction of alienation and consequent exile, God retains the power to encourage repentance through punishing the human arrogance. In mercy, moreover, God exer-

cises the power to respond to repentance with forgiveness, that is, a change of attitude evoking a counterpart change. Since, commanding its own will, humanity also has the power to initiate the process of reconciliation with God, through repentance, an act of humility, humanity may restore the perfection of that order that through arrogance it has marred.

4. God ultimately will restore that perfection that embodied his plan for creation. In the work of restoration, death that comes about by reason of sin will die; the dead will be raised and judged for their deeds in this life; and most of them, having been justified, will go on to eternal life in the world to come. In the paradigm of humanity restored to Eden is realized in Israel's return to the land of Israel. In that world or age to come, however, that sector of humanity that through the Torah knows God will encompass all of humanity. Idolaters will perish, and humanity that comprises Israel at the end will know the one, true God and spend eternity in God's light.

This account presents no surprises to those familiar with Scripture and shows why I have repeatedly insisted that Judaic monotheism derives from a rationalist reading—one in accord with the principles of natural history—of Scripture, that alone. For recorded in this way, the story told by the oral Torah proves remarkably familiar, with its stress on God's justice (to which his mercy is integral), the human correspondence with God in his possession of the power of will, humanity's sin and God's response. That is what I meant when I said that the sages read forward from the Hebrew Scriptures to the eternal present in which they lived. And in their forward-reading of Scripture, they sought for generalizations, rules of conduct and conviction critically adduced from properly classified cases. They further set forth those general rules of heaven and earth in terms that compelled credence from all reasonable persons, doing so in accord with rules of evidence and argument common to humanity at large. That is what I mean in contrasting categorical with intellectual monotheism, the one declared and imposed, the other logically demonstrated out of irrefutable facts.

The Universalistic Character of Judaic Monotheism

Now, in behalf of the universalistic character of the sages' monotheism, I have set forth two claims. The first is that through applied logic and practical reason that transcend all ethnic lines and appeal to a common rationality shared by humanity in general, the sages read in the revealed Scriptures revered by all three monotheisms. The second is that they so read Scriptures as to find in them the story of humanity writ small: the human condition embodied in the Israelite experience, Adam's sin in Israelite recalcitrance, for instance. Logic and rationality by their nature transcend the limits of space and time, and Scripture, as Judaism represents Scripture, addresses the human situation of all humanity from Adam and Eve onward. Not bound by episodic particularities of occasion and location, the governing logic of Judaism's distinctive version of monotheism is practical, its reason the applied kind. Judaism appeals to a logic that is embodied in the ordinary, workaday world.

No one can argue that, in its appeal to the written Torah (a.k.a. the Old Testament) Judaism isolates itself from the generality of humankind, because all three monotheist religions—but they alone—invoke the Scriptures of ancient Israel. So we cannot find surprising that a universalistic monotheism reworks the tales of God's self-revelation to Israel at Sinai, from Genesis through Kings, encompassing, also, the Israelite prophets. Indeed, given the character of the written Torah, one may claim that in their particular way, the sages have simply restated the universalistic vision that inheres therein. What we see in the Judaic reworking of the shared story of the monotheist religions—as much as in the Christian one—is how the narrative of Scripture from Genesis through Kings, leading humanity from Eden to death, then back upward to Sinai, but finally to exile from the holy land that realized Eden in the here and now, is taken up and completed.

But because the sages set forth a restorationist Torah, guiding humanity back to Eden, now for eternal life, the sages underscore the universalistic vision of the written Torah. The one and only God has given the Torah to show humanity embodied in Israel the way back to the land that is Eden. Then the restoration to Eden will take place with the final judgment, when those who accept God's dominion, who are called by Judaism *Israel,* will rise from the grave and, with few losses, enter upon life eternal. Then the calamities of Jerusalem and its temple in 586 B.C.E. and again in 70 C.E. are made to signify way-stations on the road from Eden to death and back to Eden and now to resurrection and eternal life.

That is the reworking of the written Torah's tale that the sages of the oral Torah in the authoritative documents of the first six centuries C.E. put forth. They tell the story of humanity from Eden to Eden via Sinai and exile. Excluded from the tale of return are only those unregenerates that do not acknowledge the will of the one and only God. And, as we shall see in rich detail, that will is shown by the sages to accord with humanity's own rules of reason and order and lays strong claim upon the status of self-evidence. So before us is monotheism in its intellectual formulation: the rationality of creation, matching the logic of revelation, embodying God's dominion—applied reason and practical logic applied to revelation.

"Israel" as Ethnic, as Supernatural: The Issue Joined

Naturally, the competing, politically successful monotheisms, Christianity and Islam, dismiss Judaic monotheism. This they find incomplete and unfulfilled, because Judaism speaks of Israel, which the world (not without cause) sees not as a holy community called into being at Sinai by the self-revealing God, but as an ethnic group. Christian apologetics (often in the guise of historical scholarship) as we saw declares that Judaism "found itself unable to separate ethnic identity from religious identity."[7] But that accusation represents willful anachronism, a reading back into the first century of the social transformation of the nineteenth and twentieth. As we shall see in these pages, the account of monotheism set forth by the sages in their reading of the Torah, oral and written, no more records the parochial history of an ethnic group than the Gospels relate the private and personal biography of a Galilean rabbi. Just as Jesus for Christianity is Christ, God incarnate, the last Adam, so Israel for the Torah is God's stake on earth, bearing the Torah, the antidote to Adam's and Eve's rebellion and sin, carrying the message and the promise here and now of life eternal for all who come under the sheltering wings of God's presence. Just as in Christianity humanity knows God through Christ, so in Judaism, humanity confronts God's vision of humanity in holy Israel's realization of the Torah.

How such a worthy rendition of monotheism, now in terms of not a single individual but an entire community, not the imitation of one Adam and Eve but the realization of an entire holy society—not the last Adam but that other, that alternative to Adam—took shape defines the task of this book. I tell the story of how monotheism made logic, reason, rationality, compelling argument into the media for the message of a single, unique God. And that God was and is the sole God conceived by all three monotheisms: creator of heaven and earth, attested to by the regularity and order of the stars in the heaven and humanity on earth. Judaism formulated monotheism in Scripture's particulars that are shown to convey universal truth. This was through the halakah, transforming the local and particular into the intimation of the universal, and the haggadah, transcending the limits of time and space that bound Scripture's account and discovering therein the paradigm of the human situation.

2. The Legal Medium: From the Particular Case to the Governing Rule

Norms of Behavior, Norms of Belief

Judaism makes its statement through norms of both behavior, called halakah, and belief, called haggadah. Thereby the Torah is set forth, a monotheist structure and system embodied by propositions of legal and theological character, respectively. The halakah describes the way of life, the haggadah the worldview, of the Israel of the one whole Torah, oral and written, that the world knows as Judaism. The norms in both halakah and haggadah derive from the sages' generalizing reading of Scripture, an effort to discern out of Scripture's cases the governing rules that are self-evidently compelling for all reasonable persons.

That the halakah serves as a medium of generalizing, universalizing thought hardly is a commonplace of general culture. Quite the opposite, the halakah is represented, and not only by Judaism's enemies, as intensely particularistic, formal, and external in character. Maintaining that salvation is gained by faith, not by keeping the law of the Torah, Christianity dismissed as ethnic and particular the entire structure of the halakah and, it goes without saying, ignored the haggadah as well. "The letter that kills" Christianity has found in the halakah, and (alas) "the spirit that gives life," it located nowhere in Judaism. On the contrary, I argue, the monotheist system of Judaism both through the halakah and through the haggadah speaks in universal terms about truths that pertain to all humanity and transcend history and circumstance. These truths moreover can be shown to be self-evident to any reasonable, logical person within universal norms of analytical thinking.

How Does the Halakah Speak
to Humanity at Large?

Accordingly, I have now to show how Judaism speaks through the halakah to humanity at large. I do so by demonstrating that in its context in the first six centuries of the Common Era the law sets down out of the facts of Scripture principles that any reasonable person will have found rational, fully within the realm of comprehension and utterly beyond all special pleading. Responding to Dunn's repulsive caricature, "God is our God and not yours, God of our way of life and not yours, God of our 'civilization' and not yours,"[1] I claim that the Judaic monotheism, no less than the Christian, is universal. But it is a monotheism that is interior and ontological, not exterior and ethnological, as I shall explain in this chapter.

The universal character (and potential appeal) of Judaic monotheism involves a definition of the unity of humanity under the one and only God that differs from Christianity's definition of the same matter. Unlike Christianity, Judaism does not merely fabricate by declaration the categorical unity of humankind in dismissing existing category formations of the social order, as I said in chapter 1. Rather, Judaism demonstrates the logical, the philosophical unity of humanity. This it does within the framework of the halakah, by showing how halakic norms of analysis and conduct accord with the inherent, interior logic of humanity's mind in the encounter with revealed Scripture. Specifically, the medium of thought and analysis represented by natural history elicits out of the facts of Scripture those rules and truths of a general character that all humanity attains in the same rational manner.

Specifically, the halakah follows universal rules of classification, in accord with the logic of analogy and contrast, meaning things are alike, therefore follow the same rule, or not alike, therefore follow the opposite rule. Indicative, intrinsic traits of things serve as the guides to classification of like and unlike. Accordingly, the halakah embodies in detail the rationality of a well-crafted system of classification, and, in the nature of classification, hierarchization. Treating facts of Scripture the way philosophers in natural history address the established facts of nature, the sages show the universal rationality of the rules of the revealed Torah. This they do by identifying the regularity, order, and sensibility—hence the hierarchical classification of things—that applied reason and practical logic discern in Scripture. And to make the case for monotheism, the sages further show how arrayed in hierarchical order all things ascend to the One, or all things descend from the

One: the ontological unity of existence.[2] So they put forth a monotheism resting on the universality of principles of order: mere intelligence makes the case for the one and only God of creation, revelation, and redemption, made manifest in the Torah. That is what I mean when I refer to the logical and ontological, not the declarative and ethnographic, address of the Judaic monotheism by contrast to the Christian.

And that general account of matters brings us to the corpus of rules called *the halakah,* meaning the way things are done and are to be done, the norms of the arrangement of things, the self-evidently valid media of classification of all being. The halakah, the statement of norms of behavior, set forth by Judaism in its formative age and normative statement emerges in two closely related documents, the Mishnah and the Tosefta.[3] Of the two, the former takes priority in the Judaic canon.[4] That is why we turn to the Mishnah to find an account of the medium of thinking about the norms, the halakah, of the Torah. And there we find the single most sustained representation of thought in universal terms, in commonly accessible reason, in a practical logic that pertains universally, that Judaism possesses. Of the two documents, the Mishnah is accorded privileged standing as the foundation of the two Talmuds, so we shall concentrate on its halakic medium.[5]

The Particular as the Medium for the General

The Mishnah, seen whole, presents a system that is in method profoundly philosophical. The Mishnah's is a mode of thought and analysis that employs numerous cases to make a single general point and that does so within the taxonomic scheme of natural history familiar to ancient philosophical science. What marks the Mishnah's system as philosophical is its focus upon not merely classification by intrinsic traits to show how things are, but also upon why things are the way they are, that is, upon the question of what it means that things are this way, rather than some other. Apart from the distinct source of facts appealed to by each—Scripture, nature—the Mishnah's philosophical method coheres with the natural history of Aristotle and aims at the hierarchical classification of all things.[6]

It follows that the Mishnah's systemic statement demonstrates that all things in place, in proper rank and position in the hierarchy of being, point to, stand for, one thing, and it is a small step indeed to identify at the apex of the unity of being the one God. The sages call to mind Murray's judgment of the Olympians, "They issued no creeds that contradicted knowledge, no commands that made man sin against his own inner light."[7] In their encounter with revealed truth, the sages did no less. They demonstrated through the halakah that all norms accord with knowledge, all laws with the inner light of self-evident rationality. Nature and Scripture conspire to reveal at their depths the one law that governs throughout.

To identify the monotheist telos of thought in the Mishnah and in the halakah as set forth by the Mishnah (and its companion, the Tosefta), I state the generative proposition of the Mishnah very simply: in the halakah of the Mishnah, many things are made to say one thing, which concerns the nature of being. So all things are teleologically hierarchized. In fact, the system of the halakah as set forth in the Mishnah registers these two contrary propositions: many things are one, one thing is many. These propositions complement each other, because, in forming matched opposites, the two provide a complete and final judgment of the whole: the one and only God the source of all, the one and only God the goal of all. The monotheism of Judaism must be deemed ontological,[8] for it is a statement of an ontological order that the system makes when it claims that all things are not only orderly, but ordered in such wise that many things fall into one classification, and one thing may hold together many things of a single classification. The nature of being—the many coming from the one, the many rising to the one—embodies monotheism.

For this philosophy rationality consists in hierarchy of the order of things and in reasoned inquiry and analysis. Reason accomplishes its task in demonstrating out of the innate traits of things the classification into which they fall and the hierarchy of the things that are then classified. That rationality is revealed by the possibility always of effecting the hierarchical classification of all things: each thing in its taxon, all taxa in correct sequence, from least to greatest, the many at the bottom, the One at the top. And showing that all things can be ordered, and that all orders can be set into relationship with one another, we transform method into message. The message of hierarchical classification is that many things really form a single thing, the many species a single genus, the many genera an encompassing and well-crafted, cogent whole. Every time we speciate, we affirm that position; each successful labor of forming relationships among species—for example, making them into a genus, or identifying the hierarchy of the species—proves it again. Not only so, but when we can show that many things are really one, or that one thing yields many (the reverse and confirmation of the former), we say in a fresh way a single immutable truth, the one of this philosophy concerning the unity of all being in an orderly composition of all things within a single taxon.

Rational Analysis of Data: Classes of Things

To show how this works, I turn to a very brief sample of the Mishnah authorship's sustained effort to demonstrate how many classes of things—actions, relationships, circumstances, persons, places—really form one class.[9] This supererogatory work of classification then works its way through the potentialities of chaos to explicit order. It is classification transformed from the how of intellection to the why, the what for, and above all the what does it all mean. Recognition that one thing may fall into several categories and many things into a single one comes to expression, for the authorship of the Mishnah, in diverse ways. One of the interesting ones is the analysis of the several taxa into which a single action may fall, with an account of the multiple consequences, for example, as to sanctions that are called into play, for a single action. The right taxonomy of persons, actions, and things will show the unity of all being by finding many things in one thing, and that forms the first of the two components of what I take to be the philosophy's teleology.

> A. There is one who plows a single furrow and is liable on eight counts of violating a negative commandment:
> B. [specifically, it is] he who (1) plows with an ox and an ass [Deut. 22:10], which are (2, 3) both Holy Things, in the case of (4) [plowing] Mixed Seeds in a vineyard [Deut. 22:9], (5) in the Seventh Year [Lev. 25:4], (6) on a festival [Lev. 23:7] and who was both a (7) priest [Lev. 21:1] and (8) a Nazirite [Num. 6:6] [plowing] in a grave-yard.
> C. Hanania b. Hakhinai says, "Also: He is [plowing while] wearing a garment of diverse kinds" [Lev. 19:19, Deut. 22:11).
> D. They said to him, "This is not within the same class."
> E. He said to them, "Also the Nazir [B8] is not within the same class [as the other transgressions]." (*m. Ker.* 3:9)

Here is a case in which more than a single set of flogging is called for. B's felon is liable to 312 stripes on the listed counts. The ox is sanctified to the altar, the ass to the upkeep of the house (B2, 3). Hanania's contribution is rejected since it has nothing to do with plowing, and the sages' position is equally flawed.

The main point, for our inquiry, is simple. The one action draws in its wake multiple consequences. Classifying a single thing as a mixture of many things then forms a part of the larger intellectual address to the nature of mixtures. But it yields a result that, in the analysis of an action, far transcends the metaphysical problem of mixtures, because it moves us toward the ontological solution of the unity of being.

The real interest in demonstrating the unity of being lies not in things but in abstractions, and among abstractions *types* of actions take center stage. Mishnah tractate *Keritot* works out how many things are really one thing. This is accomplished by showing the end or consequence of diverse actions to be always one and the same. The issue of the tractate is the definition of occasions on which one is obligated to bring a sin-offering and a suspensive guilt-offering. The tractate lists those sins that are classified together by the differentiating criterion of intention. If one deliberately commits those sins, he is punished through extirpation. If it is done inadvertently, one brings a sin-offering. In case of doubt as to whether or not a sin has been committed (hence: inadvertently), one brings a suspensive guilt offering. Leviticus 5:17-19 specifies that if one sins but does not know it, one brings a sin-offering or a guilt offering. Then a different penalty is invoked, with the suspensive guilt offering at stake as well. While we have a sustained exposition of implications of facts that Scripture has provided, the tractate also covers problems of classification of many things as one thing, in the form of a single sin-offering for multiple sins, and that problem fills the bulk of the tractate.

1:1   A. Thirty-six transgressions subject to extirpation are in the Torah . . .
1:2   A. For those [transgressions] are people liable, for deliberately doing them, to the punishment of extirpation,
       B. and for accidentally doing them, to the bringing of a sin-offering,
       C. and for not being certain of whether or not one has done them, to a suspensive guilt-offering (Lev. 5:17)—
       D. "except for the one who imparts uncleanness to the sanctuary and its Holy Things,
       E. "because he is subject to bringing a sliding scale offering (Lev. 5:6-7, 11)," the words of R. Meir.
       F. And sages say, "Also: [except for] the one who blasphemes, as it is said, 'You shall have one law for him that does anything unwittingly' (Num. 15:29)—excluding the blasphemer, who does no concrete deed."
1:7   A. The woman who is subject to a doubt concerning [the appearance of] five fluxes,
       B. or the one who is subject to a doubt concerning five miscarriages
       C. brings a single offering.

D. And she [then is deemed clean so that she] eats animal sacrifices.

E. And the remainder [of the offerings, A, B] are not an obligation for her.

F. [If she is subject to] five confirmed miscarriages,

G. or five confirmed fluxes,

H. she brings a single offering.

I. And she eats animal sacrifices.

J. But the rest [of the offerings, the other four] remain as an obligation for her [to bring at some later time].

3:2   A. [If] he ate [forbidden] fat and [again ate] fat in a single spell of inadvertence, he is liable only for a single sin-offering,

B. [If] he ate forbidden fat and blood and remnant and refuse [of an offering] in a single spell of inadvertence, he is liable for each and every one of them.

C. This rule is more strict in the case of many kinds [of forbidden food] than of one kind.

D. And more strict is the rule in [the case of] one kind than in many kinds:

E. For if he ate a half-olive's bulk and went and ate a half-olive's bulk of a single kind, he is liable.

F. [But if he ate two half-olive's bulks] of two [different] kinds, he is exempt.

3:4   A. There is he who carries out a single act of eating and is liable on its account for four sin-offerings and one guilt-offering:

B. An unclean [lay] person who ate (1) forbidden fat, and it was (2) remnant (3) of Holy Things, and (4) it was on the Day of Atonement.

C. R. Meir says, "If it was the Sabbath and he took it out [from one domain to another] in his mouth, he is liable [for another sin-offering]."

D. They said to him, "That is not of the same sort [of transgression of which we have spoken heretofore since it is not caused by eating (A)]." (*m. Ker.* 1:1, 2, 7, 3:2, 4)

Mishnah tractate *Keritot* 1:7 introduces the case of classifying several incidents within a single taxon, so that one incident encompasses a variety of cases and therefore one penalty or sanction covers a variety of instances.

The recognition that one thing becomes many does not challenge the philosophy of the unity of all being, but confirms the main point. If we can show that differentiation flows from within what is differentiated—that is, from the intrinsic or inherent traits of things—then we confirm that at the heart of things is a fundamental ontological being, single, cogent, simple, capable of diversification, yielding complexity and diversity. The upshot is to be stated with emphasis: *that diversity in species or diversification in actions follows orderly lines confirms the claim that there is that single point from which many lines come forth.* Carried out in proper order—(1) the many form one thing, and (2) one thing yields many—the demonstration then leaves no doubt as to the truth of the matter. Ideally, therefore, we shall argue from the simple to the complex, showing that the one yields the many; one thing, many things; two, four.

1:1   A. [Acts of] transporting objects from one domain to another, [which violate] the Sabbath, (1) are two, which [indeed] are four [for one who is] inside, (2) and two which are four [for one who is] outside,

B. How so?

C. [If on the Sabbath] the beggar stands outside and the householder inside,

D. [and] the beggar stuck his hand inside and put [a beggar's bowl] into the hand of the householder,

E. or if he took [something] from inside it and brought it out,

F. the beggar is liable, the householder is exempt.

G. [If] the householder stuck his hand outside and put [something] into the hand of the beggar,

H. or if he took [something] from it and brought it inside,

I. the householder is liable, and the beggar is exempt.

J. [If] the beggar stuck his hand inside, and the householder took [something] from it,

K. or if [the householder] put something in it and he [the beggar] removed

L. both of them are exempt.

M. [If] the householder put his hand outside and the beggar took [something] from it,

N. or if [the beggar] put something into it and [the householder] brought it back inside,

O. both of them are exempt. (*m. Shab.* 1:1)

This passage from Mishnah tractate *Shabbat* classifies diverse circumstances of transporting objects from private to public domain. The purpose is to assess the rules that classify as culpable or exempt from culpability diverse arrangements. The operative point is that a prohibited action is culpable only if one and the same person commits the whole of the violation of the law. If two or more people share in the single action, neither of them is subject to punishment. At stake therefore is the conception that one thing may be many things, and if that is the case, then culpability is not incurred by any one actor.

The Sabbath-exposition appears so apt and perfect for the present proposition that readers may wonder whether the authorship of the Mishnah could accomplish that same wonder of concision of complex thought more than a single time. Joining rhetoric, logic, and specific proposition transforms thought into not merely expository prose but poetry. So I must ask, have I given a proof consisting of one case? Quite to the contrary, the document contains a plethora of exercises of the same kind. My final demonstration of the power of speciation in demonstrating the opposite, namely, the generic unity of species and the hierarchy that orders them, derives from the treatment of oaths, to which we now turn. The basic topical program of Mishnah tractate *Shabuot* responds systematically to the potpourri of subjects covered by Leviticus 5 and 6 within the (to the priestly author) unifying rubric of those who bring a guilt-offering. Leviticus 5:1-6 concerns oaths, an oath of testimony, and one who touches something unclean in connection with the temple cult, and finally, one who utters a rash oath.

1:1   A. Oaths are of two sorts, which yield four subdivisions.
       B. Awareness of [having sinned through] uncleanness is of two sorts, which yield four subdivisions.
       C. Transportation [of objects from one domain to the other] on the Sabbath is of two sorts, which yield four subdivisions.
       D. The symptoms of Negaim [the skin ailment described in Leviticus 13] are of two sorts, which yield four subdivisions.

1:2   A. In any case in which there is awareness of uncleanness at the outset and awareness [of uncleanness] at the end but unawareness in the meantime—lo, this one is subject to bringing an offering of variable value.
       B. [If] there is awareness [of uncleanness] at the outset but no apprehension [of uncleanness] at the end, a goat which [yields blood to be sprinkled] within [in the Holy of Holies], and the Day of Atonement suspend [the punishment],
       C. until it will be made known to the person, so that he may bring an offering of variable value.

2:1   A. Awareness of uncleanness is of two sorts, which yield four subdivisions [Midrash 1:1B].
       B. (1) [If] one was made unclean and knew about it, then the uncleanness left his mind, but he knew [that the food he had eaten was] Holy Things,
       C. (2) the fact that the food he had eaten was Holy Things left his mind, but he knew about [his having contracted] uncleanness,
       D. (3) both this and that left his mind, but he ate Holy Things without knowing it and after he ate them, he realized it—
       E. lo, this one is liable to bring an offering of variable value.

F. (1) [If] he was made unclean and knew about it, and the uncleanness left his mind, but he remembered that he was in the sanctuary;

G. (2) the fact that he was in the sanctuary left his mind, but he
remembered that he was unclean,

H. (3) both this and that left his mind, and he entered the sanctuary
without realizing it, and then when he had left the sanctuary, he
realized it—lo, this one is liable to bring an offering of variable
value. (*m. Shabu.* 1:1-2; 2:1)

Mishnah tractate *Shabuot* 1:1-7; 2:1-5 accomplish the speciation of
oaths, on the one side, and uncleanness in regard to the cult, on the other.
That work of speciation then joins two utterly disparate subjects, oaths
and uncleanness, so showing a unity of structure that forms a metaphysical argument for the systemic proposition on the unity of being.

Natural History in Mishnaic Analysis

We do so in a way that is now to be predicted. It is by showing that
many things are one thing, now, as I said, oaths, uncleanness. When the
priestly author at Leviticus 5 joined the same subjects, it was because a
single offering was involved for diverse and distinct sins or crimes.
When the mishnaic author does, it is because a single inner structure
sustains these same diverse and distinct sins or crimes. Comparing the
priestly with the Mishnah's strategy of exposition underlines the
remarkable shift accomplished by our philosophers. Their power of formulation—rhetoric, logic together—of course, works to demonstrate
through the medium the message that these enormously diverse subjects in fact can be classified within a simple taxonomic principle: there
are two species to a genus, and two subspecies to each species, and
these are readily determined by appeal to fixed taxonomic indicators.
An abstract statement of the rule of classification (and, it must follow,
also hierarchization) will have yielded less useful intellectual experience than the remarkably well-balanced concrete exemplification of the
rule, and that is precisely what we have in Mishnah tractate *Shabuot*.

The main point of differentiation—the taxonomic indicator—derives
from the intersecting issues of a divided sequence of time frames and of
awareness. If one knows something at one point in a differentiated
process (the outset, the meantime, the end) but does not know that thing
at some other point, then we have a grid in two dimensions: sequence of
time, sequence of spells of being aware or unaware. And then the taxonomic indicators are in place, so the process of speciation and subspeciation is routine. At stake is the power of the taxonomic indicator. What

is stunning is that the same process of speciation and subspeciation is explicitly applied to utterly unrelated matters, which demonstrates for all to see that the foundations of knowledge lie in method, which makes sense of chaos; and method means correct knowledge of the classification of things and the ability to identify the taxonomic indicators that make classification possible.

The upshot may be stated very simply. The species point to the genus, all classes to one class, all taxa properly hierarchized then rise to the top of the structure and the system forming one taxon. So all things ascend to, reach one thing. All that remains is for the theologian to define that one thing: God. But that is a step that the philosophers of the Mishnah did not take. Perhaps it was because they did not think they had to. But I think there is a different reason altogether. It is because, as a matter of fact, they were philosophers. And to philosophers, as I said at the outset, God serves as premise and principle; philosophy serves not to demonstrate principles or to explore premises, but like contemporary natural science, to analyze the unknown, to answer important questions.

Where Does God Abide in Reasoned Analysis?

In such an enterprise, the premise, God, turns out to be merely instrumental, and the given principle, to be merely interesting. But for philosophers, intellectuals, God can live not in the details, but in the unknowns, in the as yet unsolved problem and the unresolved dilemma. So God lives, so to speak, in the excluded middle. God is revealed in the interstitial case. God is made known through the phenomena that form a single phenomenon. God is perceived in the one that is many. God is encountered in the many that are one. For that is the dimension of being—that, so I claim, immanent and sacramental dimension of being—that defines for this philosophy its statement of ultimate concern, its recurrent point of tension, its generative problematic. The cases are particular, the principles universal.

That then is the urgent question, the ineluctable and self-evidently truthful answer: God in the form, God in the order, God in the structure, God in the heights, God at the head of the great chain of hierarchical being. True, God is premise, scarcely mentioned. But it is because God's name does not have to be mentioned when the whole of the order of being says that name, and only that name, and always that name, the name unspoken because it is always in the echo, the silent, thin voice, the numinous in all phenomena.

Science: The Universal Knowledge

What next? I have to answer the question, is this generically philosophical or a particular philosophy? As we shall now see, among the philosophers of that time and place, which is to say, within important components of the philosophical tradition that sustained the Greco-Roman world, however arcane the subject matter of the philosophy of Judaism, the sages can claim a rightful, and honored, place. I shall now show that among the philosophers, Judaism's philosophy can and should have been perceived not merely as philosophical, but, indeed, as philosophy—rational learning, not particular to a given time or place. The basis for that claim is simple: whether or not philosophers can have understood a line of the document (and I doubt that they would have cared to try), the method and the message of the philosophy of Judaism expressed in the halakah fall into the classification of philosophical methods and messages of the Greco-Roman philosophical tradition. The method is like that of Aristotle, the message, congruent to that of neo-Platonism.[10] To state the upshot of the proposition at hand, the halakah finds its natural place within philosophy first because it appeals to the Aristotelian methods of natural philosophy—classification, comparison, and contrast—and the media of expression of philosophy—*Listenwissenschaft*—to register its position.[11]

As to method, can we classify the taxonomic method—premises and rules—of the sages in the same category as the method of Aristotle? This is the question that yields answers on the methodological context in which the philosophy of Judaism is to be located. And in this setting by *context* we mean something piquantly appropriate to our results: the classification of the philosophy. For our backcountry philosophers in a fairly primitive way replicated the method of Aristotle in setting forth the single paramount proposition of neo-Platonism.[12] As a matter of fact, in its indicative traits of message and method, the Mishnah's philosophical system through the exposition of the halakah sets forth one critical proposition of neo-Platonism, which moreover is demonstrated through a standard Aristotelian method.[13] And that is what an examination of the philosophical context will show us.

But these judgments rest upon not a claim of direct connection but an exercise of simple, inductive comparison and contrast, that is to say, of mere classification.[14] I propose now only in an entirely inductive manner to classify the system by the indicative traits of philosophical systems. In that simple way I shall show that in one of the two fundamental aspects—method, message—this system shares traits important to systems all deem to be philosophical. Therefore this system by the criteria of philosophy and in the specific and explicit context of philosophy must be classified as philosophical. That is my simple argument. But it is fundamental to my purpose, which is to show that in the Mishnah's system, both as to mode of thought and as to message, we deal with a philosophy—philosophy in an odd idiom to be sure, but philosophy nonetheless: universally accessible to the reason common to all humanity.

Let me ask the question in its simplest form: by appeal to the paramount taxonomic traits of Aristotelian method, can we classify the method as Aristotelian? If we can, then my purpose, which is to demonstrate that the halakah in its medium of thought sustains generalization like a philosophy, will have been accomplished. That is as far as we can go. But it suffices to accomplish the goal of demonstrating that, as to the method of classification, the Mishnah's is philosophical, in the way in which Greco-Roman philosophy, exemplified by Aristotle, is philosophical. True, we cannot show, and therefore do not know, that the Mishnah's philosophers read Aristotle's work on natural history or his reflections on scientific method, for example, the *Posterior Analytics*.[15] But we can compare our philosophers' method with that of Aristotle, who also set forth a system that, in part, appealed to the right ordering of things through classification by correct rules.[16]

Rules of Natural History:
Aristotle and the Sages

Now to the specific task at hand. A brief account, based upon the standard textbook picture, of the taxonomic method of Aristotle permits us to compare the philosophical method of the philosophy of Judaism with that of the methodologically paramount natural philosophy of the Greco-Roman world.[17] We begin with the simple observation that the distinction between genus and species lies at the foundation of all knowledge. Adkins states the matter in the most accessible way, "Aristotle, a systematic biologist, uses his method of classification by genera and species, itself developed from the classificatory interests of the later Plato, to place humanity among other animals . . . The classification must be based on the final development of the creature."[18] But to classify, we have to take as our premise that things are subject to classification, and that means that they have traits that are essential and indicative, on the one side, but also shared with other things, on the other. The point of direct contact and intersection between the Mishnah's philosophy of hierarchical classification and the natural philosophy of Aristotle lies in the shared, and critical, conviction concerning the true nature or character of things. Both parties concur that there *is* such a true definition—a commonplace for philosophers, generative of interesting problems, for example, about ideas, or form and substance, actual and potential, and the like—of what things really are.[19]

But how are we to know the essential traits that allow us to define the true character of, to classify, things? And this is the point at which our comparison becomes particular, since what we need to find out is whether there are between Aristotle's and Judaism's philosophies only shared convictions about the genus and the species or particular conceptions as to how these are to be identified and organized. The basic conviction on both sides is this: objects are not random but fall into classes and so may be described, analyzed, and explained by appeal to general traits or rules.

The component of Aristotelianism that pertains here is "the use of deductive reasoning proceeding from self-evident principles or discovered general truths to conclusions of a more limited import; and syllogistic forms of demonstrative or persuasive arguments."[20] The goal is the classification of things, which is to say, the discovery of general rules that apply to discrete data or instances. Minio-Paluello states,

> In epistemology . . . Aristotelianism includes a concentration on knowledge accessible by natural means or accountable for by reason; an inductive, analytical empiricism, or stress on experience in the study of nature . . . leading from the perception of contingent individual occurrences to the discovery of permanent, universal patterns; and the primacy of the universal, that which is expressed by common or general terms. In metaphysics, or the theory of Being, Aristotelianism involves belief in the primacy of the individual in the realm of existence; in correlated conceptions allowing an articulate account of reality (e.g., ten categories; genus-species-individual, matter-form, potentiality-actuality, essential-accidental; the four material elements and their basic qualities; and the four causes—formal, material, efficient, and final); in the soul as the inseparable form of each living body in the vegetable and animal kingdoms; in activity as the essence of things; and in the primacy of speculative over practical activity.

The manner in which we accomplish this work is to establish categories of traits, and these will yield the rules or generalizations that make possible both classification, and, in the nature of things, therefore also hierarchization.

Clearly, when we review some of the more obvious characteristics of Aristotle's logical and taxonomic principles, in specific terms we find only occasional points of contact with the principles we uncover in the Mishnah's philosophical structure. Only in general does the manner in which Aristotle does the work of definition through classification also characterize the way in which the sages do the same work. But there are points of intersection. For instance, while the actual and the potential form critical taxonomic categories for Aristotle, they prove subsidiary, though pertinent, in the Mishnah. While for the Mishnah, the matter of mixtures defines a central and generative problematic, for Aristotle, the same matter is subsumed into other compositions altogether. It constitutes a chapter in the story of change, which is explained by the passage of elements into one another. That will help us to account for the destruction of one element and the creation of another. In this connection Allan says, "Aristotle does not mean by 'mixture' a mere shuffling of primary particles, as if the seeds of wheat and barley were mixed in a heap, but genuine change of quality resulting in a new 'form,' towards which each component has made a contribution."[21] The consideration of the classes of mixtures plays its role in Aristotle's account of the sublunary region; it is not—as represented by Allan—a point at which Aristotle repeatedly uncovers problems that require solution, in the way in which the issue of mixtures forms the source for the Mishnah's solution of urgent problems.

Enough has been said to justify comparing Aristotle's and Judaism's philosophies, but I have yet to specify what I conceive to be the generative point of comparison. It lies in two matters: first, the paramount one of the shared principles of formal logic, which I find blatant in the Mishnah and which all presentations of Aristotle's philosophy identify as emblematic. The second, as is clear, is the taxonomic method, viewed from afar. Let us turn only briefly to the former. When we follow a simple account of the way in which we attain new truth, we find ourselves quite at home. Allan's account follows:

Induction . . . is the advance from the particular to the general. By the inspection of examples . . . in which one characteristic appears conjoined with another, we are led to propound a general rule which we suppose to be valid for cases not yet examined. Since the rule is of higher generality than the instances, this is an advance from a truth "prior for us" toward a truth "prior in nature."[22]

My representation of the mishnaic mode of presentation of halakic cases that, with our participation, yield a general rule, accords with this logic, which is inductive.

The more important of the two principles of sound intellectual method is the taxonomic interest in defining through classification. This definitive trait of natural philosophy is what we find in common between Aristotle's and the Mishnah's philosophical method, and the points in common prove far more than those yielded by the general observation that both systems appeal to the identification of genera out of species. In fact, what philosophers call the dialectical approach in Aristotle proves the same approach to the discovery or demonstration of truth as that we find in the Mishnah. Owens sets the matter forth in the following language: "Since a theoretical science proceeds from first principles that are found within the thing under investigation, the initial task of the philosophy of nature will be to discover its primary principles in the sensible thing themselves."[23] I cannot imagine a formulation more suited to the method of the Mishnah than that simple statement. For the Mishnah's philosophers compose their taxonomy by appeal to the indicative traits of things, rather than to extrinsic considerations of imposed classification, for example, by reference to Scripture.[24] The philosophers whose system is set forth in the Mishnah appeal to the traits of things, deriving their genera from the comparison and contrast of those inherent or intrinsic traits. This I take to be precisely what is stated here. In accordance with the general directives of the Aristotelian logic, the process of their discovery will be dialectical, not demonstrative. This distinction is between genuine reasoning and demonstration.

Where the Sages Part Company with Aristotle

If the parallels in method are clear, where do we find the difference between Aristotle's system and the Mishnah's? It is that the goal of Aristotle's system, the teleological argument in favor of the unmoved mover, and the goal of Judaism's system, the demonstration of the unity of being, are essentially contradictory, marking utterly opposed positions on the fundamental character of God and the traits of the created world that carries us upward to God. So we establish the philosophical character of the method of the Mishnah's system only at the cost of uncovering a major contradiction: the proposition that animates the one system stands in direct opposition, as to its premises, implications, and explicit results, with the results of the other. Aristotle's God attained through teleological demonstration accomplished through the right classification of all things and the Mishnah's monotheist God, whose workings in the world derive from the demonstration of the ontological unity of all things, cannot recognize one another. And that is the case even though they are assuredly one.

Accordingly, we must ask ourselves, cui bono? Or more precisely, not to whose advantage, but rather, against whose position, did the Judaic philosophical system propose to argue? When we realize that at stake is a particular means for demonstrating in universal terms the unity of God, we readily identify as the principal focus the pagan reading of the revealed world of the here and the now, and, it must follow, Judaism as a philosophy stood over against the pagan philosophy of the world of its time and place. The fundamental argument in favor of the unity of God in the philosophy of Judaism is by showing the hierarchical order, therefore the unity, of the world. The world therefore is made to testify to the unity of being, and—to say the obvious with very heavy emphasis—*the power of the philosophy derives from its capacity for hierarchical classification.* When we compare the pagan and the Christian philosophical ontology of God, we see that it is the pagan position, and not the Christian one, that forms the target of this system. The Christian position is simply not perceived and not considered.

The comparison of the Judaic, Christian, and pagan systems of Middle Platonism seems to me made possible, in a very preliminary way to be sure, by Armstrong:

> The difference here between pagans and Christians . . . is a difference about the degree of religious relevance of the material cosmos, and, closely connected with this, about the relative importance of general, natural, and special, supernatural, divine self-manifestation and self-communication. On the one side, the pagan, there is the conviction that a multiple self-communication and self-revelation of divinity takes place always and everywhere in the world, and that good and wise men everywhere . . . have been able to find the way to God and the truth about God in and through rational reflection on themselves and on the world, not only the heavens but the earth, and the living unity of the whole. On the other side, the Christian, there is indeed a readiness to see the goodness and beauty of the visible cosmos as a testimony to God's creation . . . but the religious emphasis lies elsewhere. Saving truth and the self-communication of the life of God come through the Incarnation of God as a man and through the human . . . society of which the God-Man is the head, the Church. . . . It is only in the Church that material things become means of revelation and salvation through being under-

stood in the light of Scripture and Church tradition and used by God's human ministers in the celebration of the Church's sacraments. It is the ecclesiastical cosmos, not the natural cosmos, which appears to be of primary religious importance for the Christian.[25]

If God is revealed in the artifacts of the world, then, so pagans in general considered, God must be multiple. No, the philosophy of Judaism is here seen to respond. Here we find a Judaic argument, within the premises of paganism, against paganism. To state—once more with emphasis—what I conceive to be that argument: *the very artifacts that* appear *multiple in fact form classes of things, and, moreover, these classes themselves are subject to a reasoned ordering, by appeal to this-worldly characteristics signified by properties and indicative traits.* Monotheism hence is to be demonstrated by appeal to those very same data that for paganism prove the opposite.

The medium of hierarchical classification, which is Aristotle's, conveys the message of the unity of being[26] in the this-worldly mode of discourse formed by the framers of the Mishnah. The way to one God, ground of being and ontological unity of the world, says Armstrong, lies through "rational reflection on themselves and on the world," this world, which yields a living unity encompassing the whole. That claim, conducted in an argument covering overwhelming detail in the Mishnah, directly faces the issue as framed by paganism. Immanent in its medium, it is transcendent in its message. And I hardly need spell out the simple reasons, self-evident in Armstrong's words, for dismissing as irrelevant to their interests the Christian reading of the cosmos. To the Mishnah's sages, it is not (merely) wrong, it is insufficient. Their conception of monotheism transcended such particularities, built as it was upon foundations of certainty that universal logic and reason sustain.

Where Material Things Become Means of Revelation

And yet, that is not the whole story. For the Mishnah's sages reach into Scripture for their generative categories, and in doing so, they address head-on a Christianity that Armstrong centers, with entire soundness, upon the life of the church of Jesus Christ, God-Man.[27] We do well here to review Armstrong's language: "It is only in the Church that material things become means of revelation and salvation through being understood in the light of Scripture and Church tradition and used by God's human ministers in the celebration of the Church's sacraments."

The framers of the Mishnah will have responded, "It is in the Torah that material things are identified and set forth as a means of revelation."

Again Armstrong: "It is the ecclesiastical cosmos, not the natural cosmos, which appears to be of primary religious importance for the Christian."

To this the philosophers of Judaism reply, "It is the scriptural account of the cosmos that forms our generative categories, which, by the power of intellect, we show to constitute an ordered, hierarchical unity of being."

So the power of this identification of "the ecclesiastical cosmos" is revealed when we frame the cosmos of the Mishnah by appeal to its persistent response to the classifications and categories of Scripture. If the church (as Armstrong portrays matters) worked out an ecclesiastical cosmos—only later producing the Bible as it did—for its part the philosophy of Judaism framed a scriptural cosmos; then Judaism read it philosophically in the way in which I have explained matters. We may therefore identify three distinct positions on the reading of the natural world: the pagan, the Christian, and the Judaic. The Judaic one reads nature as a source of revelation. The other two insist on a medium of mediation between nature and intellect. For Christianity it is, as Armstrong says, ecclesiastical, and, as I claim, for Judaism, the medium of mediation of nature lies through revelation, the Torah.

Why the difference? There is a philosophical reason, which I deem paramount, and which explains my insistence that this Judaism is a philosophy of monotheism addressed to rational humanity at large, in its message and its mode of thought accessible to all reasonable persons. It is that by not merely appealing to the authority of Scripture, but by themselves analyzing the revealed truths of Scripture, that the intellects at hand accomplished their purposes. By themselves showing the order and unity inherent within Scripture's list of topics, the philosophers on their own power meant to penetrate into the ground of being as God has revealed matters. This they did by working their way back from the epiphenomena of creation to the phenomenon of creation—then to the numinous, that is, the Creator. That self-assigned challenge forms an intellectual vocation worthy of a particular kind of philosopher, an Israelite one. And, in my view, it explains also why in the Mishnah philosophers produced their philosophy in the form that they chose.

For the form, so superficially unphilosophical in its crabbed and obsessive mode of discourse, proves in the end to form a philosophy. Judaism in the system of the Mishnah is philosophical in medium, method, and message. But then philosophy also is represented as, and within, the Torah in topic and authority. The union, then, of the Torah's classifications and topics, and philosophy's modes of thought and propositions produced as its firstfruits a philosophical Judaism—a Judaic philosophy: the Torah as Moses would have written it at God's instructions had Moses been a philosopher. So much for the monotheist method. Now to the monotheist message: the universalistic reading of the particularities of Scripture.

3. The Legal Message: Restoring Eden through Israel

God's Unity and Dominion

The key to the universalistic character of Judaic monotheism lies in its focus upon Adam and Israel, Eden and the land—and its eagerness to receive "under the wings of God's presence" all who accept God's dominion and the Torah's statement thereof. The whole is captured in the twice-daily recitation of the Shema, "Hear, Israel, the LORD is our God, the one God." That liturgical act accepts God's unity and dominion at one and the same moment, and the rest follows. But how is this "Israel" that defines itself as those who accept the dominion of one God to regain the land, this new Adam to restore Eden? Here are the ways in which the halakah answers that question, all the time building upon that same record of humanity that the two other monotheisms affirm.

Why turn to the halakah? The reason is that Judaism in the formative age through the halakah offered a restorationist program such as Scripture invites—bringing humanity back to Eden. The halakah as set forth in its formative age aims to describe how in concrete terms holy Israel—those who know God through the Torah of Sinai—is to construct a social order in the land of Israel to realize that just and perfect world order that God had in mind in creating the world. The halakah is so framed, its category-formation so constituted, as to yield an account of how humanity in paradise, Adam in Eden, ought to have lived and therefore ought now to live.

Speaking in monumental dimensions, the halakah makes a teleological[1] statement. And the promise of the halakah speaks less to Israel's messianic so much as to its restorationist aspiration: to form Eden not in time past nor in time future but in the here and now of everyday Israel—but this time we shall do it right. And here in this chapter is how—in concrete detail[2]—the sages say so. This they do in a number of large halakic statements concerning restoration and renewal. We consider three of them.

Between Israel and God: *Shebi'it*

The Torah represents God as the sole master of creation, the Sabbath as testimony to God's pleasure with, and therefore sanctification of, creation. Tractate *Shebi'it* sets forth the law that in relationship to the Land of Israel embodies that conviction. The law systematically works through Scripture's rules, treating (1) the prohibition of farming the land during the seventh year, (2) the use of the produce in the seventh year solely for eating, and (3) the remission of debts. During the sabbatical year, Israel relinquishes its ownership of the land of Israel. At that time Israelites in farming may do nothing that in secular years effects the assertion of ownership over the land.[3] Just as one may not utilize land he does not own, in the Sabbatical year, the farmer gives up ownership of the land that he does own.

What defines the particular problems that attract the sages' attention? The problematic of the tractate is the interplay between the land of Israel, the people of Israel dwelling on the land of Israel, and God's Sabbath, and what imparts energy to the analysis of the law is the particular role accorded to humanity's—Israelite humanity's—intentionality and attitude. These form the variable, to be shown able to determine what is, or is not, permitted in the holy time of the seventh year. Specifically, the focus of the law of *Shebi'it* as set forth in the Mishnah centers upon the role of the human will in bringing about the reordering of the world (of which we shall hear more in the next section). By laying emphasis upon the power of the human will, the sages express the conviction that the Israelite has the power by an act of will to restore creation to its perfection. That is why the details of the law time and again spin out the implications of the conviction at hand, that all things depend upon humanity's intentionality in a given action or humanity's likely perception of an action.

If the problematics of the halakah generate small-scale inquiries into large-bore principles, then, as a matter of fact, the reason that questions of a particular order dominate in the exposition of the law of a specific topic requires attention. Specifically, why is it that the sages identified questions that they have found urgent for sustained inquiry? Why have they defined the problematics of the law in the way that they have? Not only did they have the choice of answering questions of another order entirely, they also had reason to select this particular topic to make the statement that they have made—this and no other. And we want to know why.

To understand the answer, we turn first of all to Avery-Peck's and Newman's introductions to the halakah of *Shebi'it,* which, in both cases, turn to Scripture for perspective on how the Mishnah (we should say, how the halakah) treats the topic at hand. Both make the move from the problematics of human intentionality—in this case: how people will make sense of appearances—a problematics that can and does animate discussion of a variety of topics, to the particular topic of *Shebi'it.* The written Torah leaves no doubt that the sabbatical year finds its place in the context of creation and God's conduct thereof: perfecting the world order of creation, sanctifying the order of creation, then, celebrating the Sabbath in response thereto. Avery-Peck provides this fine statement of the paramount religious principle of the halakah of *Shebi'it.*

> In modeling their lives on the perfected character of the universe that once existed, Israelites make explicit their understanding that this order will exist again, that God's plan for the Israelite people still is in effect. . . . Israelites themselves, through their actions, participate in the creation of that perfected world. They do this through their intentions and perceptions in defining proper observance of the Sabbatical year. . . .[4]

The sabbatical year recovers that perfect time of Eden when the world was at rest, all things in place. Before the rebellion, humanity did not have to labor on the land; the first people picked and ate meals freely. And, in the nature of things, everything belonged to everybody; private ownership in response to individual labor did not exist, because humanity did not have to work anyhow. Reverting to that perfect time, the Torah maintains that the land will provide adequate food for everyone, including the flocks and herds, even if people do not work the land. But that is on condition that all claim of ownership lapses; the food is left in the fields, to be picked by anyone who wishes, but it may not be hoarded by the landowner in particular. Avery-Peck states this matter as follows:

> Scripture thus understands the Sabbatical year to represent a return to a perfected order of reality, in which all share equally in the bounty of a holy land that yields its food without human labor. The Sabbatical year provides a model through which, once every seven years, Israelites living in the here-and-now may enjoy the perfected order in which God

always intended the world to exist and toward which, in the Israelite world view, history indeed is moving. . . . The release of debts accomplishes for Israelites' economic relationships just what the agricultural Sabbatical accomplishes for the relationship between the people and the land. Eradicating debt allows the Israelite economy to return to the state of equilibrium that existed at the time of creation, when all shared equally in the bounty of the Land.[5]

The Priestly Code expresses that same concept when it arranges for the return, at the jubilee year, of inherited property to the original family ownership: "You shall count off seven weeks of years, so that the period of seven weeks of years gives you a total of forty-nine years. . . . You shall proclaim release throughout the land for all its inhabitants. It shall be a jubilee for you; each of you shall return to his holding and each of you shall return to his family" (Lev. 25:8-10). The jubilee year is observed as is the sabbatical year, meaning that for two successive years the land is not to be worked. The halakah we shall examine in due course will establish that when land is sold, it is for the span of time remaining to the next jubilee year. That then marks the reordering of landholding to its original pattern, when Israel inherited the land to begin with and commenced to enjoy its produce.

Just as the Sabbath commemorates the completion of creation, the perfection of world order, so does the sabbatical year. So too, the jubilee year brings about the restoration of real property to the original division. In both instances, Israelites so act as to indicate they are not absolute owners of the land, which belongs to God and which is divided in the manner that God arranged in perpetuity. Avery-Peck states the matter in the following way:

> On the Sabbath of creation, during the Sabbatical year, and in the Jubilee year, diverse aspects of Israelite life are to return to the way that they were at the time of creation. Israelites thus acknowledge that, in the beginning, God created a perfect world, and they assure that the world of the here-and-now does not overly shift from its perfect character. By providing opportunities for Israelites to model their contemporary existence upon a perfected order of things, these commemorations further prepare the people for messianic times, when, under God's rule, the world will permanently revert to the ideal character of the time of creation.[6]

Here we find the halakic counterpart to the restorationist theology that the oral Torah sets forth in the haggadah. Israel matches Adam; the land of Israel, Eden; and, we now see, the sabbatical year commemorates the perfection of creation and replicates it.

A further, striking point, emerges from the sages' reading of the law of *Shebi'it* in the written part of the Torah. It is that the sabbatical year takes effect at the moment of Israel's entry into the land. Then Israel reenacts the drama of creation, the seventh day marking the perfection of creation and its sanctification, so, here too, the Sabbath is observed for the land as much as for humanity. Observing the commandments of the sabbatical year marks Israel's effort at keeping the land like Eden, six days of creation, one day of rest, and so too here in this passage from *Sifra:*

2. A. "When you come [into the land which I give you, the land shall keep a Sabbath to the LORD]":

    B. Might one suppose that the sabbatical year was to take effect once they had reached Transjordan?

    C. Scripture says, "into the land."

    D. It is that particular land.

Now comes the key point: the sabbatical year takes effect only when Israel enters the land, which is to say, Israel's entry into the land marks the counterpart to the beginning of the creation of Eden. But a further point will register in a moment. It is when Eden/the land enters into stasis, each family receiving its share in the land, that the process of the formation of the new Eden comes to its climax; then each Israelite bears responsibility for his share of the land. That is when the land has reached that state of order and permanence that corresponds to Eden at sunset on the sixth day:

    E. Might one suppose that the sabbatical year was to take effect once they had reached Ammon and Moab?

    F. Scripture says, "which I give you,"

    G. and not to Ammon and Moab.

    H. And on what basis do you maintain that when they had conquered the land but not divided it, divided it among familiars but not among fathers' houses so that each individual does not yet recognize his share—

    I. might one suppose that they should be responsible to observe the sabbatical year?

    J. Scripture says, "[Six years you shall sow] your field,"

    K. meaning, each one should recognize his own field.

    L. ". . . your vineyard":

    M. meaning, each one should recognize his own vineyard.

    N. You turn out to rule:

    O. Once the Israelites had crossed the Jordan, they incurred liability to separate dough-offering and to observe the prohibition against eating the fruit of fruit trees for the first three years after planting and the prohibition against eating produce of the new growing season prior to the waving of the sheaf of new grain [that is, on the fifteenth of Nisan].

P. When the sixteenth of Nisan came, they incurred liability to wave the sheaf of new grain.

Q. With the passage of fifty days from then they incurred the liability to the offering of the Two Loaves.

R. At the fourteenth year they became liable for the separation of tithes.

The sabbatical takes over only when the Israelite farmers have asserted their ownership of the land and its crops. Then the process of counting the years begins.

S. They then began to count the years of the sabbatical cycle, and in the twenty-first year after entry into the land, they observed the sabbatical year.

T. In the sixty-fourth year they observed the first Jubilee [*t. Menah.* 6:20].

What, exactly, imposes limits on the analogy of the Sabbath for the land? Do we treat the Sabbath of the land as equivalent in all ways to the Sabbath observed by Israel? No, the metaphor has its limits:

3. A. " . . . the land shall keep a Sabbath to the LORD":
   B. might one suppose that the Sabbath should involve not digging pits, ditches, and wells, not repairing immersion-pools?
   C. Scripture says, "you shall not sow your field or prune your vineyard"—
   D. I know that the prohibition extends only to sowing.
   E. How do I know that it covers also sowing, pruning, plowing, hoeing, weeding, clearing, and cutting down?
   F. Scripture says, "your field you shall not . . . your vineyard . . . you shall not":
   G. none of the work that is ordinarily done in your field and in your vineyard.

4. A. And how do we know that farmers may not fertilize, prune trees, smoke the leaves, or cover over with powder for fertilizer?
   B. Scripture says, "your field you shall not . . ."

5. A. And how do we know that farmers may not trim trees, nip off dry shoots, trim trees?
   B. Scripture says, "your field you shall not . . ."

6. A. Since Scripture says, "you shall not sow your field or prune your vineyard,"

B. might one suppose that the farmer also may not hoe under the olive trees, fill in the holes under the olives trees, or dig between one tree and the next?

C. Scripture says, "you shall not sow your field or prune your vine-yard"—

D. sowing and pruning were subject to the general prohibition of field labor. Why then were they singled out?

E. It was to build an analogy through them, as follows:

F. what is distinctive in sowing and pruning is that they are forms of labor carried on on the ground or on a tree.

G. So I know that subject to the prohibition are also other forms of labor that are carried on on the ground or on a tree, [excluding from the prohibition, therefore, the types of labor listed at B]. (*Sifra* CCXLV:I)

So much for the systematic exploration of the enlandisement of Eden in the land of Israel, the formulation of Israel's relationship with God through Israel's use of the land of Israel and its produce, in a way analogous to Adam's use of Eden—and abuse thereof.

In relationship to God, the land of Israel, as much as the people of Israel, emerges as a principal player. The land is treated as a living entity, a participant in the cosmic drama, as well it should, being the scene of creation and its unfolding. If the perfection of creation is the well-ordered condition of the natural world, then the land of Israel, counterpart to Eden, must be formed into the model of the initial per-fection, restored to that initial condition. So the Sabbath takes over and enchants the land of Israel as much as it transforms Israel itself. Newman expresses this view in the following language:

For the priestly writer of Leviticus, the seventh year, like the seventh day, is sanctified. Just as God rested from the work of creation on the seventh day and sanctified it as a day of rest, so too God has desig-nated the seventh year for the land's rest. Implicit in this view is the notion that the Land of Israel has human qualities and needs. It must "observe a Sabbath of the Lord" because, like the people of Israel and God, it too experiences fatigue and requires a period of repose. The Land of Israel, unlike all other countries, is enchanted, for it enjoys a unique relationship to God and to the people of Israel. That is to say, God sanctified this land by giving it to his chosen people as an exclu-sive possession. Israelites, in turn, are obligated to work the Land and to handle its produce in accordance with God's wishes. . . .[7]

The counterpart in the matter of the remission of debts works out the conception that all Israelites by right share in the land and its gifts, and if they have fallen into debt, they have been denied their share; that imbalance is righted every seven years.

Now how shall we relate the problematics that direct the exposition of details of the law to the particular religious convictions inherent in the topic of the law? The halakah outlines where and how humanity participates in establishing the sanctity of the sabbatical year, expanding the span of the year to accommodate humanity's intentionality in working the land now for advantage then. It insists that humanity's perceptions of the facts, not the facts themselves, govern: what looks like a law violation is a law violation. In these and other ways the halakah of *Shebi'it* works out the problematics of humanity's participation in the sanctification of the land in the sabbatical year. The topic of the law, restoring the perfection of creation, then joins with the generative problematics of the halakah to make the point that Israel has in its power the restoration of the perfection of creation, the ordering of all things to accord with the condition that prevailed when God declared creation to be God, therefore sanctified creation and declared the Sabbath. The particular topic served as an obvious, an ideal medium to deliver in the context of that message of restoration the statement that Israel by a fulfilled act of will bore within its power the capacity to attain the perfection of the world. That is because to begin with Israel's perception of matters—and its actions consequent upon those perceptions—made all the difference. The halakah of *Shebi'it* did not define the sole arena for the detailed and practical working out of that statement. We shall find ourselves many times in the same framework of discussion. But the halakah of *Shebi'it* did frame a particularly fitting occasion to show how, in small things, that large conception was to be realized.

What of the interiorities of Israel's relationship with God? The blatant affirmation that God pays the closest attention to Israel's attitudes and intentions pervades the tractate. Otherwise there is no way to explain the priority accorded to Israelite perception of whether or not the law is kept, Israelite intention in cultivating the fields in the sixth year, and other critical components of the governing, generative problematic. God furthermore identifies the land of Israel as the archetype of Eden and model of the world to come. That is why, as we have seen, God treats the land in its perfection just as he treats Eden, by according to the land the Sabbath rest. He deems the union of Israel and the land of Israel to effect the sanctification of the land in its ascending degrees corresponding to the length of the term of Israel's possession. And, finally, he insists, as the ultimate owner of the land, that at regular intervals, the possession of the land be relinquished, signaled as null, and that at those same intervals ownership of the produce of the land at least in potentiality be equally shared among all its inhabitants. God therefore relates to Israel through the land and the arrangements that he imposes upon the land. In that context God relates to the land in response to Israel's residence thereon. But God relates to the land in a direct way, providing for the land, as he provides for Israel, the sanctifying moment of the Sabbath. So a web of relationships, direct and indirect, hold together God, land, and Israel. That is for the here and now, all the more so for the world to come. And if that is how God relates to Israel, Israel relates to God in one way above all, by exercising in ways that show love for God and acceptance of God's dominion the power of free will that God has given humanity. The universality of the message pervades the details: here the Sabbath celebrates not ethnic Israel but the creation of the world. I cannot imagine a more encompassing frame of reference than nature common to us all.

Israel's Social Order:
Sanhedrin-Makkot **and the Death Penalty**

The most profound question facing Israelite thinkers concerns the fate of the Israelites at the hands of the perfectly just and merciful God. Since essential to their thought is the conviction that all creatures are answerable to their creator, and absolutely critical to their system is the fact that at the end of days the dead are raised for eternal life, the criminal justice system encompasses deep thought on the interplay of God's justice and God's mercy: how are these reconciled in the case of the sinner or criminal? And if, as I have claimed, the purpose of the halakic system is restorationist, what has criminal justice to do with Eden?

Within Israel's social order the halakah addresses from a theological perspective the profound question of social justice: what shall we make of the Israelite sinner or criminal? Specifically, does the sin or crime which has estranged him from God close the door to life eternal? If it does, then justice is implacable and perfect. If it does not, then God shows mercy—but what of justice? We can understand the answer only if we keep in mind that the halakah takes for granted the resurrection of the dead, the final judgment, and the life of the world to come beyond the grave. From that perspective, death becomes an event in life but not the end of life. And it must follow that the death penalty too does not mark the utter annihilation of the person of the sinner or criminal. On the contrary, by paying for the crime or sin in this life, that person stands with all of the rest of supernatural Israel, ready for the final judgment. Having been judged, the sinner or criminal will "stand in judgment," meaning, will find a way to the life of the world to come along with everyone else. Within the dialectics formed by those two facts—punishment now, eternal life later on—we identify as the two critical passages in the halakah of *Sanhedrin-Makkot* (*m. Sanh.* 6:2 and 10:1): Achan pays the supreme penalty but secures his place in the world to come, all Israel, with only a few exceptions, is going to stand in judgment and enter the world to come, explicitly including all manner of criminals and sinners.

That is what defines the stakes in this critical component of the sages' account of God's abode in Israel. What the halakah wishes to explore is the question of how the Israelite sinner or criminal is rehabilitated through the criminal justice system so as to rejoin Israel in all its eternity. The answer is that the criminal or sinner remains Israelite, no matter what crime or sin has been committed—and the death penalty is exacted by the earthly court. So the halakah of Sanhedrin embodies these religious principles: (1) Israel endures forever, encompassing (nearly) all Israelites; (2) sinners or criminals are able to retain their position within that eternal Israel by reason of the penalties that expiate the specific sins or crimes spelled out by the halakah; (3) it is an act of merciful justice that is done when the sinner or criminal is put to death, for at that point, he is assured of eternity along with everyone else. God's justice comes to full expression in the penalty, which is instrumental and contingent; God's mercy endures forever in the forgiveness that follows expiation of guilt through the imposition of the penalty.

That explains why the governing religious principle of *Sanhedrin-Makkot* is the perfect, merciful justice of God, and it accounts for the detailed exposition of the correct form of the capital penalty for each capital sin or crime. The punishment must fit the crime within the context of the Torah in particular so that, at the resurrection and the judgment, the crime will have been correctly expiated. Because the halakah rests on the premise that God is just and that God has made humanity in God's image, after God's likeness, the halakah cannot deem sufficient that the punishment fit the crime. Rather, given its premises, the halakah must pursue the issue, what of the sinner once punished has been exacted? And the entire construction of the continuous exposition of *Sanhedrin-Makkot* aims at making this simple statement: the criminal, in God's image, after God's likeness, pays the penalty for the crime in this world but like the rest of Israel will stand in justice and, rehabilitated, will enjoy the world to come.

Accordingly, given their conviction that all Israel possesses a share in the world to come, meaning, nearly everybody will rise from the grave, the sages took as their task the specification of how, in this world, criminals and sinners would receive appropriate punishment in a proper procedure, so that, in the world to come, they would take their place along with everyone else in the resurrection and eternal life. So the religious principle that comes to expression in *Sanhedrin-Makkot* concerns the meaning of humanity's being in God's image. That means it is in humanity's nature to surpass the grave. And how, God's being just, does the sinner or criminal survive the sin or crime? By paying with his life in the here and now, so that at the resurrection, he may regain life, along with all Israel. That is why the climactic moment in the halakah comes at the end of the long catalog of those sins and crimes penalized with capital punishment. It is with ample reason that the Bavli, the Talmud of Babylonia, places at the conclusion and climax of its version the ringing declaration, "all Israel has a portion in the world to come, except . . ." And the exceptions pointedly do not include any of those listed in the long catalogs of persons executed for sins or crimes.

The sole exceptions, indeed, pertain to persons who classify themselves entirely outside of the criminal justice system: those who deny that the resurrection of the dead is a teaching of the Torah or (worse still) that the Torah does not come from God. Now, as we realize, these classes of persons hardly belong in the company of the sinners and criminals cataloged here. Then come specified individuals or groups: (1) three kings—Jeroboam, Ahab, and Manasseh—and (2) four ordinary folk—Balaam, Doeg, Ahithophel, and Gehazi—have no portion in the world to come. The standard trilogy follows, the generation of the flood, the generation of the dispersion, the generation of Sodom and Gomorrah. We note the difference between the individual who commits an act of idolatry and the entire community, the townsfolk of the apostate town, that does so; God punishes and forgives the individual, but not an entire generation, not an entire community. That is the point at which the criminal justice system completes its work.

That the two religious principles just now specified play a critical role in the formulation and presentation of the halakah of *Sanhedrin-Makkot* is made explicit in the context of legal exposition itself. The rite of stoning involves an admonition that explicitly declares the death penalty as the means of atoning for all crimes and sins, leaving the criminal blameless and welcome into the kingdom of heaven:

A. [When] he was ten cubits from the place of stoning, they say to him, "Confess," for it is usual for those about to be put to death to confess.

B. For whoever confesses has a share in the world to come.

C. For so we find concerning Achan, to whom Joshua said, "My son, I pray you, give glory to the LORD, the God of Israel, and confess to him, [and tell me now what you have done; hide it not from me]. And Achan answered Joshua and said, Truly have I sinned against the LORD, the God of Israel, and thus and thus I have done" (Josh. 7:19). And how do we know that his confession achieved atonement for him? For it is said, "And Joshua said, Why have you troubled us? The LORD will trouble you this day" (Josh. 7:25)—This day you will be troubled, but you will not be troubled in the world to come.

D. And if he does not know how to confess, they say to him, "Say as follows: 'Let my death be atonement for all of my transgressions.'" (*m. Sanh.* 6:2)

Within the very center of the halakic exposition comes the theological principle that the death penalty opens the way for life eternal. It follows that at stake in the tractate *Sanhedrin-Makkot* is a systematic demonstration of how God mercifully imposes justice upon sinners and criminals, and also of where the limits to God's mercy are reached: rejection of the Torah, the constitution of a collectivity—an "Israel"— that stands against God. God's merciful justice then pertains to private persons. But there can be only one Israel, and that Israel is made up of all those who look forward to a portion in the world to come: who will stand in justice and transcend death. In humanity, idolaters will not stand in judgment, and entire generations who sinned collectively as well as Israelites who broke off from the body of Israel and formed their own Israel do not enjoy that merciful justice that reaches full expression in the fate of Achan: he stole from God but shared the world to come. And so will all of those who have done the dreadful deeds cataloged here.

The upshot should not be missed. It is not merely that through the halakah at hand the sages make the statement that they make. I claim much more, specifically: the religious principle expressed here—God's perfect, merciful justice, correlated with the conviction of the eternity of holy Israel—cannot have come to systematic statement in any other area of the halakah. It is only in the present context that the sages can have linked God's perfect, merciful justice to the concrete life of ordinary Israel, and it is only here that they can have invoked the certainty of eternal life to explain the workings of merciful justice.

The sages insist that without mercy, justice cannot function. Now that we have seen how that statement is made in the halakah, let us explore some of the counterpart formulations of the same principle in the haggadah. God created the world with the attributes of mercy and justice so that in that complementary balance, the world might endure:

    A. "The Lord GOD [made earth and heaven]" (Gen. 2:4):

    B. The matter [of referring to the divinity by both the names, LORD, which stands for mercy, and God, which stands for justice] may be compared to the case of a king who had empty cups. The king said, "If I fill them with hot water, they will split. If I fill them with cold water, they will contract [and snap]."

    C. What did the king do? He mixed hot water and cold water and put it into them, and the cups withstood the liquid.

    D. So said the Holy One, blessed be he, "If I create the world in accord with the attribute of mercy, sins will multiply. If I create it in accord with the attribute of justice, the world cannot endure.

    E. "Lo, I shall create it with both the attribute of justice and the attribute of mercy, and may it endure!"

    F. "Thus: The Lord [standing for the attribute of mercy] GOD [standing for the attribute of justice] [made the earth and heavens]" (Gen. 2:4). (*Genesis Rabbah* XII:XV.1)

Just as too much justice will destroy the world, so too much mercy will ruin its coherence; each set of traits achieving complementarity must be shown, like dancers, to move in balance one with the other. Then and only then are excesses avoided, is stasis in motion attained. That brings about the world of justice at rest that the sages deemed God to have created in the beginning, to have celebrated on the original Sabbath, and to intend to restore in the end. But notice, when the haggadah makes its statement, it speaks in generalities, and, further, it addresses the world at large. It is the halakah that formulates the matter not only in specificities but well within the limits of holy Israel. Seeing how the halakah and the haggadah make the same statement, we once more see the way in which the halakah portrays the interiorities of Israelite life.

But there is more. The sages recognize that, in the setting of this life, the death penalty brings anguish, even though it assures the sinner or criminal expiation for what he has done. That matter is stated in so many words:

    A. Said R. Meir, "When a person is distressed, what words does the Presence of God say? As it were: 'My head is in pain, my arm is in pain'.

    B. "If thus is the Omnipresent distressed on account of the blood of the wicked when it is shed, how much the more so on account of the blood of the righteous!" (*m. Sanh.* 6:5)

God is distressed at the blood of the wicked, shed in expiation for sin or crime, so too humanity. So while the sages recognize the mercy and justice that are embodied in the sanctions they impose, they impute to God, and express in their own behalf, common sentiments and attitudes. They feel the same sentiments God does.

That fact alerts us to the fundamental principle embodied in the halakah: humanity is responsible for what it does, because humanity is like God. That is the basis for penalizing sins or crimes, but it also is the basis for the hope of eternal life for nearly all Israel—hope for eternal life in Eden. Like God, humanity is in command of, and responsible for, its own will and intentionality and consequent conduct. The very fact that God reveals himself through the Torah, which humanity is able to understand, there to be portrayed in terms and categories that humanity grasps, shows how the characteristics of God and humanity prove comparable. The first difference between humanity and God is that humanity sins, but the one and the just God, never; connecting God and sin yields an unintelligible result. And the second difference between creature and creator, humanity and God, is that God is God.

It is not an accident that in the setting of the category-formation of *Sanhedrin-Makkot,* the sages set forth how God's emotions correspond with humanity's. Like a parent faced with a recalcitrant child, God takes no pleasure in humanity's fall, but mourns. Not only so, but even while God protects those who love him, Israel, from his, and their, enemies, God takes to heart that he made all persons; he does not rejoice at the Sea when Israel is saved, because even then his enemies are perishing. This is said in so many words in the context of a discussion on whether God rejoices when the wicked perish:

> A. Therefore man was created alone (Gen. 4:5):
> B. "And there went out a song throughout the host" (1 Kings 22:36) [at Ahab's death at Ramoth in Gilead].
> C. Said R. Aha b. Hanina, "'When the wicked perish, there is song' (Prov. 11:10).
> D. "When Ahab, b. Omri, perished, there was song."

Does God sing and rejoice when the wicked perish? Not at all:

> E. But does the Holy One, blessed be he, rejoice at the downfall of the wicked?
> F. Is it not written, "That they should praise as they went out before the army and say, 'Give thanks to the LORD, for his mercy endures forever' (2 Chron. 20:21),

> G. and said R. Jonathan, "On what account are the words in this psalm of praise omitted, 'Because he is good'? Because the Holy One, blessed be he, does not rejoice at the downfall of the wicked."

Now we revert to the conduct of God at the very moment of Israel's liberation, when Israel sings the Song at the Sea:

> H. For R. Samuel bar Nahman said R. Jonathan said, "What is the meaning of the verse of Scripture [that speaks of Egypt and Israel at the sea], 'And one did not come near the other all night' (Exod. 14:20)?
> I. "At that time, the ministering angels want to recite a song [of rejoicing] before the Holy One, blessed be he.
> J. "Said to them the Holy One, blessed be he, 'The works of my hands are perishing in the sea, and do you want to sing a song before me?'"

Now the matter is resolved:

> K. Said R. Yosé bar Hanina, "He does not rejoice, but others do rejoice. Note that it is written, '[And it shall come to pass, as the LORD rejoiced over you to do good, so the LORD] will cause rejoicing over you by destroying you' (Deut. 28:63)—and not 'so will the LORD [himself] rejoice.'"
> L. That proves the case. (*b. Sanh.* 4:5 VI.1/39b)

God's emotions correspond, then, to those of a father or a mother, mourning at the downfall of their children, even though their children have rebelled against them. Even at the moment at which Israel first meets God, with God's act of liberation at the sea, God cannot join them in their song. In the sages' portrait, God weeps for the death of Israel's enemies. A more universalistic statement of monotheism is beyond all imagining.

Nonetheless, God and Israel then correspond, the eternal God in heaven, Israel on earth, also destined for eternal life. Israel forms on earth a society that corresponds to the retinue and court of God in heaven. The halakah in its way, in *Sanhedrin-Makkot,* says no less. But it makes the statement, as we have seen, in all of the intimacy and privacy of Israel's interior existence: when (in theory at least) Israel takes responsibility for its own condition. *Sanhedrin-Makkot,* devoted to the exposition of crime and just punishment, turns out to form an encompassing exercise in showing God's mercy, even or especially for the sinner or criminal who expiates the sin or crime: that concludes the transaction, but a great deal will follow it—and from it. Even the criminal and the sinner find their way to Eden. In the context of the Torah I cannot think of any other way of making that statement stick than through the halakah of *Sanhedrin-Makkot:* this sin, this punishment—and no more. That theology of atonement and reconciliation in eternal life in Eden, embodied in the halakah of *Sanhedrin-Makkot,* can have been made solely in the venue of the halakah of criminal justice.

Inside the Israelite Household:
Shabbat-'Erubin

The halakah of the Mishnah and Tosefta tractates *Shabbat* and *'Erubin* focuses upon the prohibition of transporting objects on the Sabbath from public to private domain. This is not a matter of labor, since trivial things are commonly at issue, a child's hair-ribbon, a woman's brooch, a man's sandal. The paramount question before us is, why do the sages devote their reading of the law of *Shabbat-'Erubin* above all to differentiating public from private domain? All of *'Erubin* and a fair component of *Shabbat* focus upon that matter, which stands at the head of the first of the two tractates and at the conclusion of the second, *'Erubin.* And, to revert to the halakah of *Shabbat* once more, the other principal focus, the definition of an act of labor that is culpable when performed on the Sabbath, defines yet another question that demands attention. Why do the sages formulate the principle that they do, that the act of labor prohibited on the Sabbath is one that fully constitutes a completed act of labor—beginning, middle, and end—in conformity with the intentionality of the actor? So the issues of the law of the Sabbath once more come to the fore in our inquiry into how the halakah formulates, out of the resources of the written part of the revealed Torah of Sinai, a statement bearing upon all the world.

The answer to both questions derives from the governing theology of the Sabbath. The written Torah represents the Sabbath as the climax of creation. The theology of the Sabbath put forth in the oral Torah's halakah derives from a systematization of definitions implicit in the myth of Eden that envelops the Sabbath in the account of Genesis. The sages' thinking about the Sabbath invokes in the formation of the normative law defining the matter the model of the first Sabbath, the one of Eden. The two paramount points of concern—(1) the systematic definition of private domain, where ordinary activity is permitted, and (2) the rather particular definition of what constitutes a prohibited act of labor on the Sabbath—precipitate deep thought and animate the handful of principles brought to concrete realization in the two tractates. "Thou shalt not labor" of the Commandments refers in a generic sense to all manner of work; but in the halakah of *Shabbat, labor* bears very particular meanings and is defined in a quite specific, and somewhat odd, manner. We can make sense of the halakah of *Shabbat-'Erubin* only by appeal to the story of creation, the governing metaphor derived therefrom, the sages' philosophical reflections that transform into principles of a general and universal character the details of the case at hand.

Given the broad range of possible points of halakic emphasis that the written Torah sustains—the dual formulation of matters in the Ten Commandments that make remarkably slight impact here, rest for animals and slaves playing no role in the articulation of the law, the focus on the rite of the day for the Day of Atonement and for Passover—we realize that the sages made choices. Why the stress on space and activity? When approaching the theme and problem of the Sabbath, they chose to answer two questions: what does it mean to remain "in his place" (Exod. 16:29) and what constitutes the theory of forbidden activity—that is, what principles that shape the innumerable rules and facts of the prohibition? Accordingly, we must ask a basic question: what is it about the Sabbath of creation that captures the sages' attention?

We work back from the large structures of the halakah to the generative thought—how the sages thought, and about what they thought—that gives definition to those structures. And, among available formulations, clearly they gave priority to the creation story of Gen. 1:1—2:3, which accounts for the origin of the Sabbath. As we shall see, the foci of their thinking turn out to locate themselves in what is implicit and subject to generalization in that story. The halakah turns out to realize in detailed, concrete terms generalizations that the sages locate in and derive from the story of creation. And what they find is a metaphor for themselves and their Israel, on the one side, and the foundation for generalization, out of the metaphor, in abstract terms susceptible to acute concretization, on the other. That is to say, the Sabbath of Eden forms the model: like this, so all else. And the sages, with their remarkable power to think in general terms but to convey thought in examples and details, found it possible to derive from the model the principles that would accomplish their goal: linking Israel to Eden through the Sabbath, the climax of their way of life, the soul of their theological system. The halakah thereby formulates Sabbath law in terms pertinent to the whole of creation, once more a universalistic focus.

Our task, then, is first of all to identify the halakah that best states in detail some of the principles that the sages derived from their reading of the story of the Genesis of Eden. Building on the definition supplied by that halakah that supplies to the Sabbath its program of legislation—the things subjected to acute exegesis, the things treated as other than generative—we may then undertake to construct an encompassing theory to find a position, within a single framework, for all of the principal halakic constructions at hand. Clearly, the halakah of *'Erubin* is not the place, since that body of halakah takes for granted layers of profound thought and speculation that have already supplied foundations for the matter at hand. Nor, for the same reason, will the halakah of *Shabbat* help, for its framers know as established principles a set of conceptions, for example, about the definition of forbidden activity, that presuppose much but articulate, in this context, remarkably little. Accordingly, when it comes to decoding the sages' reading of the story of creation culminating in the Sabbath of Eden, there is no reading the halakah of *Shabbat* or of *'Erubin* out of the context of the Sabbath as the sages defined that context.

If in *Shabbat* the sages know that the division of the world, on the Sabbath, into public and private domain precipitates the massive exegetical task undertaken both there and in *'Erubin,* and they further have in mind a powerful definition of the meaning of an act of labor—of what labor consists—those facts on their own give little direction. For neither *Shabbat* nor *'Erubin* defines its context; both presuppose analogies and metaphors that are not articulated but constantly present. Only when we know what is supposed to take place on the Sabbath—in particular in the model of the Sabbath that originally celebrated creation—to the exclusion of the model of the Sabbath that would focus the halakah upon the liberation of slaves from Egypt (Deuteronomy's version) or the cessation of labor of the household, encompassing animals and slaves (Exodus's version)—only then shall we find the key to the entire matter of the Sabbath of the halakah of the oral Torah. Then we may identify the setting in which the rules before us take on meaning and prove to embody profound religious thinking.

I find the halakah that presents the model of how the sages think about the Sabbath and accounts for the topical program of their thought—the fully articulated source of the governing metaphor—is *Shebi'it.* That tractate describes the observance of the Sabbath that is provided every seventh year for the land of Israel itself. The land celebrates the Sabbath, and then, Israel in its model. The land is holy, as Israel is holy, and the Priestly Code leaves no doubt that for both, the Sabbath defines the rhythm of life with God: the seventh day for Israel, the seventh year for the land. For both, moreover, to keep the Sabbath is to be like God. And, specifically, that is when God had completed the work of creation, pronounced it good, sanctified it—imposed closure and permanence, the creation having reached its conclusion. God observed the Sabbath, which itself finds its definition as the celebration and commemoration of God's own action. This is what God did, this is what we now do. What God did concerned creation, what we do concerns creation. And all else follows. The Sabbath then precipitates the imitation of God on a very particular occasion and for a very distinctive purpose. And given what we have identified as the sages' governing theology—the systematic account of God's perfect justice in creation, yielding an account and explanation of all else—we find ourselves at the very center of the system. The meeting of time and space on the seventh day of creation—God having formed space and marked time—finds its counterpart in the ordering of Israelite space at the advent of time, the ordering of that space through the action and inaction of the Israelites themselves.

In stating what I think is at stake, I have gotten ahead of my story. Since I have established that the traits that the Sabbath precipitates for the land guide us in our interpretation of the considerations that govern the rules of *Shabbat-'Erubin* but do not suffice to place into context those rules and their principles, where do we turn? It is to the halakah of *Shebi'it,* and I shall now explain why.

To state matters very simply, *'Erubin,* with its sustained exercise of thought on the commingling of ownership of private property for the purpose of Sabbath observance and on the commingling of meals to signify shared ownership, accomplishes for Israel's Sabbath what *Shebi'it* achieves for the land's. On the Sabbath inaugurated by the sabbatical year the land, so far as it is otherwise private property, no longer is possessed exclusively by the householder. So too, the produce of the land consequently belongs to everybody. It follows that the halakah of *'Erubin* realizes for the ordinary Sabbath of Israel the very same principles that are embodied in the halakah of *Shebi'it.* That halakah defines the Sabbath of the land in exactly the same terms: the land is now no longer private, and the land's produce belongs to everybody. The Sabbath that the land enjoys marks the advent of shared ownership of the land and its fruit. Sharing is so total that hoarding is explicitly forbidden, and what has been hoarded has now to be removed from the household and moved to public domain, where anyone may come and take it.

Here we find the Sabbath of creation overspreading the Sabbath of the land, as the Priestly Code at Genesis 1 and at Lev. 25:1-8 define matters. The latter states,

When you enter the land that I am giving you, the land shall observe a Sabbath of the LORD. Six years you may sow your field and six years you may prune your vineyard and gather in the yield. But in the seventh year the land shall have a Sabbath of complete rest, a Sabbath of the LORD; you shall not sow your field or prune your vineyard. You shall not reap the aftergrowth of your harvest or gather the grapes of your untrimmed vines; it shall be a year of complete rest for the land. But you may eat whatever the land during its Sabbath will produce—you, your male and female slaves, the hired-hand and bound laborers who live with you, and your cattle and the beasts in your land may eat all its yield.

The sabbatical year bears the message, therefore, that on the Sabbath, established arrangements as to ownership and possession are set aside, and a different conception of private property takes over. What on ordinary days is deemed to belong to the householder and to be subject to his exclusive will on the Sabbath falls into a more complex web of possession. The householder continues to use his property but not as a proprietor does. He gives up exclusive access thereto, and gains in exchange rights of access to other people's property. Private property is commingled; everybody shares in everybody's. The result is that private property takes on a new meaning, different from the secular one. So far as the householder proposes to use his private property, he must share it with others, who do the same for him. To own then is to abridge ownership in favor of commingling rights thereto, to possess is to share. And that explains why the produce of the land belongs to everyone as well, a corollary to the fundamental postulate of the Sabbath of the land.

Now the halakah of *Shebi'it* appeals to the metaphor of Eden, and, along those same lines, if we wish to understand how the sages thought about the Sabbath, we have here to follow suit. But that is hardly to transgress the character of the evidence in hand, the story of the first Sabbath as the celebration of the conclusion and perfection of creation itself. Since, accordingly, the Sabbath commemorates the sanctification of creation, we cannot contemplate Sabbath observance outside of the framework of its generative model, which is Eden. What the sages add in the halakah of the oral Torah becomes self-evident: Eden provides the metaphor for imagining the land of Israel, and the Sabbath, the occasion for the act of metaphorization.

The hermeneutics in hand, the exegesis of the halakah becomes possible. Specifically, we have found the governing question to which the details of the law respond—specifically, what is it about Eden on the Sabbath that defines the governing metaphor that the principles of the halakah work themselves out of in the articulation of acute details that our halakah yields. Working back from the details to the organizing topics, and from the topics to the principles that govern, we find ourselves able to frame the right question.

It is, what qualities of Eden impress the sages? With the halakah as the vast corpus of facts, we focus upon two matters: (1) time and space, (2) time and activity. How is space demarcated at the specified time; how is activity classified at that same time? The former works itself out in a discussion of where people may move on the Sabbath and how they may conduct themselves (carry things as they move). The latter finds its definition in the model of labor that is prohibited. With Eden as the model and the metaphor, we take a simple sighting on the matter. First, Adam and Eve are free to move in Eden where they wish, possessing all they contemplate. God has given it to them to enjoy. If Eden then belongs to God, he freely shares ownership with Adam and Eve. And— all the more so—the produce of Eden is ownerless. With the well-known exception, all the fruit is theirs for the taking. So we find ourselves deep within the halakah of *Shebi'it*. For, as we saw above, the halakah of *Shebi'it* sets forth in concrete terms what is implicit in the character of Eden. In the sabbatical year the land returns to the condition characteristic of Eden at the outset: shared and therefore accessible, its produce available to all.

It is in this context that we turn to the halakah of *Shabbat-'Erubin*, with special reference to the division of the world into private and public domain, the former the realm of permitted activity on the Sabbath, the latter not. If we may deal with an *'erub* fence or an *'erub* meal, how are we to interpret what is at stake in these matters? In both instances it is to render private domain public through the sharing of ownership. The *'erub* fence for its part renders public domain private, but only in the same sense that private domain owned by diverse owners is shared, ownership being commingled. The *'erub* fence signals the formation for purposes of the sanctification of time of private domain—but with the ownership commingled. So what is private about private domain is different on the Sabbath from in secular time. By definition, for property to be private in the setting of the Sabbath, it must be shared among householders. On the Sabbath, domain that is totally private, its ownership not commingled for the occasion, becomes a prison, the householder being unable to conduct himself in the normal manner in the courtyard beyond his door, let alone in other courtyards in the same alleyway, or in other alleyways that lead onto the same street. And the halakah, as we have seen, makes provision for those—whether Israelite or gentile—who do not offer the proprietorship of their households for commingling for the Sabbath.

What happens, therefore, through the *'erub* fence or *'erub* meal is the redefinition of proprietorship: what is private is no longer personal, and no one totally owns what is his, but then everyone (who wishes to participate, himself and his household together) owns a share everywhere. So much for the "in his place" part of "each person in his place." "His place" constitutes an area where ordinary life goes on, but it is no longer "his" in the way in which the land is subject to his will and activity in ordinary time. If constructing a fence serves to signify joint ownership of the village, now turned into private domain, or constructing the gateway, of the alleyway and its courtyards, what about the meal? The *'erub* meal signifies the shared character of what is eaten. It is food that belongs to all who wish to share it. But it is the provision of a personal meal, also, that allows an individual to designate for himself a place of Sabbath residence other than the household to which he belongs.

So the Sabbath loosens bonds, those of the householder to his property, those of the individual to the household. It forms communities, the householders of a courtyard into a community of shared ownership of the entire courtyard, the individual into a community other than that formed by the household to which he belongs—now the community of disciples of a given sage, the community of a family other than that in residence in the household, to use two of the examples common in the halakah. Just as the Sabbath redefines ownership of the land and its produce, turning all Israelites into a single social entity, "all Israel," which, all together, possesses the land in common ownership, so the Sabbath redefines the social relationships of the household, allowing persons to separate themselves from the residence of the household and designate some other, some personal, point of residence instead.

The main point of the law of private domain in *Shabbat* and *'Erubin* seen in the model of *Shebi'it* then is to redefine the meaning of *private domain,* where each man is to remain in his place. The law aims to define the meaning of *his* and to remove the ownership of the land and its produce from the domain of a householder, rendering ownership public and collective. Taking as our model *Shebi'it,* we note that in the year that is a Sabbath, the land is held to be owned by nobody and everybody, and the produce of the land belongs to everyone and no one, so that one may take and eat but thank only God. It is no one's, so everyone may take; it is everyone's, so everyone may eat, and God alone is to be acknowledged. Since, on the Sabbath, people are supposed to remain within their own domain, the counterpart to *Shebi'it* will provide for the sharing of ownership, thus for extending the meaning of private domain to encompass all the partners in a shared locus. Private domain, his place, now bears a quite different meaning from the one that pertains in profane time. The Sabbath recapitulates the condition of Eden, when Adam and Eve could go where they wished and eat what they wanted, masters of all they contemplated, along with God. Israel on the Sabbath in the land, like Adam on the Sabbath of Eden that celebrates creation, shares private domain and its produce.

Israel on the Sabbath in the land like God on the Sabbath of Eden rests from the labor of creation. And that brings us to the question: what about that other principle of the Sabbath, the one set forth by the halakah of *Shabbat?* The richly detailed halakah of *Shabbat* defines the matter in a prolix, yet simple way: on the Sabbath it is prohibited deliberately to carry out in a normal way a completed act of constructive labor, one that produces enduring results, one that carries out one's entire intention—the whole of what one planned, one has accomplished, in exactly the proper manner. That definition takes into account the shank of the halakah of *Shabbat* as set forth in the Mishnah tractate, and the amplification and extension of matters in the Tosefta and the two Talmuds in no way revises the basic principles. Here there is a curious, if obvious, fact: it is not an act of labor that itself is prohibited (as the Ten Commandments in Exodus and Deuteronomy would have it), but an act of labor of a very particular definition.

No prohibition impedes performing an act of labor in an other-than-normal way. In theory, one may go out into the fields and plow, if he does so in some odd manner. He may build an entire house, so long as it collapses promptly. The issue of activity on the Sabbath therefore is removed from the obvious context of work, conventionally defined. Now the activity that is forbidden is of a very particular sort, modeled in its indicative traits after a quite specific paradigm. A person is not forbidden to carry out an act of destruction or an act of labor that produces no lasting consequences. One may start an act of labor if one does not complete it. One may accomplish an act of labor in some extraordinary manner. None of these acts of labor is forbidden, even though, done properly and with consequence, each represents a massive violation of the halakah. Nor is part of an act of labor that is not brought to conclusion prohibited. Nor is it forbidden to perform part of an act of labor in partnership with another person who carries out the other requisite part. Nor does one incur culpability for performing an act of labor in several distinct parts, for example, over a protracted, differentiated period of time. A person may not willingly carry out the entirety of an act of constructive labor, start to finish. The issue is not why not, since we know the answer: God has said not to do so. The question is, whence the particular definition at hand?

Clearly, a definition of the act of labor that is prohibited on the Sabbath has taken over and recast the commonsense meaning of the commandment not to labor on the Sabbath. For considerations enter that recast matters from an absolute to a relative definition. One may tie a knot—but not one that stands. One may carry a package, but not in the usual manner. One may build a wall, only if it falls down. And one may do pretty much anything without penalty—if one did not intend matters as they actually happened. The metaphor of God in Eden, as the sages have reflected on the story of creation, yields the governing principles that define forbidden labor. What God did in the six days of creation provides the model.

Let us review the main principles. They involve the three preconditions: (1) the act must fully carry out the intention of the actor, as creation carried out God's intention; (2) the act of labor must be carried out by a single actor, as God acted alone in creating the world; (3) an act of labor is like one that is required in the building and maintenance of God's residence in this world, the tabernacle. The act of labor prohibited on the Sabbath involves two considerations: (1) the act must be done in the ordinary way, just as Scripture's account leaves no doubt God accomplished creation in the manner in which he accomplished his goals from creation onward, by an act of speech; and, (2) weightier still, the forbidden act of labor is one that produces enduring consequences. God did not create only to destroy, but he created the enduring world. And it goes without saying, creation yielded the obvious consequences that the act was completely done in all ways, as God himself declared. The act was one of consequence, involving what was not negligible but what humanity and God alike deemed to make a difference. The sages would claim, therefore, that the activity that must cease on the Sabbath finds its definition in the model of those actions that God carried out in making the world.

That such a mode of thought is more than a mere surmise, based on the congruence of the principles by which labor forbidden on the Sabbath spin themselves out of the creation story, emerges when we recall a striking statement. It is the one that finds the definition of forbidden labor in those activities required for the construction and maintenance of the tabernacle, which is to say, God's residence on earth. The best statement, predictably, is the Bavli's:

People are liable only for classifications of labor the like of which was done in the tabernacle. They sowed, so you are not to sow. They harvested, so you are not to harvest. They lifted up the boards from the ground to the wagon, so you are not to lift them in from public to private domain. They lowered boards from the wagon to the ground, so you must not carry anything from private to public domain. They transported boards from wagon to wagon, so you must not carry from one private domain to another. (*b. Shab.* 4:2 I.4/49B)

The sages found in the analogy of how, in theory, the tabernacle was maintained, the classifications of labor that pertain. In the tabernacle these activities are permitted, even on the Sabbath. In God's house, the priests and Levites must do for God what they cannot do for themselves—and the identification of acts of labor forbidden on the Sabbath follows.

The details of the halakah then emerge out of a process in which two distinct sources contribute. One is the model of the tabernacle. What individuals may do for God's house they may not do for their own—God is always God, the Israelite aspires only to be "like God," to imitate God, and that is a different thing. The other is the model of the creation of the world and of Eden. Hence to act like God on the Sabbath, the Israelite rests; he does not do what God did in creation. The former source supplies generative metaphors, the like of which may not be done; thus acts such as sowing, harvesting, lifting boards from public to private domain, and the like, are forbidden. The latter source supplies the generative principles, the abstract definitions involving the qualities of perfection and causation: intentionality, completion, the normality of the conduct of the action, and the like. The mode of analogical thinking governs, but a double metaphor pertains, the metaphor of God's activity in creation, the metaphor of the priests' and Levites' activity in the tabernacle. Creation yields those large principles that we have identified: the traits of an act of labor for God in creation define the prohibited conditions of an act of labor on the Sabbath. By appeal to those two metaphors, we can account for every detail of the halakah.

What then takes place inside the walls of the Israelite household when time takes over space and revises the conduct of ordinary affairs? Israel goes home to Eden. How best to make the statement that the land is Israel's Eden, that Israel imitates God by keeping the Sabbath, meaning, not doing the things that God did in creating the world but ceased to do on the Sabbath, and that to restore its Eden, Israel must sustain its life—nourish itself—where it belongs? To set forth those most basic convictions about God in relationship to humanity and about Israel in relationship to God, I can imagine no more eloquent, no more compelling and appropriate, medium of expression than the densely detailed halakah of *Shebi'it, Shabbat,* and *'Erubin.* Indeed, outside of the setting of the household, its ownership, use, and maintenance, I cannot think of any other way of fully making that statement stick. In theory implausible for its very simplicity (as much as for its dense instantiation!), in halakic fact, compelling, the oral Torah's statement accounts for the human condition. Israel's Eden takes place in the household open to others, on the Sabbath, in acts that maintain life, share wealth, and desist from creation.

The key words, therefore, are in the shift from the here and now of time in which one works like God, to the then and there when one desists from working, just as God did at the moment the world was finished, perfected, and sanctified. Israel gives up the situation of humanity in ordinary time and space, destructive, selfish, dissatisfied, and doing. Then, on the Sabbath, and there, in the household, with each one in place, Israel enters the situation of God in that initial, that perfected and sanctified then and there of creation: the activity that consists in sustaining life, sharing dominion, and perfecting repose through acts of restraint and sufficiency.

What These Cases Tell Us

These cases show how the halakah universalizes the particular, invoking Eden to govern the land, Adam to deal with Israel. In the cases provided here we have seen how Israel relates to God in the encounter of enlandisement, where Israel takes its place in the land of Israel and confronts its relationship with God in the very terms of the creation, when Adam takes his place in Eden, with catastrophic results. But now, Israel, entering the land, shows how, regenerate, the Israelite realizes repentance, confronting the occasion of the original sin but responding in obedience rather than rebellion as at the outset. Israel in the land moreover reconstructs Eden by recapitulating creation and its requirements. All of this takes on detail and forms a cogent and compelling statement through the halakah. The halakah must respond to issues posed by the monotheism of justice (1) to Israel's relationships with God when these relationships do take place within Israel's own frame of reference; (2) to Israelites' relationships with one another; and (3) to the interior life of the individual Israelite household[8] on its own, with God.

Here is how the particular embodies and exposes the universal, the halakah realizing the haggadah. The most universal message of Scripture, concerning the creation of nature and the place of humanity therein, frames the most particular requirements for correctly marking time, celebrating creation on the seventh day, as Scripture says. For the three cases we have considered, only through the particularities of the halakah did the sages find it possible to speak to humanity as God does, which is to say, through Scripture: only through *Shebi'it,* only through *Sanhedrin,* only through *Shabbat-'Erubin.* When we take up each of the native categories of the halakah in succession and identify not only the message but the reason for delivering the message through the specificities at hand, we understand the Judaism set forth through the halakah—both the religion and its theology—in their universal recasting of particulars.[9]

4. The Narrative-Exegetical Medium: Paradigmatic Thinking

Scripture's Narratives and Laws: Governing Principles of the Social Order

In the written Torah the sages inherited a very particular document, a story to be received as an account of a single nation and how it got and lost its land and could get it back and keep it. I cannot imagine a more particularistic, localized, and ethnic story than that. Then how was that unpromising tale shaped into a tale transcending the narrow limits of ethnicity? Singular events of local significance to be sure are transformed into a theological proposition, for example, by the prophets. But there was a more profound approach to the thought-problem before us.

To understand the Rabbinic sages' universalization of Scripture's narratives into exemplary accounts of the human condition, we begin with that with which they worked: Scripture itself. In its historical interpretation of the story of Israel, by cutting the present off from the past, organizing experience in a single, linear pattern of cause and effect, and focusing upon a distinct time and place, Scripture certainly does not invite a universalistic reading. Memory particularizes, and "our" past by its nature does not invite others to join in *post facto*. For receiving Scripture historically particularizes and localizes its persons, events, and cumulative message. In privileging Israel, it is then, as Dunn would have it, an "attempt to mark off some of God's people as more holy than others, as exclusive channels of divine grace."[1] That is certainly the Christian and Islamic charge against the Judaism portrayed by Scripture and recast into a model of the social order by the Rabbinic sages who received and formed Scripture into Judaism.

Rather, the sages shaped a way of receiving Scripture that transcended the local and particular by transforming the singular into the exemplary. Here we shall trace the way in which they subverted particular history into paradigmatic philosophy, and in the next chapter we shall follow the universalistic messages that that philosophy yielded. What we see is how the Rabbinic sages took a way different from the historical mode of presenting theology that characterizes Scripture from Genesis through Kings, encompassing also prophecy. In the oral Torah the sages reveal the perfection of world order through an other-than-historical mode of thought. Asking Scripture to supply the facts, the sages perceived the governing rules, the patterns that pertained to all humanity as much as do the laws of gravity or of cause and effect. They organized experience through a mode of thought I call pattern-seeking or paradigmatic, a way of identifying enduring patterns to account for how things were, are, or will be, rather than of appealing to the sequence of unique happenings—first came this, then came that—to say why the present is what it is. And these patterns or paradigms by their nature generalize beyond ethnic limits and therefore encompass the diverse experience of humanity wherever situated or of whatever origin.

Judaism Rejects Historical Thinking

To begin with, the sages explicitly reject the ordering of events historically: first this, then that, therefore this caused that. They deemed merely adventitious the sequence of events, judging as illogical the proposition that merely because one thing happened before another, therefore the prior thing caused the other (*post hoc ergo propter hoc*). Rather, they sought connections between events, patterns yielded by events of a given classification and circumstance: the laws of the social order, not the exceptional events.

Here is the one critical point at which the sages in the oral Torah part company from the written Torah, so far as people deem the written Torah to make its statement through historical narrative, as conventionally understood. Scripture narrated history in temporal sequence. The Rabbinic sages of Judaism discerned patterns in that history and identified social laws to explain those patterns. In our terms, the sages were not historians but social philosophers, in their context, social scientists. And in that context, it is entirely proper to see their formulation of events as patterns universally pertinent. For out of Scripture they derived rules that pertain to everyone everywhere, in due course.

In the sages' world beyond time as historically understood, we deal with a realm in which the past is ever present, the present a recapitulation and reformulation of the past, and the future embedded in the here and now. To understand their mode of thought requires the effort to abandon what, in our time and circumstance, is the given of social explanation: appeal to history. But history's time is rigidly differentiated into past, present, and future, and history's events are linear and sequential. History may yield patterns, but history by its particularity also violates those patterns.

Now consider the sages' view of time and paradigm. When people recapitulate the past in the present, and when they deem the future to be no different from the remote long ago and far-away, they organize and interpret experience in a framework that substitutes patterns of enduring permanence for models of historical change. Instead of history with its one time, unique events to be read in a singular manner, thought proceeds through the explanation of paradigms, events being recast as exemplars, then interpreted by the criterion of the likenesses or unlikenesses of things set forth in an original and generative pattern. That is why the familiar modes of classifying noteworthy events, the long ago and the here and now, lose currency. Universal paradigms govern instead, against which all things—now, then, anytime—are compared. That is why events lose all specificity and particularity: they supply mere examples for testing a universal rule.

The Modes of Paradigmatic Thinking

The oral Torah formulates its conception of world order in enduring paradigms that admit no distinction between past, present, and future. All things take form in a single plane of being; Israel lives not in historical time, moving from a beginning, to a middle, to an end, in a linear plan through a sequence of unique events. Nor does it form its existence in cyclical time, repeating time and again familiar cycles of events. Those familiar modes of making sense out of the chaos of change and the passage of time serve not at all. Appealing to a world of timeless permanence that takes shape in permanent patterns, the oral Torah accounts for how things are not by appeal to what was and what will be, but by invoking the criterion of what characterizes the authentic and true being of Israel, represented in cosmic and transcendent terms involving all humanity, for example, in the persons of Adam and Eve.

Paradigms respond to the question, if not change in linear sequence of unique events then what? The pattern that controls recapitulates the paradigmatic lives of the patriarchs and matriarchs, or the tale of Eden and Adam, or the story of Israel and the land, or the model of the temple built, destroyed, and rebuilt, to take principal sources of paradigmatic construction. Therein the sages find the models of the perfection of a changeless world, governed by a set of established patterns. Here history gives way to not eternity but permanence, the rules of the paradigm telling us not how to make sense of what was or how to predict what will be, but only what it is that counts. It is this conception of a timeless perfection, attained at the beginning, restored at the end, that accounts for the sages' design for death, resurrection, judgment, and the world to come.

Paradigmatic thinking, and the particular paradigms at hand, frame a world order that is fully realized and stable, a world beyond the vagaries of time and locality. Guided by the story of creation, the sages, like philosophers, conceived order to require a world at rest. Perfection entailed stasis, all things in place in a timeless realm of stability. So they thought about past, present, and future in a manner different from the familiar historical one. To the sages, then, change marked by linear time signified imperfection, a symptom that things continue in an incomplete process of realization, falling short of realizing their goal. In a completed state of order, the balanced exchanges of justice set the norm. All things in place and proportion, each will have achieved its purpose.

In this world of stasis, governed by propositions of a uniform and ubiquitous reason, people meet in a timeless plane of eternity. They are able to exchange thoughts, conduct debates, without regard to considerations of anachronism. It is a shared logic that makes possible their encounter in debate. Throughout the oral Torah, the sages construct conversations between people of widely separated periods of history; and they moreover insert on their own conversations that, by their reason, people ought to have had. Indeed, the formidable proportion of the documents that is taken up by fabricated dialogue attests to one prevailing assumption: reason is timeless, right thinking transcends circumstance, therefore, whenever or wherever people lived, they can confront one another's ideas and sort out their differences by appeal to a common mode of thought and a shared rationality. Paradigmatic thinking then comes to expression every time a sage tells a story with an ample selection of what "he said to him . . . he said to him . . . ," indeed, at every occasion at which a sage imputes a speech to God himself. All of this forms the consequence of that timeless, perfect world that the sages find in Scripture and propose in their setting to recapitulate as well. That is only possible, only conceivable, when time stands still.

How to Find Paradigms

Accordingly, a just order attains perfection—an even and proportionate balance prevailing—and therefore does not change. To the sages, the entire Torah, oral and written, portrayed a world that began in perfection at rest, an eternal Sabbath, but then changed by reason of sin. The world preserved within itself the potentiality of restoration to a state of rest. The halakic message has already shown us how the truly orderly world is represented by the Sabbath, when God completed creation and sanctified it in its perfection. The weekly Sabbath, celebrating creation perfected and accordingly at rest, thus affords a foretaste of the world to come, one sixtieth of the Garden of Eden that awaits, the Talmud says.

In the oral Torah the concept of history, coming to expression in the categories of time and change, along with distinctions between past, present, and future, therefore surrenders to an altogether different way of conceiving time and change as well as the course of noteworthy, even memorable social events. The past takes place in the present. The present embodies the past. And there is no indeterminate future over the horizon, only a clear and present path within a different paradigm, one to be chosen if people will it. With distinctions between past, present, and future time found to make no difference, and in their stead, different categories of meaning and social order deemed self-evident, the oral Torah transforms ancient Israel's history into the categorical structure of eternal Israel's society, so that past, present, and future meet in the here and now. Two basic propositions defined the sages' doctrine of time and change, one negative, the other positive.

First comes the negative. To the sages time is neither linear nor cyclical but unremarkable, that is, a minor detail, a contingency. Time subject to a paradigm yields a pattern that differentiates one period from some other. Events removed from linear, sequential time, bear their own, other-than-time-bound signification of the meaning and consequence of a given period. Thinking through paradigms, with a conception of time that elides past and present and removes all barriers between them, in fact governs the reception of the written Torah by the oral Torah. Before proceeding, let me give a single instance (from Mishnah tractate *Zebahim*) of how a paradigm forms the medium for interpreting time as contingent and merely notional:

> 14:4   A. Before the tabernacle was set up, (1) the high places were permitted, and (2) [the sacrificial] service [was done by] the first born [Num. 3:12-13, 8:16-18].

B. When the tabernacle was set up, (1) the high places were prohibited, and (2) the [sacrificial] service [was done by] priests.

C. Most Holy Things were eaten within the veils, Lesser Holy Things [were eaten] throughout the camp of Israel.

Now comes the next stage, incidentally sequential, but essentially differentiated not by sequence but by other indicators altogether:

14:5   A. They came to Gilgal.

B. The high places were permitted.

C. Most Holy Things were eaten within the veils, Lesser Holy Things, anywhere,

The paradigmatic indicators remain the same, the details now shift:

14:6   A. They came to Shiloh.

B. The high places were prohibited.

C. (1) There was no roof-beam there, but below was a house of stone, and hangings above it, and (2) it was "the resting place"[Deut. 12:9].

D. Most Holy Things were eaten within the veils, Lesser Holy Things and second tithe [were eaten] in any place within sight [of Shiloh],

The same pattern applies once more, the data of the cult being organized not sequentially but essentially:

14:7   A. They came to Nob and Gibeon.

B. The high places were permitted.

C. Most Holy Things were eaten within the veils, Lesser Holy Things, in all the towns of Israel.

Now comes the last realization of the paradigm, marked as final by its own essential traits:

14:8   A. They came to Jerusalem.

B. The high places were prohibited.

C. And they never again were permitted.

D. And it was "the inheritance" [Deut. 12:9].

E. Most Holy Things were eaten within the veils, Lesser Holy Things and second tithe within the wall. (*m. Zebah.* 14:4-8)

Here time is divided by the periods divided by indicative traits of the cult. The first division is before and after the tabernacle, the second is marked by Gilgal, then Shiloh, then Nob-Gibeon, and finally Jerusalem, which is the end time. The consequence of dividing time concerns the conduct of the sacrificial service and the character of its location, the definition of the officiating authorities, and the like. In this paradigm, as in any other, one-time events bear no consequence on their own; sequences of linear events lead nowhere; and, most important, the radical division of time into past, present, and future simply does not apply. The past is before the tabernacle, and the future is Jerusalem in timeless eternity.

How Paradigms Replace Historical Time

To extend the matter of how a paradigm replaces historical time, we see how the sages recognized no barrier between present and past. To them, the present and past formed a single unit of time, encompassing a single span of experience. That is why the liturgy, too, can say, "In all generations an Israelite is to regard himself as if he too were redeemed from Egypt" (Passover haggadah). Why was that so? It is because, to them, times past took place in the present too, on which account, the present not only encompassed the past (which historical thinking concedes) but took place in the same plane of time as the past (which, to repeat, historical thinking rejects as unintelligible). Why? It is because the sages experienced the past in the present. What happened that mattered had already happened; an event then was transformed into a series; events themselves defined paradigms, yielded rules. A simple formulation of this mode of thought from Mishnah tractate *Ta'anit* is as follows:

> A. Five events took place for our fathers on the seventeenth of Tammuz, and five on the ninth of Ab.
> B. On the seventeenth of Tammuz
>> (1) the tablets [of the Torah] were broken,
>> (2) the daily whole offering was cancelled,
>> (3) the city wall was breached,
>> (4) Apostemos burned the Torah, and
>> (5) he set up an idol in the temple.
> C. On the ninth of Ab
>> (1) the decree was made against our forefathers that they should not enter the land,
>> (2) the first temple and
>> (3) the second [temple] were destroyed,
>> (4) Betar was taken, and
>> (5) the city was plowed up [after the war of Hadrian].
> D. When Ab comes, rejoicing diminishes. *(m. Ta'an. 4:6)*

We mark time by appeal to the phases of the moon; these then may be characterized by traits shared in common—and so the paradigm, from marking time, moves outward to the formation of rules concerning the regularity and order of events.

In the formulation just now given, we see the movement from event to rule. What is important about events is not their singularity but their capacity to generate a pattern, a concrete rule for the here and now. That is the conclusion drawn from the very passage at hand:

> A. In the week in which the ninth of Ab occurs it is prohibited to get a haircut and to wash one's clothes.
> B. But on Thursday of that week these are permitted,
> C. because of the honor owing to the Sabbath.
> D. On the eve of the ninth of Ab a person should not eat two prepared dishes, nor should one eat meat or drink wine.
> E. Rabban Simeon b. Gamaliel says, "He should make some change from ordinary procedures."
> F. R. Judah declares people liable to turn over beds.
> G. But the sages did not concur with him. (*m. Ta'an.* 4:7)

Events serve to define paradigms and therefore, also, to yield rules governing the here and now: what we do to recapitulate. Here is how diverse events are shown to fall into a single category, so adhere to the same rule, thus forming a paradigm through the shared indicative traits, but then losing that very specificity that history requires for events to make sense.

Past and Present

The past is ever present. But the present takes place in the past. When we speak of the pastness of the present, we describe the consciousness of people who could open Scripture and find themselves right there, in its record. They found themselves present in not only Lamentations, but also prophecy, and, especially, in the books of the Torah. Here we deal not with the spiritualization of Scripture, but with the acutely contemporary and immediate realization of Scripture. That meant reading Scripture in the present day, the present day into Scripture. To generalize: unlike the mode of telling time familiar in the secular West, which distinguishes present from past and future, for the sages time is not marked off in a sequence of singular, unique, one-time events. Rather, time forms an entity—like space, like food, like classes of persons, like everything—that is, an entity meant to be differentiated and classified, hierarchized. The world perfected and at rest does not tell time through an account of what came first and then what happened, a clock that measures the movement of time and change. Therefore history, with its clear division established between past, present, and future, linked through sequences of singular events, does not apply. Rather, the sages defined the world by ages or periods, with no link to sequential division of past, present, and future but rather differentiated by indicative traits. Events exemplify indicative traits of the social order in relationship to God.

What, then, of the narrative of Scripture, particularly the authorized history, Genesis through Kings, which bears the traits of history as defined in a secular way: past, present, future, the changing aspects of one-time linear and sequential events teaching lessons of history? Considerations of temporal sequence play no role in the Torah. That statement, in so many words, demonstrated by the usual assembly of probative cases, simply dismisses the historical mode of thought as irrelevant to Scripture (as philosophers would find it irrelevant to natural history, as social scientists draw their data from widely separated times and places):

I.1. A. "The enemy said, ['I will pursue, I will overtake, I will divide the spoil, my desire shall have its fill of them. I will draw my sword, my hand shall destroy them]:'"

   B. This [statement was made] at the outset of the sequence of events, and why then was it stated here?

   C. It is because considerations of temporal sequence play no role in the Torah.

2. A. Along these same lines: "And it came to pass on the eighth day that Moses called" (Lev. 9:1).

   B. This [statement was made] at the outset of the sequence of events, and why then was it stated here?

   C. It is because considerations of temporal sequence play no role in the Torah.

3. A. Along these same lines: "In the year that king Uzziah died" (Isa. 6:1).

   B. This [statement was made] at the outset of the sequence of events, and why then was it stated here?

   C. It is because considerations of temporal sequence play no role in the Torah.

4. A. Along these same lines: "Son of man, stand on your feet" (Ezek. 2:1).

   B. Some say, "Son of man, put forth a riddle" (Ezek. 17:2).

   C. This [statement was made] at the outset of the sequence of events, and why then was it stated here?

   D. It is because considerations of temporal sequence play no role in the Torah.

5. A. Along these same lines: "Go and cry in the ears of Jerusalem" (Jer. 2:2).

B. This [statement was made] at the outset of the sequence of events, and why then was it stated here?

C. It is because considerations of temporal sequence play no role in the Torah.

6. A. Along these same lines: "Israel was a luxuriant vine" (Hos. 10:1).

B. This [statement was made] at the outset of the sequence of events, and why then was it stated here?

C. It is because considerations of temporal sequence play no role in the Torah.

7. A. Along these same lines: "I, Qoheleth, have been king over Israel in Jerusalem" (Qoh. 1:12).

B. This [statement was made] at the outset of the sequence of events, and why then was it stated here?

C. It is because considerations of temporal sequence play no role in the Torah. (*Mekhilta Attributed to R. Ishmael* XXXII:I.1-7)

The atemporality of Scripture's narrative is further illustrated in a still more striking statement. Here it is made explicit that considerations of time past, present, and future in no way enter. When the Israelites plunged into the sea, at that same moment, Abraham stood over Isaac, a knife in his hand—the model for Moses at that moment:

A. R. Yosé the Galilean says, "When the Israelites went into the sea, Mount Moriah had already been uprooted from its place, with the altar of Isaac that was built on it, and with the array of wood on it, and Isaac was as if bound and set on the altar, and Abraham as though his hand were stretched out, having taken the knife to sacrifice his son.

B. "Said the Omnipresent to Moses, 'Moses, my children are in trouble, with the sea shutting the way before and the enemy pursuing, and you are standing and protracting your prayer!'

C. "Moses said to him, 'And what am I supposed to do?'

D. "He said to him, 'Lift up your rod [and stretch out your hand over the sea and divide it, that the people of Israel may go on dry ground through the sea].'

E. "'You should now exalt, give glory, and praise, and break out in songs of praise, exaltation, praise and glorification of the One who possesses war.'" (*Mekhilta Attributed to R. Ishmael* XXII:I.24)

"Abraham at the sea" means that considerations of temporal division and order do not register. But even if the matter were not made explicit, we should find ample evidence of the sages' ahistorical mode of thought on nearly every page of the documents of the oral Torah, for every time the sages spoke as though Abraham and David were contemporaries of theirs, they announced their conviction that the Torah was timeless.

The only way to validate the striking proposition that temporal considerations do not affect the narrative of Scripture, which pays no attention to the order in which events took place, is through examples of atemporality. The examples of this extract show that the Torah cites later in its narrative what in fact took place earlier, and these shifts validate the claim made at the outset. The second composition makes the same point in a very different way, by claiming that the binding of Isaac was taking place at the very moment at which Israel was tested at the sea. The events then correspond and take place in the same indeterminate moment.

Philosophy Replaces History

Since historical time does not measure the meaning of Scripture, a philosophical one does, that is to say, that quest for regularity and order that transcends particularities and episodes. That quest for the rules of the social order is advanced when the Torah narrates not history—past, present, future—but rather an enduring paradigm. Accordingly, portraying a timeless world in which the past forms a principal part of the present, and the present takes place within an eternity of contemporaneity, yields an intellectually formidable reward.

If Abraham, Aqiba, and Ashi live within the same uniform plane of existence as do you and I, this morning, then we gain access to the orderly unfolding of the rules of a well-ordered world, with special emphasis upon the social rules of Israel's life instead of upon the physical rules of the natural world. That is why for the sages it was self-evident that when the Israelites descended into the sea, Moriah was uprooted from its place, with Isaac bound on the altar and Abraham's hand poised with the knife, lessons were to be learned for their Israel too. No wonder that Moses then recapitulates Abraham's gesture (at *Mekhilta* XXII:I.24)—and the rest follows. This conception of events as patterned—here the gesture is what joins the one scene to the other—defies the historical notion of events as singular, sequential, linear.

Before we proceed to a systematic presentation of how the sages portrayed the perfection of creation in its timeless present, let us take up an account of how they divided time. In their view, temporal past, present, and future, signified by the neutral and natural passage of time, bore no consequence. Rather, they maintained that all time is differentiated and classified by the indicative traits of Israel's relationship with God. Time then is contingent upon the given, when Israel is at one with God, then world order is attained, and nothing more can happen. But, as a matter of fact, that relationship, marking time, will signify the advent of the world to come, that is to say, the end of time as humanity knows it altogether as this passage from Yerushalmi tractate *Megillah* sets out:

> E. Since it is written, "From the rising of the sun to its setting the name of the LORD is to be praised!" (Ps. 113:3). What do you derive from that verse of Scripture? [The Hallel must be read in proper order.]
>
> F. Said R. Abin, "The matter of reading the Hallel in proper order involves the right order of the various sections thereof, thus:
>
> G. "'When Israel went forth from Egypt, [the house of Jacob from a people of strange language]' (Psalm 114)—this refers to times past.
>
> H. "'Not to us, O LORD, not to us, but to thy name give glory, [for the sake of thy steadfast love and thy faithfulness!]' (Ps. 115:1)—this refers to the present generations.
>
> I. "'I love the LORD, because he has heard my voice and my supplications' (Psalm 116)—this refers to the days of the messiah.
>
> J. "'[The LORD is God, and he has given us light.] Bind the festal offering with cords [up to the horns of the altar!]' (Ps. 118:27)—this refers to the days of Gog and Magog.
>
> K. "'Thou art my God, and I will give thanks to thee; [thou art my God, I will extol thee]' (Ps. 118:28)—this refers to the age to come." (*y. Meg.* 2:1 I:2)

Here is a fine example of paradigmatic organization of time, a more accessible one than the organization by appeal to the traits of Israel's sacrificial service that we saw just now. Here, predictably for the oral Torah, the differentiation of time responds to the critical component of world history, Israel's relationship with God. It follows that no boundary distinguished past from present; time was understood in a completely different way. Within the conception of time that formed consciousness and culture, the past formed a perpetual presence, the present took place on the plane of the past, and no lines of structure or order distinguished the one from the other.

With the past very present, the present an exercise in recapitulation of an enduring paradigm, therefore, time and change signify nothing but imperfection, as much as permanence beyond time and change signifies perfection. And that carries forward that quest for the perfection of the world order that the sages anticipate will justify—show the justice, meaning here the perfection, of—God's work. That is why, as I said, time in a system of perfection can be neither linear nor cyclical; time in historical dimensions simply is not a consideration in thinking about what happens and what counts. Instead, paradigms for the formation of the social order of transcendence and permanence govern, so that what was now is, and what will be is what was and is.

It follows that the two conflicting conceptions of social explanation—the historical, the paradigmatic—appeal to two different ways of conceiving of, and evaluating, time. Historical time measures one thing, paradigmatic time, another, though both refer to the same facts of nature and of the social order. For its exposition of the cogency and meaning of Israel's social experience, for its part the oral Torah possesses no concept of history and therefore produces as its statements of the sense of the life of the people neither sustained historical narrative nor biography. Rather, the oral Torah presents exemplary moments, significations of paradigm, and exemplary incidents in the lives of the saints, also indicators of a prevailing pattern. These stories yield chapters, not lives.

The Universalization of the Patriarchs and Matriarchs

An ethnic religion propagates itself in bed. A universalistic religion appeals not to genealogy but conviction. Judaism as framed by the sages preserves the tension between the ethnic and the universalistic. A child of a Jewish mother (in contemporary Reform Judaism: or father) by birth becomes "Israel," enters into the holy community. No act of conversion is required, only, for males, an act of confirmation through circumcision. But a child of an other-than-Israelite (*gentile,* meaning everybody else, undifferentiatedly) may become "Israel" and enter the holy community. This is done by accepting God's unity and dominion and the yoke of the commandments—hardly matters of ethnic assimilation, for these are not customs and ceremonies but God's requirements of all humanity of the category "Israel."

Now to return to the question addressed in this book, whether or not, as I claim, Judaic monotheism is universal in its character. To be "Israel"—God's portion of humanity—means to conform to a pattern of actions and attitudes set forth for all time and without distinction in circumstance. That pattern, or paradigm, comes to definition in the lives of the patriarchs and matriarchs, whom one adopts as one's forebears by accepting the paradigmatic heritage. It is then recapitulated in a social world that knows not change but conformity to paradigm—

or nonconformity. Since the paradigm endures, we explain happenings by appeal to its rules, and the event is not what is singular and distinctive but what conforms to the rule: we notice what is like the paradigm, not what diverges from it. To the paradigm matters of memory and hope prove monumentally irrelevant, because they explain nothing, making distinctions that stand for no important differences at all.

"Israel" as the Paradigm

To be "Israel" means to conform to a paradigm, the one defined initially by Abraham. It means to accept God's dominion, to take upon oneself the yoke of the commandments, to affirm the unity and uniqueness of God, and to do his will. These are not considerations of the moment. They are convictions for eternity. These represent choices facing all of humanity, not matters of ethnic assimilation or territorial location.

That is why, when in the oral Torah the sages want to explain what it means to be "Israel," they appeal not to time and change but eternity and permanence. Or rather, the conception of the category of time—what is measured by the passage of the sun and moon in relationship to events here on earth—altogether loses standing. In place of distinguishing happenings through the confluence of time, measured by the passage of the sun and moon, and event, distinguished by specificity and particularity, paradigmatic thinking takes another route. It finds an event in what conforms to the paradigm, what is meaningful in what confirms it. In paradigmatic thinking we examine the norms for an account of how things ought to be, finding the rule that tells us how things really are. Then past, present, future differentiate not at all, the pattern of an eternal present taking over to make sense of the social order.

It follows that in the paradigmatic mode of thinking about the social order, the categories of past, present, and future, singular event and particular life, all prove useless. In their place come the categories defined by the actions and attitudes of paradigmatic persons, Abraham and Sarah, for instance, or paradigmatic places, the temple, or paradigmatic occasions, holy time, for instance. We identify a happening not by its consequence (historical), but by its conformity to the appropriate paradigm. We classify events in accord with their paradigms as not past, present, or future, therefore, because to the indicators of eventfulness— what marks a happening as eventful or noteworthy—time and change, by definition, have no bearing at all. Great empires do not make history; they fit a pattern.

What they do does not designate an event, it merely provides a datum for classification within the right pattern. The governing categories speak not of time and change, movement and direction, but the recapitulation of a given pattern, the repetition of the received paradigm. Being then moves from the one-time, the concrete, the linear and accumulative, to the recurrent, the mythic, and the repetitive: from the historical to the paradigmatic. These modes of identifying a happening as consequential and eventful then admit no past or present or future subject to differentiation and prognostication, respectively. Time bears no meaning, nor the passage of time, any consequence. If, therefore, the historical mode of organizing shared experience into events forming patterns, its identification of events as unique and persons as noteworthy, of memory as the medium for seeking meaning, and narrative as the medium for spelling it out, paradigmatic thinking will dictate a different mode of culture.

It is one in which shared experience takes on meaning when the received paradigms of behavior and the interpretation of the consequence of behavior come to realization once again: the paradigm recapitulated is the paradigm confirmed. What takes place that is identified as noteworthy becomes remarkable because today's rules conform to yesterday's and provoke tomorrow's recapitulation as well. We notice not the unlike—the singular event—but the like, not what calls into question the ancient pattern but what confirms it. If, then, we wish to make sense of who we are, we ask not where we come from or where we are heading, but whom we resemble, and into which classification of persons or events we fit, or events that appear to repeat. The social order then finds its explanation in its resemblances, the likenesses and the unlikenesses of persons and happenings alike.

Paradigms Discerned through Particular Cases

Let me make this point concrete. The meaning of shared experience—such as history sets forth in its categories of past, present, future, and teleology through narrative of particular events or through biography of singular lives—emerges in a different way altogether. In the formulation of the social order through paradigm, past, present, future, the conception of time in general, set forth distinctions that by definition make no difference. Events contradict the paradigm; what is particular bears no sense. Then remarkable happenings, formed into teleology through history-writing, or noteworthy persons' lives, formed into memorable cases through biography, no longer serve as the media of making a statement bearing intelligible, cultural consequence.

Paradigmatic thinking like the halakic kind is never generalized, only is meant through particular cases to yield generalizations (a very different thing). Specific paradigms come into play. They define the criteria for the selection as consequential and noteworthy of some happenings but not others. They further dictate the way to think about remarkable happenings, events, so as to yield sense concerning them. They tell people that one thing bears meaning, while another does not, and they further instruct people on the self-evident meaning to be imputed to that which is deemed consequential. The paradigms are fully as social in their dimensions, entirely as encompassing in their outreach, as historical categories. Accept the rule of, and love the one and only God, and enjoy his grace; reject that rule and rebel against God and suffer: these twin propositions pertain to every social order.

And there is a third, which concerns marking time. All humanity looks to the heavens, the moon, the sun, and the stars, to tell time. What is at stake in the conception of time within paradigmatic thinking? By a paradigm time is marked off by indicators that are utterly freestanding, in no way correlated with natural time at all; a paradigm's time is time defined in units that are framed quite independent of the ephemera of time and change as we know it in this life on the one side or the cycle of natural events that define and also delineate nature's time on the other. Paradigms may be formed on a variety of bases, but all paradigmatic formulations of time have in common their autonomy of nature on the one side and events beyond their own pattern's definitions (whether by nature or by historical events) on the other. God in creation has defined the paradigms of time, Scripture that conveys those paradigms, and humanity that discovers, in things large and small, those paradigms that inhere in the very nature of creation itself.

These general definitions should be made still more concrete in the setting of the documents of the oral Torah. Let me give a single example, among numerous possibilities, of time paradigmatic, in contrast to the conceptions of time that govern in the Hebrew Scriptures. The character of paradigmatic time is captured in the following, which encompasses the entirety of Israel's being (its history in conventional language) within the conversation that is portrayed between Boaz and Ruth; I abbreviate the passage from *Ruth Rabbah* to highlight only the critical components:

1.   A. "And at mealtime Boaz said to her, 'Come here and eat some bread, and dip your morsel in the wine.' So she sat beside the

reapers, and he passed to her parched grain; and she ate until she was satisfied, and she had some left over":

B. R. Yohanan interpreted the phrase "come here" in six ways:

Ruth is the ancestress of David, who takes first place in the exposition of cases of the pattern:

C. "The first speaks of David.

D. "'Come here': means, to the throne: 'That you have brought me here' (2 Sam. 7:18).

E. "'. . . and eat some bread': the bread of the throne.

F. "'. . . and dip your morsel in vinegar': this speaks of his sufferings: 'O Lᴏʀᴅ, do not rebuke me in your anger' (Ps. 6:2).

G. "'So she sat beside the reapers': for the throne was taken from him for a time."

I. [Resuming from G:] "'and he passed to her parched grain': he was restored to the throne: 'Now I know that the Lᴏʀᴅ saves his anointed' (Ps. 20:7).

J. "'. . . and she ate and was satisfied and left some over': this indicates that he would eat in this world, in the days of the messiah, and in the age to come.

Second comes Solomon, David's son who built the temple:

2.   A. "The second interpretation refers to Solomon: 'Come here': means, to the throne.

B. "'. . . and eat some bread': this is the bread of the throne: "And Solomon's provision for one day was thirty measures of fine flour and three score measures of meal' (1 Kings 5:2).

C. "'. . . and dip your morsel in vinegar': this refers to the dirty of the deeds [that he did].

D. "'So she sat beside the reapers': for the throne was taken from him for a time."

G. [Reverting to D:] "'and he passed to her parched grain': for he was restored to the throne.

H. "'. . . and she ate and was satisfied and left some over': this indicates that he would eat in this world, in the days of the messiah, and in the age to come.

Yet another worthy heir of David is Hezekiah, in the time of the Assyrian invasion from the north, who stood firm and believed that God would protect Israel:

3.   A. "The third interpretation speaks of Hezekiah: 'Come here': means, to the throne.

B. "'. . . and eat some bread': this is the bread of the throne.

C. "'. . . and dip your morsel in vinegar': this refers to sufferings [Isa.

5:1]: 'And Isaiah said, Let them take a cake of figs' (Isa. 38:21).

D. "'So she sat beside the reapers': for the throne was taken from him for a time: 'Thus says Hezekiah, This day is a day of trouble and rebuke' (Isa. 37:3).

E. "'. . . and he passed to her parched grain': for he was restored to the throne: 'So that he was exalted in the sight of all nations from then on' (2 Chron. 32:23).

F. "'. . . and she ate and was satisfied and left some over': this indicates that he would eat in this world, in the days of the messiah, and in the age to come.

Manasseh is another embodiment of the paradigm, this time showing how one may lose the throne and regain it, just as Israel has lost Jerusalem and the temple but will be restored in the last days:

4. A. "The fourth interpretation refers to Manasseh: 'Come here': means, to the throne.

B. "'. . . and eat some bread': this is the bread of the throne.

C. "'. . . and dip your morsel in vinegar': for his dirty deeds were like vinegar, on account of wicked actions.

D. "'So she sat beside the reapers': for the throne was taken from him for a time: 'And the LORD spoke to Manasseh and to his people, but they did not listen. So the LORD brought them the captains of the host of the king of Assyria, who took Manasseh with hooks' (2 Chron. 33:10-11)."

K. [Reverting to D:] "'and he passed to her parched grain': for he was restored to the throne: 'And brought him back to Jerusalem to his kingdom' (2 Chron. 33:13).

N. "'. . . and she ate and was satisfied and left some over': this indicates that he would eat in this world, in the days of the messiah, and in the age to come.

From the restoration of the monarch, we come to the messiah who will restore Israel to the land, all within the pattern now established:

5. A. "The fifth interpretation refers to the messiah: 'Come here': means, to the throne.

B. "'. . . and eat some bread': this is the bread of the throne.

C. "'. . . and dip your morsel in vinegar': this refers to suffering: 'But he was wounded because of our transgressions' (Isa. 53:5).

D. "'So she sat beside the reapers': for the throne is destined to be taken from him for a time: For I will gather all nations against Jerusalem to battle and the city shall be taken' (Zech. 14:2).

E. "'. . . and he passed to her parched grain': for he will be restored to the throne: 'And he shall smite the land with the rod of his mouth' (Isa. 11:4)."

I. [reverting to G:] "so the last redeemer will be revealed to them and then hidden from them." (*Ruth Rabbah* XL:i.1)

The paradigm here may be formed of six units: (1) David's monarchy; (2) Solomon's reign; (3) Hezekiah's reign; (4) Manasseh's reign; (5) the messiah's reign; (6) the last redeemer. So paradigmatic time compresses events to the dimensions of its model. All things happen on a single plane of time. Past, present, future are undifferentiated, and that is why a single action contains within itself an entire account of Israel's social order under the aspect of eternity.

The foundations of the paradigm, of course, rest on the fact that David, Solomon, Hezekiah, Manasseh, and therefore also, the messiah, all descend from the union of Ruth and Boaz. Then, within the framework of the paradigm, the event that is described here—"And at mealtime Boaz said to her, 'Come here and eat some bread, and dip your morsel in the wine.' So she sat beside the reapers, and he passed to her parched grain; and she ate until she was satisfied, and she had some left over"—forms not an event but a pattern. The pattern transcends time; or more accurately, aggregates of time, the passage of time, the course of events—these are all simply irrelevant to what is in play in Scripture. Rather, we have a tableau, joining persons who lived at widely separated moments, linking them all as presences at this simple exchange between Boaz and Ruth, imputing to them all, whenever they came into existence, the shape and structure of that simple moment: the presence of the past, for David, Solomon, Hezekiah, and so on, but the pastness of the present in which David or Solomon—or the messiah for that matter—lived or would live (it hardly matters, verb tenses prove hopelessly irrelevant to paradigmatic thinking).

Taking account of both the simple example of B.C.E. and C.E. and the complex one involving the Israelite monarchy and the messiah, we ask ourselves how time has been framed within the paradigmatic mode of thought. The negative is now clear. Paradigmatic time has no relationship whatsoever to nature's time. It is time invented, not discovered; time predetermined in accord with a model or pattern, not time negotiated in the interplay between time as defined by nature and differentiated by human cognizance and recognition. Here the points of differentiation scarcely intersect with either nature's or history's time; time is not sequential, whether in natural or historical terms; it is not made up of unique events, whether in nature or in the social order; it is not differentiated by indicators of a commonplace character. Divisions between past, present, and future lie beyond all comprehension.

That is what I mean when I say that the paradigm takes its measures quite atemporally, in terms of not historical movements or recurrent cycles but rather atemporal units of experience. A model or pattern or paradigm will set forth an account of the life of the social entity (household, village, kingdom, people, territory) in terms of differentiated events—wars, reigns, for one example, building a given building and destroying it, for another—yet entirely out of phase with sequences of time. The pattern that the cases embody turns out to focus upon the loss and recovery of perfection, here, the throne, which embodies so much more for Israel in exile, either overseas or subject to gentile rule.

Clearly, in paradigmatic existence, time is not differentiated by events, whether natural or social. Time is differentiated in another way altogether, and that way so recasts what happens on earth as to formulate a view of existence to which any notion of events strung together into sequential history or of time as distinguished by one event rather than some other is not so much irrelevant as beyond all comprehension. To characterize Judaism as atemporal or ahistorical is both accurate and irrelevant. Judaism sets forth a different conception of existence, besides the historical one that depends upon nature's and humanity's conventions on the definition and division of time.

Existence takes on sense and meaning not by reason of sequence and order, as history maintains in its response to nature's time. Rather, existence takes shape and acquires structure in accord with a paradigm that is independent of nature and the givens of the social order: God's structure, God's paradigm, the sages would call it; but in secular terms, a model or a pattern that in no way responds to the givens of nature or the social order. It is a conception of time that is undifferentiated by event because time is comprised of components that themselves dictate the character of events: what is noteworthy, chosen out of the variety of things that merely happen. And what is remarkable conforms to the conventions of the paradigm.

Particular Historical Narrative to Exemplary Social Generalization

How in concrete terms does paradigmatic thinking in haggadic writing recast historical narrative into generalization, as much as halakic thinking treats cases as occasions for generalization? Here, the storyteller retrojects the destruction of the Second Temple into the events of the first, or, more to the point, finds no point in distinguishing one from the other. As at Mishnah tractate *Zebahim* 14:4-9, where we differentiate epochs in the temple's history in such a way that sequence on its own bears no message, here too patterns homogenize periods, then differentiate them by indicative traits that have no bearing upon sequence at all. And why should it, since—in the case at hand—the two events conform to a single paradigm, and, it is hoped, the second of the two will produce the same outcome as the first, repentance, atonement, forgiveness, and restoration:

1.   A. "This was for the sins of her prophets and the iniquities of her priests, who shed in the midst of her the blood of the righteous:"

        B. R. Yudan asked R. Aha, "Where did the Israelites kill Zechariah? Was it in the courtyard of women or in the courtyard of the Israelites?"

        C. He said to him, "It was neither in the women's courtyard nor in the Israelites' courtyard, but in the priests' courtyard.

        D. "But they did not dispose of his blood like the blood of a hind or a ram: 'He shall pour out the blood thereof and cover it with dust' (Lev. 17:13).

        E. "But here: 'For the blood she shed is still in her; she set it upon a bare rock; she did not pour it out on the ground to cover it with earth' (Ezek. 24:7).

        F. "'She set her blood upon the bare rock, so that it was not covered, so that it may stir up my fury to take vengeance' (Ezek. 24:8)."

From the initial narrative, we turn to a generalization:

2.   A. Seven transgressions did the Israelites commit on that day: they murdered (1) a priest, (2) prophet, (3) judge, (4) they spilled innocent blood, (5) they blasphemed the divine name, (6) they imparted uncleanness to the courtyard, and it was, furthermore, (7) a Day of Atonement that coincided with the Sabbath.

        B. When Nebuzaradan came in, he saw the blood of Zechariah begin to drip. He said to them, "What sort of blood is this dripping blood?"

        C. They said to him, "It is the blood of oxen, rams, and sheep that we offered on the altar."

        D. He forthwith sent and brought oxen, rams, and sheep and slaughtered them in his presence, but the blood continued to drip.

        E. He said to them, "If you tell the truth, well and good, but if not, I shall comb your flesh with iron combs."

        F. They said to him, "What shall we tell you? He was a prophet who rebuked us. We conspired against him and killed him. And lo, years have passed, but his blood has not stopped seething."

        G. He said to them, "I shall appease it."

        H. He brought before him the great Sanhedrin and the lesser Sanhedrin and killed them, [until their blood mingled with that of

Zechariah: "Oaths are imposed and broken, they kill and rob, there is nothing but adultery and license, one deed of blood after another (Hos. 4:2)].

I. Still the blood seethed. He brought boys and girls and killed them by the blood, but it did not stop seething.

J. He brought youngsters from the school house and killed them over it, but it did not stop seething.

K. Forthwith he took eighty thousand young priests and killed them on his account, until the blood lapped the grave of Zechariah. But the blood did not stop seething.

L. He said, "Zechariah, Zechariah, All the best of them I have destroyed. Do you want me to exterminate them all?"

M. When he said this, the blood forthwith came to rest.

The gentile draws the right conclusion, repents, and accepts the one true God and so becomes one of Israel—underscoring the accessibility of Israel, through Israel's God, to all humanity:

N. Then he considered repenting, saying, "Now if one soul matters thus, as to that man who has killed all these souls, how much the more so!" [He fled and sent a parting gift and converted.]

O. On the spot the Holy One, blessed be he, was filled with mercy and made a gesture to the blood, which was swallowed up in place.

P. To that Scripture refers when it says, "This was for the sins of her prophets and the iniquities of her priests, who shed in the midst of her the blood of the righteous." (*Lamentations Rabbati* CXIII.i.1)

In all, to the past is imputed no autonomy; between past and present is conceived no dividing line of any kind; vastly transcending the mere flaws of anachronism, the conception that time past and time present flow together yields the principle that events may be ordered in accord with a logic quite autonomous of temporal order. The point at which we started forms a fitting conclusion to this brief experiment in the testing of a null-hypothesis. Not only do we find not a trace of historical thinking, as that mode of thought is defined in the Hebrew Scriptures, we find expressions of a quite different mode of thought altogether.

The Four Principal Models for Organizing Events

Now that we recognize a different way of thinking about time past, present, and future, we come to the question: what exactly are the paradigms through which the sages set forth the world order they proposed to discern? In their view the written part of the Torah defined a set of paradigms that served without regard to circumstance, context, or, for that matter, dimension and scale of happening. A very small number of models emerged from Scripture, captured in the sets: (1) Eden and Adam, (2) Sinai and the Torah, (3) the land and Israel, and (4) the temple and its building, destruction, rebuilding.

Within these paradigms nearly the whole of human experience was organized. These paradigms served severally and jointly, for example, Eden and Adam on its own but also superimposed upon the land and Israel; Sinai and the Torah on its own but also superimposed upon the Land and Israel, and, of course, the temple, embodying natural creation and its intersection with national and social history, could stand entirely on its own or be superimposed upon any and all of the other paradigms. In many ways, then, we have the symbolic equivalent of a set of two- and three- or even four-dimensional grids. A given pattern forms a grid on its own, one set of lines being set forth in terms of, for example, Eden, timeless perfection, in contrast against the other set of lines, Adam, temporal disobedience; but upon that grid, a comparable grid can be superimposed, the land and Israel being an obvious one; and upon the two, yet a third and fourth, Sinai and Torah, temple and the confluence of nature and history.

By reference to these grids, severally or jointly, the critical issues of existence, whether historical or contemporary, played themselves out in the theology of the oral Torah. I identify four models by which, out of happenings of various sorts, consequential or meaningful events would be selected, and by reference to which these selected events would be shown connected (or meaningful) and explicable in terms of that available logic of paradigm that governed both the making of connections and the drawing of conclusions.

1. How shall we organize (mere) happenings into events? On the largest scale the question concerns the division into periods of not sequences but mere sets of happenings. Periodization involves explanation, of course, since even in a paradigmatic structure, once matters are set forth as periods, then an element of sequence is admitted into the processes of description and therefore analysis and explanation.

2. How does Israel relate to the rest of the world? This involves explaining not what happened this morning in particular, but what always happens, that is, defining the structure of Israel's life in the politics of this world, explaining the order of things in both the social, political structure of the world and also the sequence of actions that may occur and recur over time (the difference, paradigmatically, hardly matters).

3. How do we explain the pattern of events, making connections and drawing conclusions from what happens? Paradigmatic thinking, no less than historical, explains matters. But the explanation derives from the character of the pattern rather than the order of events, which governs historical explanation. Connections then drawn between one thing and something else serve to define a paradigm, rather than to convey a temporal explanation based on sequences, first this, then that, therefore this explains why that happened. The paradigm bears a different explanation altogether, one that derives from its principle of selection, and therefore the kinds of explanations paradigmatic thinking sets forth, expressed through its principles of selection in making connections and drawing conclusions, will demand rich instantiation.

4. How do we anticipate the future history of Israel? That concerns not so much explaining the present as permitting informed speculation about what will happen in the future. And that speculation will appeal to those principles of order, structure, and explanation that the paradigm to begin with sets forth. So future history in historical thinking and writing projects out of past and present a trajectory over time to come, and future history in paradigmatic thinking forms projects along other lines altogether.

Here is how the entire history of Israel, beginning to end, is to be portrayed in a systematic narrative of an other-than-historical character. The exegesis of "remember the days of yore" leads us to a review of God's relationship with the world through Israel. "Remember" here does not precipitate a review of times perceived as past—not at all. Memory is an act that is contemporary, calling up the past as a player in the acutely present tense of today's world. Not only so, but the climax focuses not on the past but on the future. The catalog is complete, the message clear. The past is now invoked as a model for the messianic future, which is to be anticipated.

I abbreviate the passage to highlight the structure of the paradigm that takes the place of history in the description of the existence of Israel.

1.   A. ["He found him in a desert region, in an empty howling waste. He engirded him, watched over him, guarded him as the pupil of his eye. Like an eagle who rouses his nestlings, gliding down to his young, so did he spread his wings and take him, bear him along on his pinions; the LORD alone did guide him, no alien god at his side" (Deut. 32:10-12).] (*Sifré to Deuteronomy* CCCXIII:I)

Abraham is our first exemplary figure, establishing the paradigm:

      B. "He found him in a desert region:"

      C. This refers to Abraham.

2.   A. ". . . He engirded him:"

      B. In line with this verse: "The LORD said to Abram, 'Go from your land'" (Gen. 12:1).

3.   A. ". . . watched over him:"

      B. Before Abraham came into the world, it was as if the Holy One, blessed be he, was king only over heaven alone, as it is said, "The LORD, God of heaven, who has taken me. . ." (Gen. 24:7).

      C. But when Abraham our father came into the world, he made him king over heaven and also over earth, as it is said, "I impose an oath upon you, by the LORD, God of heaven and God of earth" (Gen. 24:2).

4.   A. ". . . guarded him as the pupil of his eye:"

      B. Even if the Holy One, blessed be he, had asked from our father Abraham the pupil of his eye, he would have given it to him, and not only the pupil of his eye, but even his soul, which was the most precious to him of all things.

      C. For it is said, "Take your son, your only son, Isaac" (Gen. 22:2).

      D. Now was it not perfectly self-evident to him that it was his son, his only son.

      E. But this refers to the soul, which is called "only," as it is said, "Deliver my soul from the sword, my only one from the power of the dog" (Ps. 22:21). (*Sifré to Deuteronomy* CCCXIII:II)

From Abraham we turn for our second exemplary figure to Israel:

1.   A. Another teaching concerning, "He found him in a desert region:"

      B. This refers to Israel, as it is said, "I found Israel like grapes in a desert" (Hos. 9:10).

2.   A. "...in an empty howling waste:"

      B. It was in a difficult situation, a place in which were marauding bands and thugs.

3.   A. "He engirded him:"

      B. Before Mount Sinai, as it is said, "And you shall set a boundary for the people round about" (Exod. 19:12).

4.   A. ". . . watched over him:"

      B. Through the Ten Commandments.

      C. This teaches that when the act of speech went forth from the mouth of the Holy One, blessed be he, the Israelites saw it and understood it and knew how much amplification was contained therein, how much law was contained therein, how many possibilities for lenient rules, for strict rulings, how many analogies were contained therein.

5.   A. ". . . guarded him as the pupil of his eye:"
      B. They would fall back twelve mils and go forward twelve mils at the sound of each and every act of speech,
      C. yet they did not take fright on account of the thunder and lightning.

We have dealt with a particular person, then the entire group, and now, in a category shift, we move on to a particular epoch, a spell defined by its own enchantment, so to speak:

1.   A. Another teaching concerning, "He found him in a desert region:"
      B. This refers to the age to come.
      C. So Scripture says, "Therefore behold, I will seduce her and bring her into the wilderness and speak tenderly to her" (Hos. 2:16).
2.   A. ". . . in an empty howling waste:"
      B. This refers to the four kingdoms, as it is said, "Who led you through the great and dreadful wilderness" (Deut. 8:15).
3.   A. "He engirded him:"
      B. with elders.
4.   A. "...watched over him:"
      B. with prophets.
5.   A. ". . . guarded him as the pupil of his eye:"
      B. He guarded them from demons, that they not injure them, in line with this verse: "Surely one who touches you touches the apple of his eye" (Zech. 2:12). (*Sifré to Deuteronomy* CCCXIII:IV)

The paradigm then covers Abraham, Israel, and the world to come—person, community, age. It is not a historical paradigm, since it does not organize and classify sequential periods of the same character. What is set into relationship are three modes of being: Abraham, the model; Israel, to conform to the model; the world to come, to mark the fruition of the model.

Supernatural Israel Transcending the Tides of Time

How is Israel's place in world affairs to be accounted for—if not by reference to history? Elected by God, Israel's this-worldly fate contradicted its supernatural standing. Now that question is readily framed in this-worldly, historical terms, and a variety of conventional historical writing did just that. What makes the following important is its demonstration of the way in which paradigmatic thinking takes over historical events. The paradigm defines that which counts, among the variety of events at hand—defines, but then explains:

7.   A. Rabban Gamaliel, R. Joshua, R. Eleazar b. Azariah, and R. Aqiba
         were going toward Rome. They heard the sound of the city's traf-
         fic from as far away as Puteoli, a hundred and twenty mil away.
         They began to cry, while R. Aqiba laughed.

      B. They said to him, "Aqiba, why are we crying while you are
         laughing?"

      C. He said to them, "Why are you crying?"

      D. They said to him, "Should we not cry, since gentiles, idolaters,
         sacrifice to their idols and bow down to icons, but dwell securely
         in prosperity, serenely, while the house of the footstool of our
         God has been put to the torch and left [Hammer:] a lair for beasts
         of the field?"

      E. He said to them, "That is precisely why I was laughing. If this is
         how he has rewarded those who anger him, all the more so [will
         he reward] those who do his will."

8.   A. Another time they went up to Jerusalem and to Mount Scopus.
         They tore their garments.

      B. They came to the mountain of the house [of the temple] and saw
         a fox go forth from the house of the Holy of Holies. They began
         to cry, while R. Aqiba laughed.

      C. They said to him, "You are always giving surprises. We are cry-
         ing when you laugh!"

      D. He said to them, "But why are you crying?"

      E. They said to him, "Should we not cry over the place concerning
         which it is written, 'And the common person who draws near
         shall be put to death' (Num. 1:51)? Now lo, a fox comes out of it.

      F. "In our connection the following verse of Scripture has been car-
         ried out: 'For this our heart is faint, for these things our eyes are
         dim, for the mountain of Zion which is desolate, the foxes walk
         upon it' (Lam. 5:17-18)."

      G. He said to them, "That is the very reason I have laughed. For
         lo, it is written, 'And I will take for me faithful witnesses to
         record, Uriah the priest and Zechariah the son of Jeberechiah'
         (Isa. 8:2).

      H. "And what has Uriah got to do with Zechariah? What is it that
         Uriah said? 'Zion shall be plowed as a field and Jerusalem shall
         become heaps and the mountain of the Lord's house as the high
         places of a forest' (Jer. 26:18).

      I. "What is it that Zechariah said? 'Thus says the Lord of hosts,
         "Old men and women shall yet sit in the broad places of
         Jerusalem"' (Zech. 8:4).

      J. "Said the Omnipresent, 'Lo, I have these two witnesses. If the
         words of Uriah have been carried out, then the words of
         Zechariah will be carried out. If the words of Uriah are nullified,
         then the words of Zechariah will be nullified.

> K. "'Therefore I was happy that the words of Uriah have been carried
> out, so that in the end the words of Zechariah will come about.'"
> L. In this language they replied to him: "Aqiba, you have given us
> comfort." (*Sifré to Deuteronomy* XLIII:III)

Here the paradigm that Aqiba finds in Scripture tells him what data
require attention and what do not. The prosperity of the idolaters matters only because the paradigm explains why to begin with we may take
account of their situation. The destruction of the temple matters also
because it conforms to an intelligible paradigm. In both cases, we both
select and also understand events by appeal to the pattern defined by the
working of God's will. The data at hand then yield inferences of a particular order—the prosperity of idolaters, the disgrace of Israel in its
very cult. We notice both facts because they both complement one
another and illustrate the workings of the model: validating prophecy,
interpreting experience in light of its message.

The passages just now reviewed leave no doubt about the character
of the explanations of the paradigms of Israel's experience. Explanation
will derive from whether or not Israel obeys the Torah, whether or not
Israel studies the Torah, the character of Israel's moral condition,
Israel's separating itself from the ways of the gentiles, and the like.
None of these explanations will have surprised or even much puzzled
the framers of the authorized history. A single case suffices to show
the character of paradigmatic explanation. Here we have quite a
remarkable statement, that the great figures of the nation, and the
nation as a whole, are punished for their sins in such a way that the
punishment derives from them themselves; we move along a rather
strange line of people who sinned through their arrogance—Adam,
Esau, Sennacherib, Hiram, Nebuchadnezzar—then Israel. But the
part of Israel under discussion is the part punished through the afflic-
tion, through natural, internal causes, of leprosy or flux. This then
yields a comprehensive theory of Israel's history. I have abbreviated
the passage as much as possible:

1.   A. "Dread and terrible are they; their justice and dignity proceed
      from themselves" (Hab. 1:7).
     B. "Dread and terrible" refers to the first Man.
     G. "Their justice and dignity proceed from themselves" (Hab. 1:7).
     H. This refers to Eve.
     I. That is in line with the following verse of Scripture: "The woman
      whom you gave to be with me is the one who gave me of the tree,
      and I ate" (Gen. 3:2).
2.   A. Another interpretation: "Dread and terrible" refers to Esau.

B. That is in line with the following verse of Scripture: "And Rebecca took the most coveted garments of Esau, her elder son" (Gen. 27:15). [This clothing came from Nimrod, so Esau was more of a hunter than he, hence, "dread and terrible."]

C. "Their justice and dignity proceed from themselves" (Hab. 1:7).

D. This refers to [the prophet] Obadiah.

E. Said R. Isaac, "Obadiah was a proselyte of Edomite origin, and he gave a prophecy concerning Edom, 'And there shall not be any remnant of the house of Esau for the mouth of the LORD has spoken it'" (Obad. 1:18).

3. A. Another interpretation: "Dread and terrible" refers to Sennacherib.

B. "Who among all the gods of the lands has saved their country from my hand" (Isa. 36:20).

C. "Their justice and dignity proceed from themselves" (Hab. 1:7).

D. This refers to his sons: "And it came to pass, as Sennacherib was worshiping in the house of Nisroch, his god, [that Adrammelech and Sarezer, his sons, smote him with the sword]" (2 Kings 19:37). (*Leviticus Rabbah* XVIII:II.1)

Once more, we notice that the appeal to one paradigm obliterates lines of structure and order that we should have anticipated, for example, differentiation between the personal and the public, or the social and the natural. As much as lines of differentiation among spells of time (past, present, future) are obscured, so all other indicators of classification are set aside by the ones that are in play here. Indeed, the power of paradigmatic thinking is not only to order what should be classified, but also to treat as lacking all differentiation what does not require classification. What we have is a reordering of all of the lines of existence, nature's and humanity's, as much as an obliteration of conventional points of differentiation, for example, of time or space for that matter.

The Purpose of Paradigmatic Thinking

The purpose of paradigmatic thinking, as much as historical, thus points toward the future. History is important to explain the present, also to help peer into the future; and paradigms serve precisely the same purpose. The choice between the one model and the other, then, rests upon which appeals to the more authentic data. In that competition, Scripture, treated as paradigm, met no competition in linear history, and it was paradigmatic, not historical, thinking that proved compelling for a thousand years or more. The future history of Israel is written in Scripture, and what happened in the beginning is what is going to happen at the end of time. That sense of order and balance prevailed.

The restorationist theology that infuses the sages' expression of paradigmatic thinking with its structure and system comes to expression in a variety of passages, of which a severely truncated selection will have to suffice:

2.   A. Said R. Abin, "Just as [Israel's history] began with the encounter with four kingdoms, so [Israel's history] will conclude with the encounter with the four kingdoms.

   B. "'Chedorlaomer, king of Elam, Tidal, king of Goiim, Amraphel, king of Shinar, and Arioch, king of Ellasar, four kings against five' (Gen. 14:9).

   C. "So [Israel's history] will conclude with the encounter with the four kingdoms: the kingdom of Babylonia, the kingdom of Medea, the kingdom of Greece, and the kingdom of Edom." (*Genesis Rabbah* XLII:II)

Another pattern serves as well, resting as it does on the foundations of the former. It is the familiar one that appeals to the deeds of the founders. The lives of the patriarchs stand for the history of Israel; the deeds of the patriarchs cover the future historical periods in Israel's destiny.

A single formulation of matters suffices to show how the entire history of Israel was foreseen at the outset:

1.   A. R. Hiyya taught on Tannaite authority, "At the beginning of the creation of the world the Holy One, blessed be he, foresaw that the temple would be built, destroyed, and rebuilt.

   B. "'In the beginning God created the heaven and the earth' (Gen. 1:1) [refers to the temple] when it was built, in line with the following verse: 'That I may plant the heavens and lay the foundations of the earth and say to Zion, You are my people' (Isa. 51:16).

   C. "'And the earth was unformed'—lo, this refers to the destruction, in line with this verse: 'I saw the earth, and lo, it was unformed' (Jer. 4:23).

   D. "'And God said, Let there be light'—lo, it was built and well constructed in the age to come." (*Pesiqta de Rab. Kahana* XXI:V)

A single specific example of the foregoing proposition suffices. It is drawn from that same mode of paradigmatic thinking that imposes the model of the beginning upon the end. In the present case the yield is consequential: we know what God is going to do to Rome. What God did to the Egyptians foreshadows what God will do to the Romans at the end of time.

We have now to ask why the sages rejected the linear sequence of unique events that Scripture sets forth in the authorized history in favor of the kind of paradigmatic thinking that has now been amply instantiated. Historical thinking yielded an unintelligible result, paradigmatic thinking, a rational one. The reason is that historical thinking—sequential narrative of one-time events—presupposes order, linearity, distinction between time past and time present, and teleology, among data that—for the sages, struggling with the secular facts of Israel's condition—do not self-evidently sustain such presuppositions. Questions of chaos, disorder, and disproportion naturally intervene; the very possibility of historical narrative meets a challenge in the diversity of story lines, the complexity of events, the bias of the principle of selection of what is eventful, of historical interest, among a broad choice of happenings: why this, not that. Narrative history first posits a gap between past and present but then bridges the gap; why not entertain the possibility that to begin with there is no such gap? These and similar considerations invite a different way of thinking about how things have been and now are, a different tense structure altogether.

A way of thinking about the experience of humanity, whether past or contemporary, that makes distinctions other than the historical ones between past and present and that eschews linear narrative and so takes account of the chaos that ultimately prevails, now competes with historical thinking. Paradigmatic thinking, a different medium for organizing and explaining things that happen, deals with the same data that occupy historical thinking, and that is why when we refer to paradigmatic thinking, the word *history* gains its quotation marks: it is not a datum of thought, merely a choice; contradicting to its core the character of paradigmatic thinking, the category then joins its opposite, paradigm, only by forming the oxymoron before us: paradigmatic thinking about "history."

From Scripture to Torah

What Scripture yields for the Torah that is Judaism, therefore, is not one-time events, arranged in sequence to dictate meaning, but models or patterns of conduct and consequence. These models are defined by the written Torah. No component of the paradigm we have reviewed emerges from other than the selected experience set forth by Scripture. But the models or paradigms pertain not to one time alone—past time—but to all times equally—past, present, and future. Then time itself no longer forms an organizing category of understanding and interpretation. Nor does nature, except in a subordinated role. The spells marked out by moon and sun and fixed stars bear meaning, to be sure. But that meaning has no bearing upon the designation of one year as past, another as present. The meaning imputed to the lunar and solar marking of time derives from the cult, on the one side, and the calendar of holy time, on the other: seven solar days, a Sabbath; a lunar cycle, a new month to be celebrated; the first new moon after the vernal equinox, the Passover, and after the autumnal, Tabernacles. The oral Torah tells time the way nature does and only in that way; events deemed worth recording in time take place the way events in nature do. What accounts for the difference between history's time and paradigmatic time as set forth here, I maintain, is a conception of time quite different from the definition of historical time that operates in Scripture—the confluence of nature's time and history's way of telling time: two distinct chronographies brought together, the human one then imposed upon the natural one.

Israel kept time with reference to events, whether past or present, that also were not singular, linear, or teleological. These were, rather, reconstitutive in the forever of here and now—not a return to a perfect time but a recapitulation of a model eternally present. Israel could treat as comparable the creation of the world and the exodus from Egypt (as the Judaic liturgy commonly does, for example, in connection with the Sabbath) because Israel's paradigm (not "history") and nature's time corresponded in character, were consubstantial and not mutually contradictory. And that consubstantiality explains why paradigm and natural time work so well together. Now, *time* bears a different signification. It is not limited to the definition assigned by nature— yet also not imposed upon natural time but treated as congruent and complementary with nature's time. How so? Events—things that happen that are deemed consequential—are eventful, meaningful, by a criterion of selection congruent in character with nature's own.

The Character of the Torah's Paradigms

To conclude: to understand why, we must recall the character of the Torah's paradigms:

1. Scripture set forth certain patterns, which, applied to the chaos of the moment, selected out of a broad range of candidates some things and omitted reference to others.

2. The selected things then are given their structure and order by appeal to the paradigm or described without regard to scale.

3. That explains how some events narrated by Scripture emerged as patterns, imposing their lines of order and structure upon happenings of other times.

And this yields the basis for the claim of consubstantiality:

4. Scripture's paradigms—Eden, the land—appealed to nature in another form.

The upshot, then, is that the rhythms of the sun and moon are celebrated in the very forum in which the land, Israel's Eden, yields its celebration to the creator. The rhythmic quality of the paradigm then compares with the rhythmic quality of natural time: not cyclical, but also not linear. Nature's way of telling time and the Torah's way meet in the temple: its events are nature's, its story a tale of nature too. Past and present flow together and join in future time too because, as in nature, what is past is what is now and what will be. Out of that presence of eternity in time, the world is ordered in perfection, quietly singing in its perfect orbit a hymn of praise to the creator. And that world, within the paradigmatic mode of thought and analysis, encompasses all humanity.

5. The Narrative-Exegetical Message: Restoring Adam to Eden, Israel to the Land

The universalizing method of paradigmatic thinking about matters of scriptural narrative yielded a universalistic message concerning the destiny of humanity. All humanity will come together, now in death, then at the end of days, in judgment and resurrection for those who stand in judgment. Consequence of humanity's fall from grace, death does not mark the end of the life, nor—correspondingly—exile the last stop in the journey of holy Israel. Israelites will live in the age or the world to come, all Israel in the land of Israel. Then all things depend upon who and what is "Israel." The universality of Judaic monotheism emerges when we realize that that "Israel" will encompass all who know the one true God. The restorationist theology provides for an eternal life matching the promise of Eden at the outset; to be Israel means to live and not die—Adam redivivus. And every human being has the opportunity of eternal life. By *Israel* then is meant those who know God and accept his dominion, and by *gentiles* or *non-Israel,* those who worship idols. There are no other lines of differentiation in common humanity.

Restoring Israel to the Land, Humanity to Eden

But the message that Scripture yields for Judaism involves the comparison of Adam and Israel, each having possessed paradise—the Garden of Eden, the land of Israel, respectively—and each having lost it. The last things are to be known from the first. In the just plan of creation humanity was meant to live in Eden, and Israel in the land of Israel in time without end. Humanity sinned and lost Eden. Israel sinned and lost the land. So the sages state, had Israel not sinned, Scripture would have closed with the book of Joshua: the people settled in the land. Then, at the other end of time, the eschatological restoration of humanity to Eden, Israel to the land, will bring about that long and tragically postponed perfection of the world order, sealing the demonstration of the justice of God's plan for creation. Risen from the dead, having atoned through death, humanity will be judged in accord with its deeds. Israel for its part, when it repents and conforms its will to God's, recovers its Eden. So the consequences of rebellion and sin having been overcome, the struggle of humanity's will and God's word having been resolved, God's original plan will be realized at the last. The simple, global logic of the system, with its focus on the world order of justice established by God but disrupted by humanity, leads inexorably to this eschatology of restoration, the restoration of balance, order, proportion—eternity for all who worship the one true God. Islam and Christianity say no less, and not much more.

That is because resurrection is a necessary doctrine for a system that insists upon the rationality and order of the universe under the rule of the unique, just, and merciful God. Monotheism that posits an ethical and just God without an eschatology of judgment and the world to come leaves unresolved the tensions inherent in the starting point: God is one, God is just. The basic logic of the monotheist system of Judaism requires the doctrine of personal resurrection. Indeed, without the conception of life beyond the grave, the system as a whole yields a mass of contradictions and anomalies: injustice to the righteous, prosperity to the wicked, never recompensed. That explains why at one point after another, the path to the future passes through, and beyond, the grave and arrives at the judgment that, for all Israel with few exceptions, leads to eternity. God's justice governs even in the chaos of private life, despite the clear disruption brought about by dreadful actualities: the prosperous wicked, the penurious righteous, in all the many variations that the imperfect world presents. Monotheism in this formulation requires the theodicy that promises resurrection and eternal life in the world to come to those who live out their years in accord with God's will, even suffering here to expiate sin, so as to enjoy a sinless eternity. The doctrine of resurrection proved integral to, an absolute necessity for, the account of the world's justice as the sages recorded matters. Without the doctrine of resurrection for eternal life, the theology can have found no solution to the crisis of everyday life, which hardly confirms the logic of a system of a just order.

For Israel judgment is not left to the end of days, when the dead will rise from their graves. For holy Israel judgment takes place in this world and in this age. The written Torah laid down the principle that Israel suffers for its sins, and everything that has happened since the closure of the written Torah only confirms that principle. The very continuation of Scripture beyond the Pentateuch and the account of the inheritance of the land makes that point, as we noted earlier.

Not only so, but the very heart of the doctrine of paradigmatic as against historical time, set forth in chapter 4—the explanation of Israel's subjugation to the gentiles and their idolatry—carries within itself a profound statement about Israel's identity, its enduring presence, from this age to the world to come, without interruption. Israel is judged and suffers its punishment in the here and now. That conviction animates the entire theological system before us. Then that same Israel, the never-dying people, emerges in the world to come fully at one with God. Indeed, that is the meaning of the advent of the world to come: "today if all Israel will it," "today if all Israel keeps a single Sabbath." To Israel the resurrection of the dead forms the beginning of the restoration of Eden, now meaning the restoration of Israel to the land of Israel, as we have noted many times.

The Resurrection of the Dead and Judgment

Paradigmatic thinking in monotheism necessarily generates the conviction of resurrection. This is stated in so many words. The certainty of resurrection derives from a simple fact of restorationist theology: God has already shown that he can do it, so *Genesis Rabbah* LXXVII:I.1: "You find that everything that the Holy One, blessed be he, is destined to do in the age to come he has already gone ahead and done through the righteous in this world. The Holy One, blessed be he, will raise the dead, and Elijah raised the dead." The sages deem urgent the task of reading outward and forward from Scripture, and at the critical conclusion of their theological system the oral Torah focuses upon Scripture's evidence, the regularization of Scripture's facts.

But the doctrine of resurrection as defined by the principal (and huge) composite of the Talmud of Babylonia contains a number of components: (1) origin of the doctrine in the written Torah; (2) the gentiles and the resurrection of the dead; (3) the distinction between the days of the messiah and the world to come; and (4) the restoration of Israel to the land of Israel. Here is the systematic exposition from Bavli tractate *Sanhedrin:*

I.22   A. R. Simeon b. Laqish contrasted [these two verses]: "It is written, 'I will gather them . . . with the blind and the lame, the woman with child and her that trail travails with child together' (Jer. 31:8), and it is written, 'Then shall the lame man leap as a hart and the tongue of the dumb sing, for in the wilderness shall waters break out and streams in the desert' (Isa. 35:6). How so [will the dead both retain their defects and also be healed]?

B. "They will rise [from the grave] bearing their defects and then be healed."

The first inquiry deals with the problem of the condition of the body upon resurrection and finds its resolution in the contrast of verses, yielding the stated doctrine: the dead rise in the condition in which they died and then are healed. Next comes the question of what happens to the gentiles, and the answer is given:

I.23   A. Ulla contrasted [these two verses]: "It is written, 'He will destroy death forever and the Lord God will wipe away tears from all faces' (Isa. 25:9), and it is written, 'For the child shall die a hundred years old . . . there shall no more thence an infant of days' (Isa. 65:20).

B. "There is no contradiction. The one speaks of Israel, the other of idolaters."

But then after the resurrection, the gentiles—meaning, in so many words, the idolaters—have no role except in relationship to Israel:

C. But what do idolaters want there [after the resurrection]?

D. It is to those concerning whom it is written, "And strangers shall stand and feed your flocks, and the sons of the alien shall be your plowmen and your vine-dressers" (Isa. 61:5).

Idolaters represent those alienated from the one and only God, and by no stretch of the imagination can that be represented, in contemporary categories, as an ethnic category. The clear distinction between the days of the messiah, involving, as we have seen, the resurrection of the dead, and the world to come, is now drawn:

I.24   A. R. Hisda contrasted [these two verses]: "It is written, 'Then the moon shall be confounded and the sun ashamed, when the Lord of hosts shall reign' (Isa. 24:23), and it is written, 'Moreover the light of the moon shall be as the light of seven days' (Isa. 30:26).

B. "There is no contradiction. The one refers to the days of the messiah, the other to the world to come."

The world to come demands attention in its own terms. Samuel's doctrine, that the world to come is marked solely by Israel's return to the land of Israel—that is, the restoration of humanity to Eden—requires attention in its own terms:

> C. And in the view of Samuel, who has said, "There is no differ-
>   ence between the world to come and the days of the messiah,
>   except the end of the subjugation of the exilic communities of
>   Israel"?
> D. There still is no contradiction. The one speaks of the camp of the
>   righteous, the other the camp of the Presence of God.
>
> I.25 A. Raba contrasted [these two verses]: "It is written, 'I kill and I
>   make alive' (Deut. 32:39) and it is written, 'I wound and I heal'
>   (Deut. 32:39). [The former implies that one is resurrected just as
>   he was at death, thus with blemishes, and the other implies that at
>   the resurrection all wounds are healed].
>   B. "Said the Holy One, blessed be he, 'What I kill I bring to life,'
>   and then, 'What I have wounded I heal.'" (b. Sanh. 11:1-2
>   I.22ff/91b)

Since people will enjoy individual existence beyond death, at the resurrection, death itself must be fated to die. We simply complete the exposition of the principle by encompassing an important detail.

The first component of the doctrine of the resurrection of the dead—belief both that the resurrection of the dead will take place and that it is the Torah that reveals that the dead will rise are fundamental to the oral Torah—is fully exposed in a fundamental composition devoted by the framers of the Mishnah to that subject. The components of the doctrine fit together, in that statement, in a logical order. First, in a predictable application of the governing principle of measure for measure, those who do not believe in the resurrection of the dead will be punished by being denied what they do not accept. Some few others bear the same fate. Second, but to be Israel means to rise from the grave, and that applies to all Israelites. That is to say, the given of the condition of Israel is that the entire holy people will enter the world to come, will enjoy the resurrection of the dead and eternal life. "Israel" then is anticipated to be the people of eternity. Third, excluded from the category of resurrection and the world to come, then, are only those who by their own sins have denied themselves that benefit. These are those who deny that the teaching of the world to come derives from the Torah, or who deny that the Torah comes from God, or hedonists. Exegesis of Scripture also yields the names of three kings who will not be resurrected, as well as four commoners; also specified generations: the flood, the dispersion, and Sodom, the generation of the wilderness, the party of Korah, and the ten tribes:

> A. All Israelites have a share in the world to come,
> B. as it is said, "Your people also shall be all righteous, they shall

inherit the land forever; the branch of my planting, the work of
my hands, that I may be glorified" (Isa. 60:21).

That single statement serves better than any other to define Israel in
the oral Torah. Now we forthwith take up exceptions:

> C. And these are the ones who have no portion in the world to come:
> D. He who says, the resurrection of the dead is a teaching which
> does not derive from the Torah, and the Torah does not come from
> Heaven; and an Epicurean.
> E. R. Aqiba says, "Also: He who reads in heretical books,
> F. "and he who whispers over a wound and says, 'I will put none of
> the diseases upon you which I have put on the Egyptians, for I am
> the LORD who heals you' (Exod. 15:26)."
> G. Abba Saul says, "Also: He who pronounces the divine Name as
> it is spelled out." (*m. Sanh.* 10:1 [=*b. Sanh.* 11:1])

From classes of persons, we turn to specified individuals who are
denied a place within Israel and entry in the world to come; all but one
are Israelites, and the exception, Balaam, has a special relation to Israel,
as the gentile prophet who came to curse but ended with a blessing:

> A. Three kings and four ordinary folk have no portion in the world
> to come.
> B. Three kings: Jeroboam, Ahab, and Manasseh.
> C. R. Judah says, "Manasseh has a portion in the world to come,
> D. "since it is said, 'And he prayed to him and he was entreated of
> him and heard his supplication and brought him again to
> Jerusalem into his kingdom' (2 Chron. 33:13)."
> E. They said to him, "To his kingdom he brought him back, but to
> the life of the world to come he did not bring him back."
> F. Four ordinary folk: Balaam, Doeg, Ahitophel, and Gehazi (*m.
> Sanh.* 10:2)

Then come entire generations of gentiles before Abraham, who
might have been considered for eternal life outside of the framework of
God's self-manifestation, first to Abraham, then in the Torah. These are
the standard sets, the generation of the flood, the generation of the dispersion, and the men of Sodom:

> A. The generation of the flood has no share in the world to come,
> B. and they shall not stand in the judgment,
> C. since it is written, "My spirit shall not judge with man forever"
> (Gen. 6:3)
> D. neither judgment nor spirit.
> E. The generation of the dispersion has no share in the world to come,

F. since it is said, "So the LORD scattered them abroad from there upon the face of the whole earth" (Gen. 11:8).

G. "So the LORD scattered them abroad"—in this world,

H. "and the LORD scattered them from there"—in the world to come.

I. The men of Sodom have no portion in the world to come,

J. since it is said, "Now the men of Sodom were wicked and sinners against the LORD exceedingly" (Gen. 13:13)

K. "Wicked"—in this world,

L. "And sinners"—in the world to come.

M. But they will stand in judgment.

N. R. Nehemiah says, "Both these and those will not stand in judgment,

O. 'for it is said, 'Therefore the wicked shall not stand in judgment [108A], nor sinners in the congregation of the righteous' (Ps. 1:5)

P. 'Therefore the wicked shall not stand in judgment'—this refers to the generation of the flood.

Q. 'Nor sinners in the congregation of the righteous'—this refers to the men of Sodom."

R. They said to him, "They will not stand in the congregation of the righteous, but they will stand in the congregation of the sinners."

S. The spies have no portion in the world to come,

T. as it is said, "Even those men who brought up an evil report of the land died by the plague before the LORD" (Num. 14:37)

U. "Died"—in this world.

V. "By the plague"—in the world to come. (*m. Sanh.* 10:3)

What about counterparts in Israel, from the Torah forward? The issue concerns the generation of the wilderness, which rejected the Land; the party of Korah; and the ten tribes. These match the gentile contingents. But here there is a dispute, and no normative judgment emerges from the Mishnah's treatment of the matter:

A. "The generation of the wilderness has no portion in the world to come and will not stand in judgment,

B. "for it is written, 'In this wilderness they shall be consumed and there they shall die' (Num. 14:35)," The words of R. Aqiba.

C. R. Eliezer says, "Concerning them it says, 'Gather my saints together to me, those that have made a covenant with me by sacrifice' (Ps. 50:5)."

D. "The party of Korah is not destined to rise up,

E. "for it is written, 'And the earth closed upon them'—in this world.

F. "'And they perished from among the assembly'—in the world to come," the words of R. Aqiba.

G. And R. Eliezer says, "Concerning them it says, 'The LORD kills and resurrects, brings down to Sheol and brings up again' (1 Sam. 2:6)." (*m. Sanh.* 10:4)

> A. "The ten tribes [of northern Israel, exiled by the Assyrians] are not destined to return [with Israel at the time of the resurrection of the dead],
> B. "since it is said, 'And he cast them into another land, as on this day' (Deut. 29:28). Just as the day passes and does not return, so they have gone their way and will not return," the words of R. Aqiba.
> C. R. Eliezer says, "Just as this day is dark and then grows light, so the ten tribes for whom it now is dark—thus in the future it is destined to grow light for them." (*m. Sanh.* 10:5)

Scripture thus contributes the details that refine the basic proposition; the framer has found the appropriate exclusions. But the prophet, in Scripture, also has provided the basic allegation on which all else rests, that is, "Israel will be entirely righteous and inherit the land forever." Denying the stated dogmas removes a person from the status of "Israel," in line with the opening statement, so to be Israel means to rise from the dead, and Israel as a collectivity is defined as those persons in humanity who are destined to eternal life, a supernatural community.

Among the components of that doctrine, that resurrection of the dead is a doctrine set forth by the written Torah and demonstrable within the framework of the Torah occupies a principal place in the oral Torah's exposition of the topic. That proposition is demonstrated over and over again. Evidence from the Torah concerning the resurrection of the dead is ubiquitous:

> A. And so did R. Simai say, "There is no passage [in the Torah] which does not contain [clear evidence concerning] the resurrection of the dead, but we have not got the power of exegesis [sufficient to find the pertinent indication].
> B. "For it is said, 'He will call to the heaven above and to the earth, that he may judge his people' (Ps. 50:4).
> C. "'He will call to the heaven above': this refers to the soul.
> D. "'and to the earth': this refers to the body.
> E. "'that he may judge his people': who judges with him?
> F. "And how on the basis of Scripture do we know that Scripture speaks only of the resurrection of the dead?
> G. "As it is said, 'Come from the four winds, O breath, and breathe upon these slain, that they may live' (Ezek. 37:9)." (*Sifré to Deuteronomy* CCCVI:XXVIII.3)

Further proofs of the same proposition are abundant, with the following instances representative of the larger corpus. First, we note the recurrent formula, "how on the basis of the Torah do we know . . . ?" Then we are given a sequence of cases, each one of them, as noted earlier, deriving from an individual, none of them appealing to the eternity of the collectivity of Israel. We start with the case of Aaron (from Bavli tractate *Sanhedrin*):

> I.2   A. How, on the basis of the Torah, do we know about the resurrection of the dead?
>
> B. As it is said, "And you shall give thereof the LORD's offering to Aaron the priest" (Num. 18:28).
>
> C. And will Aaron live forever? And is it not the case that he did not even get to enter the Land of Israel, from the produce of which the LORD's offering is given? [So there is no point in Aaron's life at which he would receive the priestly rations.]
>
> D. Rather, this teaches that he is destined once more to live, and the Israelites will give him the LORD's offering.
>
> E. On the basis of this verse, therefore, we see that the resurrection of the dead is a teaching of the Torah.

Now come the patriarchs, who also will rise from the dead:

> I.4   A. It has been taught on Tannaite authority:
>
> B. R. Simai says, "How on the basis of the Torah do we know about the resurrection of the dead?
>
> C. "As it is said, 'And I also have established my covenant with [the patriarchs] to give them the land of Canaan' (Exod. 6:4).
>
> D. "'With you' is not stated, but rather, 'with them,' indicating on the basis of the Torah that there is the resurrection of the dead."

The question is then reframed, no longer in terms of proof based on the facts of Scripture, but now in more general terms. Sectarians ask how we know that God will do this thing:

> I.5   A. Minim asked Rabban Gamaliel, "How do we know that the Holy One, blessed be he, will resurrect the dead?"

Proofs from Scripture will not serve when dealing with outsiders to the community of the Torah:

> B. He said to them, "It is proved from the Torah, from the Prophets, and from the Writings." But they did not accept his proofs.

In each of the three matched demonstrations, a verse is adduced but interpreted in some way other than the proposed one:

C. "From the Torah: for it is written, 'And the LORD said to Moses, Behold, you shall sleep with your fathers and rise up' (Deut. 31:16)."

D. They said to him, "But perhaps the sense of the passage is, 'And the people will rise up' (Deut. 31:16)?"

E. "From the Prophets: as it is written, 'Thy dead men shall live, together with my dead body they shall arise. Awake and sing, you that live in the dust, for your dew is as the dew of herbs, and the earth shall cast out its dead' (Isa. 26:19)."

F. "But perhaps that refers to the dead whom Ezekiel raised up."

G. "From the Writings, as it is written, 'And the roof of your mouth, like the best wine of my beloved, that goes down sweetly, causing the lips of those who are asleep to speak' (Song of Sol. 7:9)."

H. "But perhaps this means that the dead will move their lips?"

I. That would accord with the view of R. Yohanan.

J. For R. Yohanan said in the name of R. Simeon b. Yehosedeq, "Any authority in whose name a law is stated in this world moves his lips in the grave,

K. "as it is said, 'Causing the lips of those that are asleep to speak.'"

Finally, Gamaliel is able to find a pertinent verse that the sectarians could accept; why this proof served and the prior ones did not would yield insight into the sages' characterization of their critics:

L. [The minim would not concur in Gamaliel's view] until he cited for them the following verse: "'Which the LORD swore to your fathers to give to them' (Deut. 11:21)—to them and not to you, so proving from the Torah that the dead will live."

M. And there are those who say that it was the following verse that he cited to them: "'But you who cleaved to the LORD your God are alive, everyone of you this day' (Deut. 4:4). Just as on this day all of you are alive, so in the world to come all of you will live." (b. Sanh. 11:1/I.2—14/90b-91b)

The successful proof involves little more than a dismissal of the others, at L, or a reaffirmation of the faith—Israel cleaves to the Lord—at M.

What about enduring the last judgment? Within the documents of the oral Torah, we have little narrative to tell us how the judgment will be carried on. Even the detail that through repentance and death humanity has already atoned, which is stated in so many words in the context of repentance and atonement, plays no role that I can discern in discussions of the last judgment. What we do know concerns two matters: (1) when does the judgment take place? And (2) by what criteria does God decide who inherits the world to come? As to the former, the judgment is comparable to the annual judgment for humanity's fate in the following year. It will happen either at the beginning of the New Year on the first of Tishré, when, annually, humanity is judged, or on the fifteenth of Nisan, when Israel celebrates its freedom from Egyptian bondage and begins its pilgrimage to Sinai. The final judgment lasts for a period of time, not forever, and at that point the resurrected who have endured in judgment pass to the world to come or eternal life.

Standing under God's Judgment

How does one stand in judgment, go through the process of divine review of one's life and actions and emerge in the world to come, restored to the land that is Eden? Proper conduct and study of Torah lead to standing in judgment and to the life of the world to come, and not keeping the one and studying the other deny entry into that life. What is striking is the appeal to Eden for just this message about reentry into the land.

1. A. Said R. Abba b. Eliashib, "[The reference at Lev. 26:3 to statutes is to] statutes that bring a person into the life of the world to come.
    B. "That is in line with the following verse of Scripture: 'And he who is left in Zion and remains in Jerusalem will be called holy, everyone who has been recorded for life in Jerusalem' [Isa. 4:3]—for he is devoted to [study of] Torah, which is called the tree of life."

Now comes the reference to Eden:

2. A. It has been taught in the name of R. Eliezer, "A sword and a scroll wrapped together were handed down from heaven, as if to say to them, 'If you keep what is written in this [scroll], you will be saved from the sword,
    B. "'and if not, in the end [the sword] will kill you.'"
    C. "Whence is that proposition to be inferred? 'He drove out the man, and at the east of the Garden of Eden he placed the cherubim, and a flaming sword which turned every way, to guard the way to the tree of life' [Gen. 3:4].
    D. "The [first] reference to 'the way' refers to the rules of proper conduct, and the second reference, '[the way to] the tree of life' refers to the Torah."

The same message is given in a different framework:

3. A. It was taught in the name of R. Simeon b. Yohai, "A loaf and a rod wrapped together were given from heaven.

  B. "It was as if to say to them, 'If you keep the Torah, lo, here is bread to eat, and if not, lo, here is a staff with which to be smitten.'

  C. "Whence is that proposition to be inferred? 'If you are willing and obedient, you shall eat the good of the land; but if you refuse and rebel, you shall be devoured by the sword'" (Isa. 15:19-20). (*Leviticus Rabbah* XXXV:VI:1f.)

The world to come, involving resurrection and judgment, will be attained through the Torah, which teaches proper conduct. That simple doctrine yields the proposition here.

When the sages speak of the world to come, their language signifies a final change in relationship between God and humanity, a model of how God and humanity relate that marks the utter restoration of the world order originally contemplated. That is the way humanity and God conduct their cosmic transaction that God had intended from the beginning and for eternity—time having no place in God's category-formation for ordering creation. The point, specifically, is that Israel enjoys a set of relationships with God that are not differentiated temporally and certainly not organized in causal patterns of sequence, in ordered, causative sequence through time, but in other ways. How then are these relationships classified in this governing model? They are either rebellious or obedient, selfish and arrogant, or selfless and humble. Since at issue are patterns of relationship, the circumstance and context, whether temporal or singular in some other way, make no impact. That is because they make no difference, the relationship transcending circumstance. Therefore it is entirely reasonable that the world to come match the world that has been—why not? The one, like the other, will find its definition in how God and humanity relate. That is what I mean when I claim that we deal with modes of thought of an other-than-historical and temporal character. The restorationist character of the theology of the oral Torah explains what the sages mean. That theology, by reason of the modes of thought that define its logic of making connections and drawing conclusions, requires that endings match beginnings, the relationships of God and humanity at the one point matching those at the other.

When the sages set forth their theological eschatology, what exactly do they mean by *'olam habba,* the world or the age that is coming? The world or the age to come (the Hebrew, *'olam,* may sustain a translation of either the locative "world," or the temporal-ordinal "age" to come) completes the story. It necessarily forms the final chapter of the theology of the oral Torah. The age that is coming will find Adam's successor in Eden's replacement, that is, resurrected, judged, and justified Israel—comprising nearly all Israelites who ever lived—now eternally rooted in the land of Israel. When Israel returns to God, God will restore their fortunes. The sentence remains brief enough with the added adjectival clause—in the model of Adam and Eve in Eden. Everything else amplifies details. That simple sentence is explicitly built on the verb-root for return, encompassing restore, *shub,* yielding *teshubah,* repentance as well as the causative form of the verb, *hashib,* thus return or restore. It thereby defines the condition, (intransitive) return or repentance, for the advent of the age to come, which encompasses the action, (transitively) to return matters to their original condition.

The Restoration of Humanity to Eden

How, exactly, do the sages envisage restoration? Predictably, because they think paradigmatically and not in historical (let alone cyclical) sequences, the sages find models of the end in beginnings. That is why in this context they cluster, and systematically review, the two principal ones, liberation, restoration. First is the account of Israel's liberation from Egypt, the initial act of redemption, which will be recapitulated in the end. Second comes the story of Adam and Eden for their picture of the world to come, the return of Adam to Eden, now in the form of Israel to Zion. (A secondary motif in the latter paradigm contains the complementary category, Gehenna, to which gentiles—those who deny God—and Israelites who sufficiently sin are consigned when they are denied life.) In the latter case the important point for paradigmatic thinking is that there is no meaningful difference between the world to come and the Garden of Eden. We go over, once more in so many words, an explicit statement that the two are not to be distinguished, here in a formulation we shall more fully see again later on in a different context:

> A. "He who performs mostly good deeds inherits the Garden of Eden, but he who performs mostly transgression inherits Gehenna." (*y. Pe'a* 1:1 XXXII.1)

The Garden of Eden is the opposite of Gehenna, and the context—Mishnah tractate *Pe'a's* picture of how good deeds store up merit for the world to come—explains the rest. Since *Pe'a* at the outset speaks of the world to come, so inheriting the Garden of Eden in context bears precisely the meaning of inheriting the world to come; there is no difference, and the two, Eden and world to come, are interchangeable when the sages speak of what happens after death, on the one side, or after resurrection and judgment, on the other. For humanity entering the world to come, on the other side of resurrection and judgment, marks a homecoming. At the moment of return to Eden, entry into the world to come, humanity returns to its original condition, in God's image, after God's likeness, complement and conclusion of creation. Here is the ultimate complementarity, the final point of correspondence.

Whatever model serves out of Scripture, that restorationist eschatology (a word that in the context now established can be used only in a loose way, as I shall explain) is stated in so many words in the following passage from *Lamentations Rabbati,* which appeals to the rhetoric of return, restoration, and renewal:

1. A. "Restore us to yourself, O LORD, that we may be restored!"
   B. Said the Community of Israel before the Holy One, blessed be he, "LORD of the world, it all depends on you: 'Restore us to yourself, O LORD.'"
   C. Said to them the Holy One, blessed be he, "It all depends on you: 'Return to me and I will return to you, says the Lord of hosts' (Mal. 3:7)."
   D. Said the Community of Israel before the Holy One, blessed be he, "LORD of the world, it all depends on you: 'Restore us, O God of our salvation' (Ps. 85:5)."
   E. Thus it says, "Restore us to yourself, O LORD, that we may be restored!"

Israel insists that restoration depends on God, but God repays the compliment, and the exchange then is equal: God restores Israel when Israel returns to God, just as we learned when we examined the category of repentance and atonement.

Now we see a sequence of models of redemption. First, as anticipated, comes the explicit comparison of Adam's Eden with the coming restoration, part of a sequence of recapitulated paradigms:

2. A. "Renew our days as of old:"
   B. As in the days of the first Adam: "So he drove out the man and he placed at the east of the Garden of Eden the cherubim" (Gen. 3:24). [The word for "east" and the word for "of old," which use the same letters; the sense, is this: "Renew our days like those of him in connection with whom *kedem* is stated." After being driven out, Adam repented of his sin.]

The restoration involves the temple offerings as well, which later on are defined in particular; this also is "as in the days of old:"

3. A. Another interpretation of the phrase, "Renew our days as of old:"

    B. That is in line with this verse: "Then shall the offering of Judah and Jerusalem be pleasant to the LORD as in the days of old and as in ancient years" (Mal. 3:4)

But the restoration is multidimensional, since it also involves the figures of Moses and Solomon:

    C. "as in the days of old:" this refers to Moses: "Then his people remembered the days of old, the days of Moses" (Isa. 63:11)

    D. "and as in ancient years:" this refers to the time of Solomon.

Noah and Abel now are introduced; they are necessary for the reason given at the end:

4. A. [Another interpretation of the phrase, "Renew our days as of old:"]

    B. Rabbi says, "'as in the days of old' refers to the time of Noah: 'For this is as the waters of Noah unto me' (Isa. 54:9)

    C. "'and as in ancient years' refers to the time of Abel, prior to whose time there was no idolatry in the world." (*Lamentations Rabbati* CXLIII:i.1ff.)

Noah represents the moment at which God made peace with humanity, even in humanity's flawed condition. Of intense interest for my analysis, within the restorationist pattern, Abel stands for the time before idolatry, so explicitly excluding idolaters from the world to come. While Noah, representing all of humanity, and Abel, standing even for antediluvian humanity, make their appearance, the upshot remains exclusionary. The restoration to perfection involves the exclusion of imperfection, and so idolaters cannot enter the new Eden. But we shall see other, inclusionary dimensions that logically complete the doctrine of the gentiles in the world to come.

Exile and Return

As the reference to the Exodus has already alerted us, the pattern that is adumbrated in these statements encompasses not only restoration, but the recapitulation of the paradigm of oppression, repentance, and reconciliation. For restoration cannot stand by itself but must be placed into that context in which the restoration takes on heavy weight. So not only Adam and Eden, but the entire past of suffering and finally of salvation, is reviewed in the same context. Many salvations, not only one, are recorded for Israel, all of them conforming to a single pattern, which imparts its definition upon the final act of salvation as well, the one that comes with personal resurrection and all Israel's entry into the world to come. That is the claim explicitly set forth in the following composition from Yerushalmi tractate *Berakhot:*

> A. Ben Zoma says, "Israel is destined not to mention the exodus from Egypt in the future age."
>
> B. What is the basis for this statement? "And thus the days are coming says the LORD, you shall no longer say, 'God lives, who took us out of the Land of Egypt'; but 'God lives, who took out and who brought the seed of the House of Israel from the Land in the North'" [Jer. 23:7-8].

The point that is argued is that a pattern of salvation is established, and it is incremental, one salvation being added to the record already written of its predecessor:

> C. "This does not mean that the exodus from Egypt will be removed [and no longer mentioned]. Rather [mention of the redemption from] Egypt will be added to the [mention of] the redemption from the Kingdom [of the North]. The [mention of the redemption from the] Kingdom [of the North] will be primary and [the mention of the redemption from] Egypt will be secondary."
>
> D. And so it says, "Your name shall no longer be called Jacob. Israel shall be your name."
>
> E. They said, "That does not mean that the name Jacob will be removed. Rather Jacob will be added to Israel. Israel will be the primary name and Jacob will be secondary."

Now the war of Gog and Magog recurs, a detail of the eschatological program that is neither bypassed nor much developed in the oral Torah:

> F. And so it says, "Do not mention the first [redemption]"—this refers to [the redemption from] Egypt. "And pay no heed to the early [redemption]"—this refers to [the redemption from] the Kingdom of the North. "Lo, I am making a new [redemption]"—this refers to [the redemption to come in the time of] Gog.

Where a paradigm is rehearsed, a parable serves to realize the matter in a clear way, because it moves from the particular to the general:

> G. They gave a parable. To what case is this matter similar? To the case of a person who was walking by the way and he met up with a wolf and was saved from it. He began to tell the story of [his salvation from] the wolf.

H. Afterwards he met up with a lion and was saved from it. He forgot the story of [his salvation from] the wolf and began to tell the story of [his salvation from] the lion.

I. Afterwards he met up with a serpent and was saved from it. He forgot both the previous incidents and began to tell the story of [his salvation from] the serpent.

Now comes the explicit application of the parable:

J. Just so was the case for Israel. Their [salvation from] the later troubles caused them to forget [to mention the story of their salvation from] the earlier troubles. (*y. Berakhot* 1:6 I:7)

So the paradigm of trouble but salvation for Israel works itself out, and it gives reassurance that God will redeem Israel in the future, as he did in the past; a pattern governs throughout. Indeed, the surest evidence of the coming redemption is the oppression that now takes place.

This point is stated in a variety of ways, taking an important place in the set of doctrines set forth around the theme of the world to come. Here is the simplest statement of why suffering and oppression present cause for renewed hope:

1.   A. "The punishment of your iniquity, O daughter of Zion, is accomplished, he will keep you in exile no longer."

Now comes the point that the very condition of Israel, its life in exile, serves as guarantee of the redemption that God is going to bring about. That relationship of complementarity—oppression, redemption—is why the act of oppression, now realized, validates the hope for the messiah to signal the advent of the redemption fulfilled in the world to come. The theology not only accommodates the dissonant fact of Israel's subjugation but finds reassurance in it, as is stated in so many words:

B. R. Helbo in the name of R. Yohanan said, "Better was the removing of the ring by Pharaoh [for the sealing of decrees to oppress the Israelites] than the forty years during which Moses prophesied concerning them, because it was through this [oppression] that the redemption came about, while through that [prophesying] the redemption did not come about."

C. R. Simeon b. Laqish said, "Better was the removing of the ring by Ahasueros decreeing persecution of Israel in Media than the sixty myriads of prophets who prophesied in the days of Elijah, because it was through this [oppression] that the redemption came about, while through that [prophesying] the redemption did not come about."

D. Rabbis said, "Better was the Book of Lamentations than the forty years in which Jeremiah prophesied over them, because in it the Israelites received full settlement of their iniquities on the day the temple was destroyed.

E. "That is in line with the following verse: 'The punishment of your iniquity, O daughter of Zion, is accomplished.'" (*Lamentations Rabbati* CXXII:i.1)

In narrative form the statement sets forth the proposition that Israel's future is already clear from its present. Here the prophets provide the key to interpreting the one and anticipating the other. Just as the prophetic prediction of the ruin of Jerusalem has been realized, so the same prophets' promises of ultimate salvation will also come about. That yields a certainty about what is going to happen. The whole then forms a coherent pattern, one that reveals what will happen through what has happened.

If we deal with so-called last things, for the oral Torah, *last* does not define a temporal category, or even an ordinal one in the exact sense. By *last things,* the sages' theology means the model of things that applies at the last, from now on, for eternity. By that, in the sages' case, they mean to say, the last, the final realization or recapitulation of the ever-present and enduring paradigm(s), creation and exodus, for instance, as we just noticed.[1] That is, I cannot sufficiently stress, a paradigm organizes and classifies relationships, treats concrete events as merely exemplary. So the actualities of this one's conduct with, and attitude toward, God are restated in generalizations, laws, or rules. To "love God" defines a relationship, and actions and attitudes that express that relationship then may be exemplified by incidents that show what happens when Israel loves God, or what happens when Israel does not love God. These further may be captured, many cases unified by a single pattern.

Redemption from Egypt, for the World to Come

In concrete terms that means intense interest will focus on the way in which the redemption of Israel from Egypt compares with the advent of the world to come. This point is made explicitly. The fall of the oppressor at the start of Israel's history and the fall of the nations at the end, characteristic of the redemption of that time and of the coming time, will be matched by the fall of the other at the end and the traits of the redemption that is coming. To see how this is made concrete is to enter into the theological workshop of the sages. No passage more clearly exposes the character of their thought—both its method and its message—than the one from *Pesiqta de Rab. Kahana* that requires them to select paradigmatic moments out of the detritus of history:

2. A. R. Levi, son-in-law of R. Zechariah, in the name of R. Berekhiah said, "As at the news concerning Egypt, so they shall be startled at the fall of the adversary (Isa. 23:5)."

    B. Said R. Eliezer, "Whenever the name of Tyre is written in Scripture, if it is written out [with all of the letters], then it refers to the province of Tyre. Where it is written without all of its letters [and so appears identical to the word for enemy], the reference of Scripture is to Rome. [So the sense of the verse is that Rome will receive its appropriate reward.]"

Now the fall of Egypt is matched by the fall of Rome, which, we surely should anticipate, is a precondition for the advent of the world to come, at which point, at a minimum, the subjugation of Israel to the pagan empire ceases:

3. A. R. Levi in the name of R. Hama bar Hanina: "He who exacted vengeance from the former [oppressor] will exact vengeance from the latter.

Now the first redemption, from Egypt, is shown to match point by point the final redemption, from Edom/Rome. Each detail finds its counterpart in an amazing selection of consequential facts, properly aligned—ten in all:

    B. "Just as, in Egypt, it was with blood, so with Edom [=Rome] it will be the same: 'I will show wonders in the heavens and in the earth, blood, and fire, and pillars of smoke' (Job 3:3).

    C. "Just as, in Egypt, it was with frogs, so with Edom it will be the same: 'The sound of an uproar from the city, an uproar because of the palace, an uproar of the Lord who renders recompense to his enemies' (Isa. 66:6).

    D. "Just as, in Egypt, it was with lice, so with Edom it will be the same: 'The streams of Bosrah will be turned into pitch, and the dust thereof into brimstone, and the land thereof shall become burning pitch (Isa. 34:9). Smite the dust of the earth that it may become lice' (Exod. 8:12).

    E. "Just as, in Egypt, it was with swarms of wild beasts, so with Edom it will be the same: 'The pelican and the bittern shall possess it' (Isa. 34:11).

    F. "Just as, in Egypt, it was with pestilence, so with Edom it will be the same: 'I will plead against Gog with pestilence and with blood' (Ezek. 38:22).

G. "Just as, in Egypt, it was with boils, so with Edom it will be the same: 'This shall be the plague wherewith the Lord will smite all the peoples that have warred against Jerusalem: their flesh shall consume away while they stand upon their feet' (Zech. 14:12).

H. "Just as, in Egypt, it was with great stones, so with Edom it will be the same: 'I will cause to rain upon Gog . . . an overflowing shower and great hailstones' (Ezek. 38:22).

I. "Just as, in Egypt, it was with locusts, so with Edom it will be the same: 'And you, son of man, thus says the Lord GOD: Speak to birds of every sort . . . the flesh of the mighty shall you eat . . . blood shall you drink . . . you shall eat fat until you are full and drink blood until you are drunk' (Ezek. 39:17-19).

J. "Just as, in Egypt, it was with darkness, so with Edom it will be the same: 'He shall stretch over Edom the line of chaos and the plummet of emptiness' (Isa. 34:11).

K. "Just as, in Egypt, he took out their greatest figure and killed him, so with Edom it will be the same: 'A great slaughter in the land of Edom, among them to come down shall be the wild oxen' (Isa. 34:6-7)." (*Pesiq. R. Kah.* VII:XI.2)

Merely juxtaposing "Egypt" and "Edom" suffices to establish that we shall compare the one and the other, and the paradigm of redemption emerges. The known, Egypt, bears the distinguishing trait of marking Israel's initial redemption; then the unknown can be illuminated. Therefore, say "Edom" (= Rome) and no one can miss the point. The stakes are sufficiently identified through the combination of the native categories, and all the rest spells out what is clear at the very outset. I do not think the method of paradigmatic thinking finds more lucid expression than in this articulate statement that the redemption that is coming replicates the redemption that is past in a world that conforms to enduring paradigms. And that must encompass, also, the return to Eden that we have many times considered.

Within the theory of paradigmatic thinking about the received facts of Scripture that is set forth here, a given paradigm should come to expression in a broad variety of exemplary cases (matched events, arrangements of symbols whether verbal or actual). In theory, therefore, once we fix upon a restorationist paradigm to account for the sages' classification of data and interpretation thereof, we should find more than a single case that embodies the paradigm. In fact, as we shall now see, a number of patterns is adduced to explain how the world to come will come about and to define its character. Our next case is a pattern that once more involves the liberation of Israel from Egypt, this time as the liberation is celebrated at the Passover Seder by the drinking of four cups of wine. These four cups drunk at the Passover Seder correspond to the redemption of Israel, four instances of the same pattern: the retribution carried out against Pharaoh, the retribution to be carried out against the Four Kingdoms, and the nations of the world generally, and the consolation of Israel; there is then a balance between Israel's and the nations' fate.

All of these events represent embodiments of a single pattern, as much as the drinking of the four cups at the celebration of the liberation from Egypt marks a single event that recurs as a pattern over the ages. As the Yerushalmi tractate *Pesahim* puts it:

> A. Whence [did they derive the requirement] for four cups?
> B. R. Yohanan [said] in the name of R. Benaiah, "[They] correspond to the four redemptions [or acts of redemption, mentioned in reference to Egypt]: 'Say, therefore, to the Israelite people: I am the LORD. I will take you out' ['from under the burdens of the Egyptians and deliver you from their bondage. I will redeem you with an outstretched arm and through extraordinary chastisements']. 'And I will take you to be my people,' (Exod. 6:6-7). [These verses contain the four terms:] 'I will take out,' 'I will deliver,' 'I will redeem,' 'I will take.'"

Here is an explicit treatment of the rite as paradigmatic, and the purpose of the pattern is to go over the acts of redemption that God carried out in bringing Israel out of Egypt. But, as we should expect, others read the same symbols in the same context of liberation in a different way, each version going over the same basic pattern and saying the same thing, all versions distinct and enriching. Here we deal with how the cups of wine form the precondition of redemption of Israel or salvation for an Israelite, in this case, Joseph:

> C. R. Joshua b. Levi said, "[They] correspond to the four cups of [wine mentioned in reference to] Pharaoh: 'Pharaoh's cup was in my hand, [and I took the grapes,] and I pressed them into Pharaoh's cup, and placed the cup in Pharaoh's hand' (Gen. 40:11) . . . 'and you will place Pharaoh's cup in his hand' (Gen. 40:13). ['But think of me when all is well with you again . . . so as to free me from this place' (Gen. 40:14).]" [The four cups in the dream and its interpretation brought or preceded a redemption, in this instance that of Joseph.]

The four cups further correspond to the four kingdoms that have ruled Israel and that Israel will succeed in the age to come:

D. R. Levi said, "[They] correspond to the four [world] kingdoms [that have oppressed Israel and that precede the kingdom of God—Babylonia, Media, Greece, and Rome, with each cup perhaps marking the release of Israel from a different oppressor]."

The Rabbis at the end take a position entirely in harmony with the preceding ones, but they state the whole in its fullness by matching retribution for the nations of the world with consolation for Israel, thus encompassing all the other matters set forth in individual names. The introduction of the gentiles into the eschatological theology presents no surprise, since in the theory of complementarity, in any paradigm in which Israel plays the principal part, the gentiles will make an appearance. Here is one account of the gentiles at the advent of the world to come:

E. And rabbis say, "[They] correspond to the four cups of retribution that the Holy One Praised be he will give the nations of the world to drink: 'For thus said the LORD, the God of Israel, to me: "Take from my hand this cup of wine—of wrath [—and make all the nations to whom I send you drink of it]"' (Jer. 25:15); '[Flee from the midst of Babylon. . . . for this is a time of vengeance for the LORD, he will deal retribution to her]. Babylon was a golden cup in the LORD's hand; it made the whole earth drunk' (Jer. 51:[6-]7); 'For in the LORD's hand there is a cup [with foaming wine fully mixed; from this he pours; all the wicked of the earth drink, draining it to the very dregs]' (Ps. 75:9); 'He will rain down upon the wicked blazing coals and sulfur, a scorching wind shall be the portion of their cup' (Ps. 11:6)."

F. [Continuing the words of the Rabbis in E:] "And corresponding to them [to the four cups of retribution], the Holy One, Praised be he, will give Israel four cups of consolation to drink: 'The LORD is my allotted share and cup' (Ps. 16:5); '[You spread a table for me in full view of my enemies;] You anoint my head with oil; my drink is abundant' (Ps. 23:5); and this [verse:] 'I raise the cup of deliverances' (Ps. 116:13) [provides an additional two cups (as "deliverances" is plural), each of which represents a separate act of deliverance]." (y. Pesah. 10:1 II:3)

So we see how the symbolic system evoked by the restorationist paradigm encompasses the received organization of the coming ages, matching past and future. The opinions complement one another. We begin with the redemption in Egypt, as is appropriate at the commemoration of that event; then comes the role of Pharaoh. This introduces the world kingdoms that correspond at the end of time to Pharaoh, Babylonia, Media, Greece, and Rome, and, in more general terms, the retribution that will overtake the nations. Here we have the working of a paradigm, a single action repeated, the meaning always the same, the moments alone differentiated one from the other by reason of a teleology out of all phase with the linear sequence, past to future, that forms the foundation of the historical understanding.

Creation the Model of Redemption

Now in this set of checks and balances that forms the architectonics of the governing theology, what at the outset matches the act of redemption at the end can only be the initial act of creation. Creation reaches its complement and completion in redemption, a somewhat jarring match. Here, when the sages speak of "the world to come," they refer to the realization of a paradigm that is established "of old," meaning that redemption of Israel that is built into the very structure of creation, a presence in the past, as much as the past of creation is present in redemption and the world to come. That is why God himself not only participated in Israel's affairs, going into exile, as we noted in connection with God's abandoning the temple, but also participates in the return to the land.

> B. R. Simeon ben Yohai says, "Come and see how dear [the nation of] Israel is before the Holy One, blessed be he, for wherever they were exiled, the Divine Presence was with them.
>
> C. "[When] they were exiled to Egypt, the Divine Presence was with them, as is said, 'was I not exiled to your father's house when they were in Egypt' (1 Sam. 2:27).
>
> D. "[When] they were exiled to Babylonia, the Divine Presence was with them, as is said, 'for your sake I sent to Babylonia' (Isa. 43:14).
>
> E. 'And also when they will be redeemed [in the future], the Divine Presence will be with them, as is said, 'and the LORD your God will return your return' (Deut. 30:3).
>
> F. "It does not say 'and he will cause to return' (ve-heshib) but 'and he will return' (ve-shab). This teaches that the Holy One, blessed be he, will return with them from among the places of exile." (b. Megillah 4:4/I.10/29a)

Specifically, God redeems Israel and saves the individual Israelite, and *when* that act of redemption or salvation takes place bears no consequence for the meaning of the act or the consequences thereof. It is an act that embodies a relationship, and relationships take place unmediated by time or circumstance. That, sum and substance, embodies the result of paradigmatic thinking, extending beginnings to endings, creation to the world to come.

The salvation of Israel in the world to come then represents the final instance of a recurrent pattern. This is portrayed through an account of the variety of occasions of redemption celebrated by the recitation of the Hallel Psalms, Psalms 113–118, which are sung on celebratory occasions. This account (from Bavli tractate *Pesahim*) homogenizes the like and distinguishes like from unlike:

> II.10 A. Our rabbis have taught on Tannaite authority:
>   B. Who recited this Hallel [Psalms 113–118]?

The answer to that question indicates that the attitude of supplication and thanks transcends all considerations of time and circumstance. The same pattern of supplication and divine response may impose itself upon any and all contexts, which is another way of saying that considerations of time and sequence play no role in the Torah. Thus the paradigm is realized by Moses and Israel, Joshua and Israel, Deborah and Barak, Hezekiah, and onward.

> II.10 C. R. Eliezer says, "Moses and Israel said it at the time that they stood at the sea. They said, 'Not unto us, not unto us' (Ps. 115:1), and the Holy Spirit responded, 'For my own sake will I do it' (Isa. 48:11)."
>   D. R. Judah says, "Joshua and Israel said it when the kings of Canaan attacked them. They said, 'Not unto us, not unto us' (Ps. 115:1), and the Holy Spirit responded, 'For my own sake will I do it' (Isa. 48:11)."
>   E. R. Eleazar the Modiite says, "Deborah and Barak said it when Sisera attacked them. They said, 'Not unto us, not unto us' (Ps. 115:1), and the Holy Spirit responded, 'For my own sake will I do it' (Isa. 48:11)."
>   F. R. Eleazar b. Azariah says, "Hezekiah and his allies said it when Sennacherib attacked them. They said, 'Not unto us, not unto us' (Ps. 115:1), and the Holy Spirit responded, 'For my own sake will I do it' (Isa. 48:11)."
>   G. R. Aqiba says, "Hananiah, Mishael, and Azariah said it when Nebuchadnezzar the wicked attacked them. They said, 'Not unto us, not unto us' (Ps. 115:1), and the Holy Spirit responded, 'For my own sake will I do it' (Isa. 48:11)."
>   H. R. Yosé the Galilean says, "Mordecai and Esther said it when Haman the wicked attacked them. They said, 'Not unto us, not unto us' (Ps. 115:1), and the Holy Spirit responded, 'For my own sake will I do it' (Isa. 48:11)."
>   I. And the sages say, "The prophets among them ordained that the Israelites should say it at every turning point and on the occasion

of every sorrow—may such not come upon them, and when they are redeemed, they are to recite it in thanks for their redemption.

So much for "all Israel," as distinct from the Israelite. If what happens to the holy people bears no relationship to time or change but recapitulates a single pattern through eternity, all the more so the affairs of the private person, Israel the Israelite. It follows that Israel is saved from Egypt, the exiles from the rule of the pagan kingdoms, the righteous from the fiery furnace or the souls of the righteous from Gehenna, one paradigm ordering all events and encounters. In that last detail the resurrection and the judgment are placed into alignment with the world to come. A further formulation now carries matters forward:

II.12 A. Now that there is the great Hallel, how come we recite this one ?
       [Ps. 113–18]
    B. It is because it contains these five references: the exodus from Egypt, dividing the Reed Sea, giving of the Torah, resurrection of the dead, and the anguish of the messiah.
    C. The exodus from Egypt: "When Israel came forth out of Egypt" (Ps. 114:1);
    D. dividing the Reed Sea: "the sea saw it and fled" (Ps. 114:3);
    E. giving of the Torah: "the mountains skipped like rams" (Ps. 114:4);
    F. resurrection of the dead: "I shall walk before the LORD in the land of the living" (Ps. 116:9);
    G. and the anguish of the messiah: "not to us, LORD, not to us" (Ps. 115:1).
II.13 A. And said R. Yohanan, "'The phrase, 'not to us, LORD, not to us' refers to the subjugation to the kingdoms."
    B. There are those who say, said R. Yohanan, "The phrase, 'not to us, LORD, not to us' refers to the war of Gog and Magog."

Now Israel the Israelite, as distinct from Israel the people, is fully subjected to the same paradigm that governs the community. That carries us to the matter of Gehenna:

II.14 A. [Reverting to II.12.A], R. Nahman bar Isaac said, "It is because it alludes to the deliverance of the souls of the righteous from Gehenna: 'I beseech you, LORD, deliver my soul' (Ps. 116:4)."
    B. Hezekiah said, "It is because it contains a reference to the descent of the righteous into the fiery furnace and their ascent from it. Their descent: 'not unto us, LORD, not to us' was said by Hananiah; 'but to your name give glory' was said by Mishael; 'for your mercy and for truth's sake' was said by Azariah; 'wherefore should the nations say' was said by all of them. It refers to

their ascent: 'praise the LORD all you nations' was said by
Hananiah; 'laud him all you peoples' was said by Mishael; 'for
his mercy is great toward us' was said by Azariah; 'and the truth
of the LORD endures forever' was said by all of them."

C. And there are those who say, "'And the truth of the LORD endures
forever' was said by Gabriel. When wicked Nimrod threw our
father Abraham into the fiery furnace, said Gabriel before the
Holy One, blessed be he, 'LORD of the world, let me go down and
cool it off and save that righteous man from the fiery furnace.'
Said to him the Holy One, blessed be he, 'I am unique in my
world and he is unique in his world. It is worthy for the unique to
save the unique.' And since the Holy One, blessed be he, doesn't
withhold a reward from any creature, he said to him, 'You will
have the merit of saving three of his descendants.'" (*b. Pesah.*
10:5-6 II.6/116A)

Salvation of the individual, redemption of the whole people—each
takes many forms but elicits only a single response to what is, in the
end, a uniform relationship, the encounter with God's love. And to
that love, time and change, history and destiny, are monumentally
irrelevant, as much as are intentionality and teleology to the laws of
gravity.

Humanity at Large in the Eschatology of Judaism

What about the charge that Judaism is an ethnic, particularistic religion,
not a universalistic one? We now realize full well that, in Judaic
monotheism, eschatology forms a category that encompasses all
humanity. The world to come marks the final condition of world order.
It signifies the realization of correct and perfect relationships between
God and humanity, God and Israel in particular. Israel encompasses all
those who worship the one God, and the rest are classified as idolaters.
It would be a long time before that interstitial category, gentiles who
are not idolaters, that is, Christians and Muslims, would require thought
on the part of the sages of Judaism. For Judaism in its canonical writings, gentiles are simply those who reject God

Those who reject God having been disposed of, we realize, the age
to come finds its definition in the time of total reconciliation between
God and humanity. It is the age when humanity loves God and accepts
God's dominion and completes the work of repentance and atonement
for acts of rebellion. While, clearly, that reconciliation of God and

humanity takes place in individual life, in which case we may use the language of salvation, it also governs the public life of Israel, in which case we may speak of redemption.

So we reasonably ask, what indeed do the sages have in mind when they speak of the world to come—concrete actualities, or intangible feelings and attitudes, impalpable matters of the spirit? May we suppose that we deal with a mere narration, in mythic form, of what in fact represents an inner, other-worldly, intangible, and spiritual encounter? That is to say, if all that is at stake is abstract patterns of relationships that happen to come to expression in tales of the eschaton, one might suppose that the conception "the world to come" simply serves as another way of saying, "humanity reconciled with God." Then, through paradigmatic thinking, the sages should be represented as finding in the myth a vivid and palpable way of speaking of the inner life of intentionality and attitude. That is a possible reading of the character of the discourse at hand. But I think that that would drastically misrepresent the worldly reality, the concrete actuality, of the sages' account of matters, their intent to speak to the here and now—"today, if you will it"! We contemplate what is palpable and real in an ordinary, everyday sense, not what is intangible or merely "spiritual," in the vulgar sense.

Who and What Then Is Israel?

We should not miss the delicate balance that is preserved by Judaism between ethnicity and universality. Israel forms a universalistic category: those who know God and rejoice in God's kingdom. It also refers to a particular group of people in the here and now. For God's kingdom is not spiritual and intangible alone, but realized in the here and now of actions and words, attitudes and emotions.

First, while the sages' Israel is the holy people, living in the plane of transcendence, their Israel truly lives in the trenchant world of marketplace and farm, and engages in the material and physical transactions of farming and love. Not a single line in the entire oral Torah would sustain the reading of "Israel" as other than (in a different theology's language) "after the flesh." The sages found no cause to differentiate an "Israel after the spirit" from their "Israel after the flesh," since when they referred to Israel, they meant all those who know God as God made manifest in the Torah, and at the end, that Israel, shorn of the handful of aliens (those who deny God, the resurrection of the dead, the resurrection of the dead as a fact set forth by God in the Torah, and so on), all together, in the flesh, sees God and enters into eternal life.

Second, their Israel does constitute a political entity—this world's embodiment of the locus of God's rule—and as we have already noted, God's intervention at the very least will bring about a radical change in the politics of world order, Rome giving way to Israel. The sages, like philosophers, were public intellectuals, undertaking the work of the community of holy Israel (the sages) or of the polis (philosophers). They thought about concrete, practical things, and at no point can we identify an area of the law or lore of the oral Torah that has no bearing upon the everyday world of the here and now. That, indeed, is the very upshot of the point-by-point match of halakah and haggadah, law and lore, that we have had occasion to review here and there.

Third, when they speak of the world to come, the sages mean a world that is public and shared, not private and inner-facing. It is not a world of relativities and relationships as these intangibles are concretely symbolized, but a world of real encounter. The sages know a palpable God who punishes arrogance and rewards humility, in both instances in worldly ways. Prayers are answered with rain or healing, virtue responded to with grace bearing material benefit, acts of generosity with miracles. Heaven intervenes in matters of health and sickness, in the abundance or scarcity of crops, in good fortune and ill. The sages insist upon an exact correspondence between practicalities and transcendent relationships.

Since humanity corresponds to God ("in our image, after our likeness") and in important ways serves God's purpose, the spiritualization of matters earthly would seriously misinterpret what is at stake here. When the sages see the world to come as the climax and conclusion of the processes of creation that commenced with Eden, they envisage the world that comes within their everyday gaze—the people they see out there in the street, not only imagine in the heart. Take the resurrection for instance. When the dead are raised from the grave, they will stink and need new clothes:

> A. Raba contrasted [these two verses]: "It is written, 'I kill and I make alive' (Deut. 32:39) and it is written, 'I wound and I heal' (Deut. 32:39). [The former implies that one is resurrected just as he was at death, thus with blemishes, and the other implies that at the resurrection all wounds are healed.]
>
> B. "Said the Holy One, blessed be he, 'What I kill I bring to life,' and then, 'What I have wounded I heal.'" (*b. Sanh.* 11:1-2 I.25.91b)

That humble fact captures the dialectic of paradigmatic, as against historical, thinking. History produces the dialectic of past against present, resolved in the future (thesis, antithesis, synthesis). Paradigms set the past within the present, Abraham or Moses consorting with the here and now and Jacob shaping public policy today—a considerable tension not to be resolved at all. On the one hand, the advent of the world to come is represented as part of an ordinal sequence, though, for reasons fully exposed, that sequence should not be treated as identical with temporal, historical happenings. On the other hand, the paradigm is fully as palpable in its shaping of the everyday world and workaday experience as history. So, as I said, at the resurrection, the corpse will need a bath.

From Concrete Event to Evocative Symbol

And yet what is tangible is relationship, not the singular and exemplary event, as I have amply explained earlier. Paradigmatic thinking transforms the concrete into evocative symbol, the unique into the exemplary. But the sages' mode of paradigmatic thinking insists upon the here-and-now quality of relationships and events, the actuality of transactions with God as much as with humanity. And why think otherwise, when Scripture is clear and rich in instances. Both in the written and in the oral Torah God and humanity correspond, and humanity is in God's image, after God's likeness. So a theology that does not "spiritualize," that does not represent as intangible God in heaven any more than humanity on earth, will insist upon the material and physical character of resurrection and the life of the Garden of Eden that is the world to come. That theology will have no motive to treat the transformation of relationships represented by the resurrection of the dead and the judgment and the world or age to come as other than consubstantial with the experienced world of the moment—if marvelously different.

Thinking paradigmatically, rather than historically, the sages envisaged matters not temporally but through epochs divided by the indicative traits of Israel's relationship with God, as we noted at Yerushalmi tractate *Megillah* 2:1 I:2. There, we saw, "past" is marked by Israel's exodus from Egypt; "present" by God's mercy as a mark not of Israel's deserts but God's own love; the days of the messiah as God's responding to Israel's supplication; the days of Gog and Magog as the embodiment of the verse, "[The LORD is God, and he has given us light.] Bind the festal offering with cords [up to the horns of the altar!]" (Ps. 118:27), and the age to come as the age of thanks to God for being God. The same matter is made still more explicit. Egypt, Sinai, Gog and Magog, and messiah—locations, events, moments, persons—mark the four epiphanies of God to Israel:

A. "He appeared from Mount Paran [and approached from Ribeboth-kodesh, lightning flashing at them from his right, lover, indeed, of the people, their hallowed are all in your hand]":

B. There are four epiphanies.

C. The first was in Egypt: "Give ear, O Shepherd of Israel, you who lead Joseph like a flock, you who are enthroned on the cherubim, shine forth" (Ps. 80:2).

D. The second at the time of the giving of the Torah: "he shone upon them from Seir."

E. The third in the days of Gog and Magog: "O LORD, your God to whom vengeance belongs, you God to whom vengeance belongs, shine forth" (Ps. 94:1).

F. And the fourth in the days of the messiah: "Out of Zion the perfection of beauty, God has shown forth" (Ps. 50:2). (*Sifré to Deuteronomy* CCCXLIII:VII.1)

The list of these native categories on its own suffices to register the intent, which is to identify, compare, and contrast, the epiphanies. Just as God was at Egypt and Sinai with Israel, so God will be at the eschatological war and at the climactic moment of the messiah as well. And, it goes without saying, in the age or world to come, the final epiphany will find God and Israel at one, as we shall see, celebrating the beneficence of God, studying the Torah, enjoying dance and song and feasting, for all eternity. Thinking paradigmatically, these events represent relationships with God. Israel in the here and now and Israel at the age to come differ only in relationship with God.

Now, after elaborately justifying the asking, we turn to a set of practical questions. With the advent of the world or age to come, exactly what happens, in the process of restoration of world order to the condition of Eden, and of Israel to the land of Israel? The third-century Babylonian sage Samuel's minimalist view, Bavli tractate *Sanhedrin* 91b, cited above, "There is no difference between the world to come and the days of the messiah, except the end of the subjugation of the exilic communities of Israel," alerts us to the breadth of opinion on how the days of the messiah will differ from the world to come. But it is clear that a sequence governs. First comes salvation in the aspect of resurrection and judgment for individuals, and then, immediately following judgment, the world or age to come marks the time of redemption for the holy people, Israel. And the bulk of the evidence supports the view that the age to come differs from this age, as well as from the time of the messiah, in more ways than the political one that Samuel (within the theory of the regnant theology set forth here) rightly selects as primary.

Life in the World to Come

This brings us to the actualities of the world to come, what people are supposed to be doing then. What is going to happen in the age to come? Israel will eat and drink, sing and dance, and enjoy God, who will be lord of the dance. What about the restored temple? The war of Gog and Magog having concluded, the dead having been returned to the land and raised, the next stage in the restoration of world order requires the reconstruction of the temple, where, as we recall, God and humanity, heaven and earth, meet.

> A. "Then Jacob called his sons and said, 'Gather yourselves together, that I may tell you what shall befall you in days to come:'"
>
> B. R. Simon said, "He showed them the fall of Gog, in line with this usage: 'It shall be in the end of days . . . when I shall be sanctified through you, O Gog' (Ezek. 38:16). 'Behold, it shall come upon Edom' (Isa. 34:5)."
>
> C. R. Judah said, "He showed them the building of the house of the sanctuary: 'And it shall come to pass in the end of days that the mountain of the LORD's house shall be established' (Isa. 2:2)."
>
> D. Rabbis say, "He came to reveal the time of the end to them, but it was hidden from him." (*Genesis Rabbah* XCVIII:II.7)

So in the now-familiar sequence of restoration, (1) final war, (2) advent of the messiah and the resurrection and judgment, and (3) the age to come, next in sequence must be (4) the restoration of Israel to the land, and (5) rebuilding the temple, destroyed by reason of Israel's sin.

But what purpose would now be fulfilled by the restoration of the temple cult—the priesthood to the altar, the Levites to the platform, and all Israel to their courtyards, men's and women's respectively? Since the bulk of offerings in the temple set forth by Moses in the written Torah had focused upon atonement for sin and guilt, what purpose would the temple, and its surrogate, the synagogue, now serve? There is only a single one. In the age to come, responding to redemption, all offerings but the thanksgiving offering, appropriately, will cease, all prayers but thanksgiving prayers will cease. So it stands to reason:

> A. R. Phineas and R. Levi and R. Yohanan in the name of R. Menahem of Gallia: "In time to come all offerings will come to an end, but the thanksgiving offering will not come to an end.
>
> B. "All forms of prayer will come to an end, but the thanksgiving prayer will not come to an end.

C. "That is in line with that which is written, 'The voice of joy and the voice of gladness, the voice of the bridegroom and the voice of the bride,

D. "'the voice of them that say, "Give thanks to the Lord of hosts"' [Jer. 33:11]. This refers to the thanksgiving prayer.

E. "'Who bring a thanksgiving offering to the house of the LORD' [Jer. 33:11]. This refers to the offering of thanksgiving sacrifice.

F. "And so did David say, 'Your vows are incumbent upon me, O God [I will render thanksgivings to you]' [Ps. 56:13].

G. "'I shall render thanksgiving to you' is not written here, but rather, 'I shall render thanksgivings [plural] to you' [Ps. 56:13].

H. "The reference [of the plural usage], then, is to both the thanksgiving prayer and the thanksgiving offering." (*Leviticus Rabbah* IX:VII.1)

Predicting the character of the temple offerings in the future presents no difficulty when we recall that at that time, judgment will have taken place, sin have been removed, and atonement completed. So much of the work of the cult will have been accomplished, leaving only the one thing that remains: to give thanks. And it is not to be missed that the offering that will go forward is the offering that gentiles as much as Israelites may present, yet another mark of the eschatological universalism that characterizes the Judaic monotheism.

In concrete terms, exactly how does the eternal life of the world to come form that complement and recompense for life in the here and now? By their deeds the righteous define themselves now and gain their reward then. This conviction, absolutely inevitable within the logic of a theology of world order defined by God's justice, comes to expression in a simple way. Since life continues beyond the grave, what we do in the initial life goes to our account, one way or the other, upon which we draw when we rise from death to eternal life. Scripture itself is explicit that benefits accrue both now and in the age to come as this passage from Tosefta tractate *Hullin* shows:

A. A man should not take a dam with the young, and even to purify a person afflicted with the skin ailment [as is required at Leviticus 14] [*m. Hul.* 12:5A] therewith,

B. because a transgression will have been committed therewith.

C. R. Jacob says, "You find no [other] commandment in the Torah, the specification of the reward for which is (not) located by its side,

D. "and the [promise of the] resurrection of the dead is written alongside it [as well],

E. "as it is said, 'If along the road you find a bird's nest . . . with fledglings or eggs and the mother sitting over the fledglings or on the eggs, to not take the mother together with her young. Let the mother go and take only the young, in order that you may be well and have a long life' (Deut. 22:6-7).

F. "If this one went up to the top of a tree and fell and died, or to the top of a building and fell and died, where has the good of this one gone, and where is the prolonging of his life?

G. "One must therefore conclude: 'So that it will be good for you'— in this world. 'And so that your days may be prolonged'—in the world of endless time." *(t. Hul. 10:16)*

Here, as in many other settings of the written Torah, the sages of the oral Torah identify a case in which one's conduct in this age affects one's standing in the age to come.

Idolaters = Gentiles and the World to Come

What of gentiles, meaning idolaters? As we realize full well, gentiles with their idolatry simply will cease to exist; some will perish, just as Israelites will perish, just as the generation of the flood, the generation of the dispersion, the men of Sodom, and certain Israelites will perish. But some—a great many—will give up idolatry and thereby become part of Israel. The gentiles as such are not subject to redemption; they have no choice at the advent of the world to come but to accept God or become extinct. But that is not the precise formulation that the system as I see it will set forth. Rather, the correct language is not, the gentiles will cease to exist, but rather, the category "gentiles with their idolatry," will cease to function. Idolatry having come to an end, God having been recognized by all humankind, everyone will enter the category "Israel."

Predictably, the sages seek analogies and patterns to work out in concrete terms the result of their compelling logic. In the present matter, the future of gentiles is worked out by analogy to holy things—the opposite, and the match in context, of gentiles. Some can be redeemed, some not, as this passage from *Mekhilta Attributed to R. Ishmael* says.

B. As to Holy Things, there are those that are subject to redemption and there are those that are not subject to redemption;

C. as to things that may not be eaten, there are those that are subject to redemption and there are those that are not subject to redemption;

D. as to things that may not be used for any sort of benefit, there are those that are subject to redemption and there are those that are not subject to redemption;

    E. as to fields and vineyards, there are those that are subject to
       redemption and there are those that are not subject to redemption;
    F. as to bondmen and bondwomen, there are those that are subject to
       redemption and there are those that are not subject to redemption;
    G. as to those subject to the death penalty by a court, there are those
       that are subject to redemption and there are those that are not sub-
       ject to redemption . . .

Now, the paradigm having established the possibilities, we come to
the critical point.

    H. [S]o in the age to come, there are those that are subject to
       redemption and there are those that are not subject to redemption.

The nations cannot be redeemed. That is by definition: their idolatry
in the end does them in.

    I. The nations of the world are not subject to redemption: "No man
      can by any means redeem his brother nor give to God a ransom for
      him, for too costly is the redemption of their soul" (Ps. 49:8-9).
    J. Precious are the Israelites, for the ransom of whose lives the Holy
      One, blessed be he, has given the nations of the world:
    K. "I have given Egypt as your ransom" (Isa. 43:4).
    L. Why so?
    M. "Since you are precious in my sight and honorable, and I have
      loved you, therefore I will give men for you and peoples for your
      life" (Isa. 43:3-4) (*Mekhilta Attributed to R. Ishmael* LXVII:I.31)

Once more the past forms a presence in the immediate age, as much
as the present participates in the past. Here the future of the gentiles
realizes their present. They are idolaters—that is why to begin with
they are classified as gentiles—and therefore they will not be
redeemed, meaning they will not stand in judgment or enjoy the eternal
life of the world to come.

What of gentiles in general, apart from those self-selected by their
conduct toward Israel for eternal Gehenna? In the age to come gentiles
will renounce idolatry and accept the one God. There simply will be no
more gentiles, everyone will serve God and come under the wings of
God's presence, within Israel.

    A. "Who is like you, O *Lord*, among gods? [Who is like you, majes-
      tic in holiness, terrible in glorious deeds, doing wonders?]:"
    B. When the Israelites saw that Pharaoh and his host had perished at
      the Red Sea, the dominion of the Egyptians was over, and judg-
      ments were executed on their idolatry, they all opened their
      mouths and said, "Who is like you, O LORD, among gods? [Who

is like you, majestic in holiness, terrible in glorious deeds, doing wonders?]"

Now the nations participate in praising the one, true God of all creation:

> C. And not the Israelites alone said the song, but also the nations of the world said the song.
> D. When the nations of the world saw that Pharaoh and his host had perished at the Red Sea, the dominion of the Egyptians was over, and judgments were executed on their idolatry, they all renounced their idolatry and opened their mouths and confessed their faith in the LORD and said, "Who is like you, O LORD, among gods? [Who is like you, majestic in holiness, terrible in glorious deeds, doing wonders?]"

Once more the selected paradigm finds the future in the past, the pattern that governs in the quality of the relationship:

> E. So too you find that in the age to come the nations of the world will renounce their idolatry: "O LORD, my strength and my stronghold and my refuge, in the day of affliction to you the nations shall come . . . shall a man make himself gods" (Jer. 16:19-20); "In that day a man shall cast away his idols of silver . . . to go into the clefts of the rocks" (Isa. 2:20-21). "And the idols shall utterly perish" (Isa. 20:18) (*Mekhilta Attributed to R. Ishmael* XXXIII:I.1)

The final step in the unfolding of creation according to plan will be the redemption of the nations of the world, their renunciation of idolatry and acceptance of God's rule. That will bring to perfect closure the drama that began with Adam. The nations' response to Israel's Exodus and redemption from Egypt prefigures what is to come about at the end.

What accounts for the condition of the gentiles? It is that they have rejected the Torah, which God offered to all humanity for their salvation, and which only Israel accepted. No picture of the universalistic eschatology of Judaism will be complete without the system's explanation of the condition of the gentiles. By their own action set outside the redeeming framework of the Torah, they attest to divine justice, just as the salvation of the righteous among the gentiles attests to divine mercy. The gentiles deprived themselves of the Torah because they rejected it, and, showing the precision of justice, they rejected the Torah because the Torah deprived them of the very practices or traits that they deemed characteristic, essential to their being. That circularity marks the tale of how things were to begin with in fact describes how things always are; it is not historical but philosophical. The gentiles' own character, the shape of their conscience, then, now, and always, accounts for their condition—which, by an act of will, as we have noted, they can change. What they did not want, that of which they were by their own word unworthy, is denied them. And what they do want condemns them. So when each nation comes under judgment for rejecting the Torah, the indictment of each is spoken out of its own mouth; its own-self-indictment then forms the core of the matter. Given what we know about the definition of Israel as those destined to live and the gentiles as those not, we cannot find surprising that the entire account is set in that age to come to which the gentiles are denied entry.

When they protest the injustice of the decision that takes effect just then, they are shown the workings of the moral order, as the following quite systematic account of the governing pattern from Bavli tractate *'Abodah Zarah* explains:

> A. R. Hanina bar Pappa, and some say, R. Simlai, gave the following exposition [of the verse, "They that fashion a graven image are all of them vanity, and their delectable things shall not profit, and their own witnesses see not nor know" (Isa. 44:9)]: "In the age to come the Holy One, blessed be he, will bring a scroll of the Torah and hold it in his bosom and say, 'Let him who has kept himself busy with it come and take his reward.' Then all the gentiles will crowd together: 'All of the nations are gathered together' (Isa. 43:9). The Holy One, blessed be he, will say to them, 'Do not crowd together before me in a mob. But let each nation enter together with [2B] its scribes, 'and let the peoples be gathered together' (Isa. 43:9), and the word 'people' means 'kingdom': 'and one kingdom shall be stronger than the other' (Gen. 25:23)."

We note that the players are the principal participants in world history: the Romans first and foremost, then the Persians, the other world rulers of the age:

> C. "The kingdom of Rome comes in first."
> H. "The Holy One, blessed be he, will say to them, 'How have you defined your chief occupation?'
> I. "They will say before him, 'LORD of the world, a vast number of marketplaces have we set up, a vast number of bathhouses we have made, a vast amount of silver and gold have we accumulated. And all of these things we have done only in behalf of Israel, so that they may define as their chief occupation the study of the Torah.'

J. "The Holy One, blessed be he, will say to them, 'You complete idiots! Whatever you have done has been for your own convenience. You have set up a vast number of marketplaces to be sure, but that was so as to set up whorehouses in them. The bathhouses were for your own pleasure. Silver and gold belong to me anyhow: "Mine is the silver and mine is the gold, says the LORD of hosts" (Hag. 2:8). Are there any among you who have been telling of "this," and "this" is only the Torah: "And this is the Torah that Moses set before the children of Israel (Deut. 4:44)." So they will make their exit, humiliated.

The claim of Rome—to support Israel in Torah-study—is rejected on grounds that the Romans did not exhibit the right attitude, always a dynamic force in the theology. Then the other world rule enters in with its claim:

K. "When the kingdom of Rome has made its exit, the kingdom of Persia enters afterward."

M. "The Holy One, blessed be he, will say to them, 'How have you defined your chief occupation?'

N. "They will say before him, 'Lord of the world, We have thrown up a vast number of bridges, we have conquered a vast number of towns, we have made vast number of wars, and all of them we did only for Israel, so that they may define as their chief occupation the study of the Torah.'

O. "The Holy One, blessed be he, will say to them, 'Whatever you have done has been for your own convenience. You have thrown up a vast number of bridges, to collect tolls, you have conquered a vast number of towns, to collect the corvée, and, as to making a vast number of wars, I am the one who makes wars: "The LORD is a man of war" (Exod. 19:17). Are there any among you who have been telling of "this," and "this" is only the Torah: "And this is the Torah that Moses set before the children of Israel" (Deut. 4:44).' So they will make their exit, humiliated.

R. "And so it will go with each and every nation." (*b. 'Abod. Zara* 1:1 I.2/2a-b)

As native categories, Rome and Persia are singled out, "all the other nations" play no role, for reasons with which we are already familiar. Once more the theology reaches into its deepest thought on the power of intentionality, showing that what people want is what they get.

But matters cannot be limited to the two world empires of the present age, Rome and Persia, standing in judgment at the end of time. The theology values balance, proportion, seeks complementary relationships, and therefore treats beginnings along with endings, the one going over the ground of the other. Accordingly, a recapitulation of the same event—the gentiles' rejection of the Torah—chooses as its setting not the last judgment but the first encounter, that is, the giving of the Torah itself. In the timeless world constructed by the oral Torah, what happens at the outset exemplifies how things always happen, and what happens at the end embodies what has always taken place. The basic thesis is identical—the gentiles cannot accept the Torah, because to do so they would have to deny their very character. But the exposition retains its interest because it takes its own course.

Now the gentiles are not just Rome and Persia but others; and of special interest, the Torah is embodied in some of the ten commandments—not to murder, not to commit adultery, not to steal; then the gentiles are rejected for not keeping the seven commandments assigned to the children of Noah. The upshot is that the reason that the gentiles rejected the Torah is that the Torah prohibits deeds that the gentiles do by their very nature. Israel ultimately is changed by the Torah, so that Israel exhibits traits imparted by their encounter with the Torah. So too with the gentiles, by their nature they are what they are; the Torah has not changed their nature. Once more a single standard applies to both components of humanity, but with opposite effect (from *Sifré to Deuteronomy*):

1.   A. Another teaching concerning the phrase, "He said, 'The LORD came from Sinai'":
        B. When the Omnipresent appeared to give the Torah to Israel, it was not to Israel alone that he revealed himself but to every nation.
        C. First of all he came to the children of Esau. He said to them, "Will you accept the Torah?"
        D. They said to him, "What is written in it?"
        E. He said to them, "'You shall not murder' (Exod. 20:13)."
        F. They said to him, "The very being of 'those men' [namely, us] and of their father is to murder, for it is said, 'But the hands are the hands of Esau'"(Gen. 27:22). 'By your sword you shall live' (Gen. 27:40)."

At this point we cover new ground: other classes of gentiles that reject the Torah; now the Torah's own narrative takes over, replacing the known facts of world politics, such as the earlier account sets forth, and instead supplying evidence out of Scripture as to the character of the gentile group under discussion:

        G. So he went to the children of Ammon and Moab and said to them, "Will you accept the Torah?"
        H. They said to him, "What is written in it?"

I. He said to them, "'You shall not commit adultery' (Exod. 20:13)."

J. They said to him, "The very essence of fornication belongs to them [us], for it is said, 'Thus were both the daughters of Lot with child by their fathers' (Gen. 19:36)."

K. So he went to the children of Ishmael and said to them, "Will you accept the Torah?"

L. They said to him, "What is written in it?"

M. He said to them, "'You shall not steal' (Exod. 20:13)."

N. They said to him, "The very essence of their [our] father is thievery, as it is said, 'And he shall be a wild ass of a man' (Gen. 16:12)."

O. And so it went. He went to every nation, asking them, "Will you accept the Torah?"

P. For so it is said, "All the kings of the earth shall give you thanks, O LORD, for they have heard the words of your mouth" (Ps. 138:4).

Q. Might one suppose that they listened and accepted the Torah?

R. Scripture says, "And I will execute vengeance in anger and fury upon the nations, because they did not listen" (Mic. 5:14).

At this point we turn back to the obligations that God has imposed upon the gentiles; these obligations have no bearing upon the acceptance of the Torah; they form part of the ground of being, the condition of existence, of the gentiles. Yet even here, the gentiles do not accept God's authority in matters of natural law:

S. And it is not enough for them that they did not listen, but even the seven religious duties that the children of Noah indeed accepted upon themselves they could not uphold before breaking them.

T. When the Holy One, blessed be he, saw that that is how things were, he gave them to Israel.

Now comes another parable, involving not a king but a common person:

2.   A. The matter may be compared to the case of a person who sent his ass and dog to the threshing floor and loaded up a letekh of grain on his ass and three seahs of grain on his dog. The ass went along, while the dog panted.

B. He took a seah of grain off the dog and put it on the ass, so with the second, so with the third.

C. Thus was Israel: they accepted the Torah, complete with all its secondary amplifications and minor details, even the seven religious duties that the children of Noah could not uphold without breaking them did the Israelites come along and accept.

D. That is why it is said, "The Lord came from Sinai; he shone upon them from Seir." (*Sifré to Deuteronomy* CCCXLIII:IV.1ff.)

In the conclusion at hand we see how the Judaic version of monotheism forms a complete system, making provision for all humanity within the framework of the revealed Torah.

When I said at the outset that Judaism reads from Scripture forward, this is what I meant. So far as monotheism rests on the initial revelation of the one and only God, Judaism is the natural outcome—for all humanity, so the sages maintained, and so Judaism has affirmed through all of time. But what unites humanity before one God is what differentiates humanity from animals. Humanity is "like God," "in our image, after our likeness," and what Judaism finds, in humanity, to compare to God is the capacity to reason, to respond to the same rationality, to use the mind in a way common to heaven and earth. And that is embodied in the certainty that Abraham expresses when he says, "Shall not the Judge of all the world do justice?" (Gen. 18:24).

6. Rational Israel: God's Justice, Humanity's Reason

At the heart of the Judaic monotheism in its appeal to all humanity we find the insistence upon a uniform justice that prevails universally. That marks what all persons have in common. And therein we find the key to the transcendent rationality that the halakah and the haggadah alike set forth. That shared power to reason forms a coherent system that addresses reason common to all humanity and accounts in a single way for all things, however diverse in character. Let me explain how, in my view, in its universalistic discourse Judaic monotheism realizes the full logic of the monotheist conception of God and draws its dynamism and vitality from the dialectics that inhere in that conception. Stated simply: since there is only one God, who is unique, omnipotent, and just, all humanity—"in our image, after our likeness"—can know that one and only God through the self-manifestation of the Torah and, therefore, can ask the same question that animates Abraham's case at Sodom: "Will the Judge of all the world not do justice?" That single sentence suffices to demonstrate the universality of Judaism, its fundamental premise that God is one and the same for all humanity. But that sentence is recapitulated through the books of the Torah, the Prophets, and the writings of the written Torah and reworked in generative ways in the works of the oral Torah written down by the Rabbinic sages as well.

Humanity Explains the Reason Why

A religion of numerous gods finds many solutions to one problem; a religion of only one God presents one to many. But then, within monotheism, life is seldom both fair and reasonable. Rules rarely work. To explain why, polytheisms adduce multiple causes of chaos, a god per anomaly. Diverse gods do various things, so, it stands to reason, ordinarily their outcomes conflict. Monotheism by nature explains many things in a single way. One God rules. Life is meant to be fair, and just rules are supposed to describe what is ordinary, all in the name of that one and only God. So in monotheism a simple logic governs to limit ways of making sense of things. But that logic contains its own dialectics. If one true God has done everything, then, since that God is all-powerful and omniscient, all things are credited to, and blamed on, God. In that case God can be either good or bad, just or unjust—but not both.

Responding to the generative dialectics of monotheism, the Torah as the sages read it systematically reveals the justice of the one and only God of all creation. God is not only God but also good. Appealing to the facts of Scripture, the written part of the Torah, in the documents of the oral part of the Torah, the sages ("our sages of blessed memory") in the first six centuries of the Common Era constructed a coherent theology, a cogent structure and logical system, to expose the justice of God. The sages' Torah conveys the picture of world order based on God's justice and equity. The categorical structure of the oral Torah encompasses the components, God and humanity; the Torah; Israel and the nations. The working system of the oral Torah finds its dynamic in the struggle between God's plan for creation—to create a perfect world of justice—and humanity's will. That dialectics embodies in a single paradigm the events contained in the sequences, rebellion, sin, punishment, repentance, and atonement; exile and return; or the disruption of world order and the restoration of world order.

Everyone Has the Power to Understand

What (within its logic) renders the Judaic monotheism universally accessible is that—in the Torah's view—all humanity has the same capacity to apprehend and understand the one and only God, because a common rationality reigns. What God does and what humanity understands—and *understanding* means to grasp the justice and good sense of something—correspond. So the Judaic monotheism sets forth a message that is universal not only in eschatological but also intellectual character. The Torah's one and only God speaks in the same way to all humanity, and that way is reasonable within humanity's grasp of things. That is to say, within humanity's understanding of reason, God's will is just. And by *just,* sages understood the commonsense meaning: fair, equitable, proportionate, commensurate. In place of fate or impersonal destiny, chance, or simply irrational, inexplicable chaos, God's plan and purpose everywhere come to realization. So the oral Torah identifies God's will as the active and causative force in the lives of individuals and nations. The answer to Abraham, pleading for Sodom, affirms: the Judge of all the world indeed does justice—in the sight of all humanity.

In that same context, nothing surprises God, for all things conform to his plan even from the very beginning. That is why, the sages maintain, even at the moment of creation God foresaw the future deeds of righteousness and sin that would be committed, and the day of judgment was prepared at the very outset. What is important in the following statement is the allegation that, built into the very construction of creation is the plan for all things to come. God created humanity and knew at the outset that, because humanity exercised freedom of will, the righteous and the wicked would exercise that freedom, each group in its own way. Each component of creation then is recapitulated in the here and now, the darkness and the light, by the wicked and the righteous. And it is self-evident, the statement refers not to the Israelite righteous and wicked, but to those of humanity at large. In the end of time, Eden will be regained and restored, wholly in light, entirely illuminated by God (as in this passage from *Genesis Rabbah*):

1.   A. Said R. Yannai, "At the beginning of the creation of the world the Holy One, blessed be he, foresaw the deeds of the righteous and the deeds of the wicked.

   B. "'And the earth was unformed and void' refers to the deeds of the wicked.

   C. "'And God said, "Let there be light"' refers to the deeds of the righteous.

   D. "'And God saw the light, that it was good,' refers to the deeds of the righteous."

Now the creation narrative is systematically divided, as indicated, between light and darkness, the righteous and the wicked:

   E. "'And God divided between the light and the darkness' means, [he divided] between the deeds of the righteous and the deeds of the wicked.

   F. "'And God called the light day' refers to the deeds of the righteous.

   G. "'And the darkness he called night' refers to the deeds of the wicked.

   H. "'And there was evening' refers to the deeds of the wicked.

   I. "'And there was morning' refers to the deeds of the righteous.

   J. "'One day,' for the Holy One, blessed be he, gave them one day, [and what day is that]? It is the day of judgment." (*Genesis Rabbah* III:VIII.1)

I can imagine no more explicit statement that justice, leading to judgment, rules through the very foundations of creation to the end of time.

The urgent question is, how do the sages know that God's will is realized in the moral order of justice, involving reward and punishment? They turned to Scripture for the pertinent facts; that is where God is manifest. But of the various types of scriptural evidence—explicit commandments, stories, prophetic admonitions—that they had available to show how the moral order prevailed in all being, what type did the sages prefer? The one bearing the greatest probative weight derived from the exact match between sin and punishment. Here is their starting point; from here all else flows smoothly and in orderly fashion. World order is best embodied when sin is punished, merit rewarded. And here, once more, we find an argument for God's reasoned justice set forth in terms that pertain to all humanity, not only Israel.

That body of evidence that Scripture supplied recorded human action and divine reaction on the one side, and meritorious deed and divine response and reward on the other. It was comprised by consequential cases, drawn from both private and public life, to underscore the sages' insistence upon the match between the personal and the public, all things subject to the same simple rule. That demonstration of not only the principle but the precision of measure for measure, deriving from Scripture's own record of God's actions, takes priority of place in the examination of the rationality of the sages' universe. That is because it permeates their system and frames its prevailing modes of explanation and argument. The principle that all being conforms to rules, and that these rules embody principles of justice through exact punishment of particular sin, precise reward of singular acts of virtue defined the starting point of all rational thought and the entire character of the sages' theological structure and system.

God's Justice: The Reason

That is why, without appeal to that fundamental principle of a just order, no question that the sages investigate, no dilemma their inquiry produces, no basic challenge to the absolute given of their worldview makes any sense at all. Whatever they propose to account for the situation of Israel in public or the individual in private, whether the resolution of the historical crisis in the coming of the messiah and the nations' standing in judgment by the criterion of the Torah or the advent of the world to come and individuals' standing in judgment by the same criterion—all of these massive presences in the sages' thinking about the here and now, the past and the future, rested on the same foundation of conviction: that an exact, prevailing justice explained the meaning of all things. Of that principle all thought formed a systematic exegesis, first of Scripture for the explanation of the here and the now, then of the workaday realities to be shaped into a midrash upon Scripture. It was a reciprocal process because the same reasonable justice ruled small and great transactions without distinction. Not only so, but for the sages, that conviction required an act not of faith but of rational inquiry into the record of reality, Scripture.

The teleological theory of natural history of philosophy here finds its counterpart. The sages' confidence in the sense, order, and the reasonable, because just, character of all reality matched philosophers' conviction that all things serve an assigned purpose. We might conceive that philosophy asked the teleological question of purpose, Judaic theology responded with the revealed answer: to achieve a just world order. The one posited a goal or end, the other defined what that purpose was: all things serve the purpose of taking part in a just and equitable order.

So the sages defined reason and rationality—despite the contrary evidence of everyday reality, beginning with Israel's own situation, subordinated as it was after its loss of great wars to Rome in the first and second centuries. That bedrock certainty identified as the fact of every life and the building block of every society the moral order of a world founded on justice. The sages deemed it a fact that humanity lived in a world in which good is rewarded and evil punished. Since the world in which they lived knew better, and since the sages framed a system that coheres solely as an explanation of why, though justice is supposed to prevail, present matters are chaotic, we may take for granted the sages themselves too knew better, so far as knowing formed a secular act. It was their theology—the logic of God, systematically expounded—that taught them to see matters as they did.

That is why we seek to identify the sources for their conviction of the order of society, natural and supernatural alike. Since few in the history of humanity have offered as a simple fact of everyday reality such a principle of natural justice, but many have found the opposite, we are forced to ask why our sages conceived matters as they did. Exactly what endowed them with certainty that they along with all Israel and humanity at large lived in a trustworthy world of reason and order defined by justice? What we shall see is that their own systematization of the facts of the written Torah nourished that conviction. Concurring on the teleological character of creation—everything with its goal and end—the sages found in Scripture that pervasive purpose in the rule of justice, resting on reason and on equity. From that generative principle—a fact of revealed Scripture really—all else followed. Then the structure stood firm, the system worked.

Scripture: God Obeys the Rules of Justice

What captures our interest therefore is not the conviction but the way in which the sages set forth that conviction. What they found to overcome the doubt that everyday life surely cast upon their insistence upon the governing of a moral order was the facts of Scripture as they ordered those facts. Now, were we on our own to open Scripture and locate pertinent evidence that God is just and that the world conforms to rules of equity, we should find Scripture states it in so many words. It is not merely that when God contemplated the world that he had made, he pronounced it good as Yannai says, specifically referring to the righteous. That surely represents a subjective judgment that can refer to anything, not only to what Yannai thought self-evident. Scripture leaves no doubt about God's definitive trait of justice, justice understood as humanity does, in a different context altogether.

Now to the main point of Judaic universalism, which we have already encountered. When humanity represented by the first monotheist, Abraham, undertook to dispute God's decision and construct an argument against it, God bound himself by the same rule of commonsense equity that Abraham deemed self-evident: "Will you sweep away the innocent along with the guilty? Far be it from you to do such a thing, to impose death upon the innocent as well as the guilty, so that innocent and guilty fare alike. Far be it from you! Shall not the Judge of all the earth deal justly?" (Gen. 18:23, 25). Far be it from thee to do such a thing, to slay the righteous with the wicked, so that the righteous fare as the wicked! Far be that from thee! Shall not the Judge of all the earth do right?" Then God does not reply, but merely responds by accepting Abraham's premise and proceeding to the negotiation. Silence bears assent: God is not only answerable, but is answerable on exactly the counts that humanity deems consequential: justice, reason, commonsense rationality. The sages did not have to search deeply into obscure traditions or difficult passages to uncover the evidence of God's justice. Wherever, in Scripture, they looked, they found ample testimony—especially in the very premise of Job's complaint!

Perhaps in that paradigmatic moment before Sodom the sages identified the principle of the moral order that sustained the world: justice distinguishes the innocent from the guilty and punishes the guilty alone. And Sodom presents the ideal venue: justice for the worst of the gentiles, as much as for holy Israel. I do not think they could have framed more eloquently their conviction concerning the universal rationality of God's creation. But as a matter of fact, as we recall from our inquiry into the halakic mode of thought, that is not how they demonstrated the validity of that principle. They had their own approach, which required them to establish proof through patterning well-analyzed facts, compared and contrasted. Like natural historians, they assembled evidence of a like kind—in this case, the administration of exact justice through appropriate, proportionate reward and punishment—and they then compared and contrasted the evidence they assembled. The concrete evidence on its own, properly arrayed, then established as fact what to begin with was entered as a postulate or hypothesis to be demonstrated—with no given axiom except the facticity of Scripture.

It is at this point that we turn directly to the method and the message of the governing theology of the oral Torah in particular. What we want to know is not how we *might* find in Scripture the basis for a position the sages maintained, but how they *did* find that basis. What satisfied them as necessary and sufficient demonstration of that fact of world order? While their theology systematically expounded the results of their disciplined study of the written Torah—we might call the process their exegesis of, or midrash upon, the written Torah—the concrete and particular types of proof alone reveal to us the workings of their minds viewed as a single, cogent intellect: the theological system.

To answer the question of the source of probative evidence for the principle that the world is reliable and orderly by reason of justice, we turn to the concrete evidence that they held demonstrated their point. Now when the sages opened Scripture to find out how, in the detail of concrete cases, the judge of all the world bound himself by the rules of justice and systematically does justice, like philosophers in natural history they looked not for the occasional but the enduring, not for the singular moment but the routine pattern. Exegesis without a guiding hermeneutics bore little appeal to them. One-shot proof-texts mattered less than governing paradigms. The sages were theologians before they were exegetes, and they were exegetes because they were theologians. So proof from specific texts they showed emerge from details, but hermeneutics holds details together in a single coherent whole. That is why they composed their account of the workings of the principle of measure for measure—whether for divine punishment or for divine reward—out of cases in which God does not intervene, but in which the very nature of things, the ordinary course of events, showed the workings of the principle.

What would suffice, then, to make a point that—we must assume—people in general deem counterintuitive? For who from Job onward—no one had to wait for Voltaire's *Candide*—assumed that the ordinary course of everyday events proves the justice (and the goodness) of God? More lost the faith because the here and now violated the rule of justice than gained the faith because it did. So, to begin with, the sages framed for themselves what we might call a null-hypothesis, that is to say, a hypothesis that they would test to prove the opposite of what they sought to show. They asked themselves this question: if justice did not govern, how should we know it? The answer is, we should find not a correlation but a disproportion between sin and consequent result, or penalty, between crime and punishment.

The Reason Why Not

The null-hypothesis framed the question of order through justice in its most palpable, material form. It is not enough to show that crime provokes divine response, that God penalizes sin. Justice in the here and now counts. The penalty must fit the crime, measure must match measure, and the more exact the result to the cause, the more compelling the proof of immediate and concrete justice as the building block of world order that sages would put forth out of Scripture. That is the point at which justice is transformed from a vague generality—a mere sentiment—to a precise and measurable dimension of the actual social order of morality: how things hold together when subject to tension, at the pressure-points of structure, not merely how they are arrayed in general. Here, in fact, is how God made the world, what is good about the creation that God pronounced good, as Yannai says.

That is why, when the sages examined the facts of Scripture to establish that principle of rationality and order in conformity to the requirements of justice and equity, what impressed them was not the inevitability but the precision of justice. Scripture portrays the world order as fundamentally just and reasonable, and it does so in countless ways. But Scripture encompasses the complaint of Job and the reflection of Qoheleth. The sages for their part identified those cases that transcended generalities and established the facticity of proportionate justice, treating them as not only exemplary but probative. They set forth their proposition and amassed evidence in support of it.

Let us turn to a systematic statement of the starting and main point: when God judges and sentences, not only is the judgment fair but the penalty fits the crime with frightening precision. But so too, when God judges and awards a decision of merit, the reward proves equally exact. These two together, the match of sin and penalty, meritorious deed and reward, then are shown to explain the point and purpose of one detail after another, and all together add up to the portrait of a world order that is fundamentally and essentially just—the starting point and foundation of all else.

Here is the sages' account of God's justice, which is always commensurate, both for reward and punishment, in consequence of which the present permits us to peer into the future with certainty of what is going to happen, so the passage from Mishnah tractate *Sotah* following. What we note is the sages' identification of the precision of justice, the exact match of action and reaction, each step in the sin, each step in the response, and, above all, the immediacy of God's presence in the entire transaction. They draw general conclusions from the specifics of the law that Scripture sets forth, and that is where systematic thinking about cases takes over from exegetical learning, or, in our own categories, philosophy from history:

> A. By that same measure by which a man metes out [to others], do they mete out to him:
> B. She primped herself for sin, the Omnipresent made her repulsive.
> C. She exposed herself for sin, the Omnipresent exposed her.
> D. With the thigh she began to sin, and afterward with the belly, therefore the thigh suffers the curse first, and afterward the belly.
> E. But the rest of the body does not escape [punishment]. (*m. Sotah* 1:7)

We begin with the sages' own general observations based on the facts set forth in Scripture. The course of response of the woman accused of adultery to her drinking of the bitter water that is supposed to produce one result for the guilty, another for the innocent, is described in Scripture in this language: "If no man has lain with you . . . be free from this water of bitterness that brings the curse. But if you have gone astray . . . then the LORD make you an execration . . . when the LORD makes your thigh fall away and your body swell; may this water . . . pass into your bowels and make your body swell and your thigh fall away" (Num. 5:20-22). This is amplified and expanded, extended to the entire rite, where the woman is disheveled; then the order, thigh, belly, shows the perfect precision of the penalty. What Scripture treats as a case, the sages transform into a generalization, so making Scripture yield governing rules.

The same passage proceeds to further cases, which prove the same point: where the sin begins, there the punishment also commences; but also, where an act of virtue takes its point, there divine reward focuses as well. Merely listing the following names, without spelling out details, for the cognoscenti of Scripture will have made that point: Samson, Absalom, Miriam, Joseph, and Moses. Knowing how Samson and Absalom match, also Miriam, Joseph, and Moses, would then suffice to establish the paired and matched general principles:

> A. Samson followed his eyes [where they led him], therefore the Philistines put out his eyes, since it is said, "And the Philistines laid hold on him and put out his eyes" (Judg. 16:21).
>
> B. Absalom was proud of his hair, therefore he was hung by his hair [2 Sam. 14:25-26].
>
> C. And since he had sexual relations with ten concubines of his father, therefore they thrust ten spear heads into his body, since it is said, "And ten young men that carried Jacob's armor surrounded and smote Absalom and killed him" (2 Sam. 18:15).
>
> D. And since he stole three hearts—his father's, the court's, and the Israelite's—since it is said, "And Absalom stole the heart of the men of Israel" (2 Sam. 15:6)—therefore three darts were thrust into him, since it is said, "And he took three darts in his hand and thrust them through the heart of Absalom" (2 Sam. 18:14). (*m. Sotah* 1:8)

Justice requires not only punishment of the sinner or the guilty but reward of the righteous and the good, and so the sages find ample, systematic evidence in Scripture for both sides of the equation of justice:

> A. And so is it on the good side:
>
> B. Miriam waited a while for Moses, since it is said, "And his sister stood afar off" (Exod. 2:4), therefore, Israel waited on her seven days in the wilderness, since it is said, "And the people did not travel on until Miriam was brought in again" (Num. 12:15). (*m. Sotah* 1:9)
>
> A. Joseph had the merit of burying his father, and none of his brothers was greater than he, since it is said, "And Joseph went up to bury his father . . . and there went up with him both chariots and horsemen" (Gen. 50:7, 9).
>
> B. We have none so great as Joseph, for only Moses took care of his [bones].
>
> C. Moses had the merit of burying the bones of Joseph, and none in Israel was greater than he, since it is said, "And Moses took the bones of Joseph with him" (Exod. 13:19).

D. We have none so great as Moses, for only the Holy One, blessed be he took care of his [bones], since it is said, "And he buried him in the valley" (Deut. 34:6).

E. And not of Moses alone have they stated [this rule], but of all righteous people, since it is said, "And your righteousness shall go before you. The glory of the LORD shall gather you [in death]" (Isa. 58:8). (*m. Sotah* 1:10)

Scripture provides the main probative evidence for the anticipation that when God judges, he will match the act of merit with an appropriate reward and the sin with an appropriate punishment. The proposition begins, however, with general observations as to how things are, in *m. Sotah* 1:7, and not with specific allusions to proof-texts; the character of the law set forth in Scripture is reflected upon. The accumulated cases yield the generalization.

When punishing, God starts with that with which the transgression commenced, which the sages see as a mark of the precision of divine justice, and, as we shall now see in a passage from *Sifré to Numbers,* that justice encompasses all humanity, from Adam forward, encompassing also the Israelites:

A. "And when he has made her drink the water, [then, if she has defiled herself and has acted unfaithfully against her husband, the water that brings the curse shall enter into her and cause bitter pain,] and her body shall swell, and her thigh shall fall away, [and the woman shall become an execration among her people. But if the woman has not defiled herself and is clean, then she shall be free and shall conceive children]" (Num. 5:23-28).

B. I know only that her body and thigh are affected. How do I know that that is the case for the rest of her limbs?

C. Scripture states, " . . . the water that brings the curse shall enter into her."

D. So I take account of the phrase, " . . . the water that brings the curse shall enter into her."

E. Why [if all the limbs are affected equally] then does Scripture specify her body and her thigh in particular?

F. As to her thigh, the limb with which she began to commit the transgression—from there the punishment begins.

But the sages represented by *Sifré to Numbers,* exegetes of Scripture and the Mishnah, like the commentators whom we shall meet in the Tosefta that follows, wish to introduce their own cases in support of the same proposition:

G. Along these same lines:

H. "And he blotted out everything that sprouted from the earth, from man to beast" (Gen. 7:23).

I. From the one who began the transgression [namely Adam], the punishment begins.

Adam sinned first, therefore the flood began with Adam. Now comes a different sort of proportion: the exact match. The Sodomites are smitten with piles:

J. Along these same lines:

K. " . . . and the men who were at the gate of the house they smote with piles" (Gen. 19:11).

L. From the one who began the transgression the punishment begins.

In the third instance, Pharaoh is in the position of Adam; with him the sin began, with him the punishment starts:

M. Along these same lines:

N. " . . . and I shall be honored through Pharaoh and through all of his force" (Exod. 14:4).

O. Pharaoh began the transgression, so from him began the punishment.

P. Along these same lines:

Q. "And you will most certainly smite at the edge of the sword the inhabitants of that city" (Deut. 34:15).

R. From the one who began the transgression, the punishment begins.

S. Along these same lines is the present case:

T. the limb with which she began to commit the transgression—from there the punishment begins.

Here comes a point important to the system: God's mercy vastly exceeds his justice, so the measure of reward is far greater than the measure of punishment—and, if possible, still more prompt:

U. Now does this not yield an argument a fortiori:

V. If in the case of the attribution of punishment, which is the lesser, from the limb with which she began to commit the transgression—from there the punishment begins,

W. in the case of the attribute of bestowing good, which is the greater, how much the more so! (*Sifré to Numbers* XVIII:I.1)

Punishment is rational in yet a more concrete way: it commences with the very thing that has sinned, or with the person who has sinned. So the principles of reason and good order pervade the world. We know that fact because Scripture's account of all that matters has shown it.

Is reward measured out with the same precision? Not at all; reward many times exceeds punishment. So if the measure of retribution is exactly proportionate to the sin, the measure of reward exceeds the contrary measure by a factor of five hundred. Later on we shall see explicit argument that justice without mercy is incomplete; to have justice, mercy is the required complement. Here in the passages from Tosefta tractate *Sotah* we address another aspect of the same matter, that if the measure of punishment precisely matches the measure of sin, when it comes to reward for merit or virtue, matters are not that way:

> A. I know only with regard to the measure of retribution that by that same measure by which a man metes out, they mete out to him [*m. Sotah* 1:7A]. How do I know that the same is so with the measure of goodness [*m. Sotah* 1:9A]?
>
> B. Thus do you say:
>
> C. The measure of goodness is five hundred times greater than the measure of retribution.
>
> D. With regard to the measure of retribution it is written, "Visiting the sin of the fathers on the sons and on the grandsons to the third and fourth generation" (Exod. 20:5).
>
> E. And with regard to the measure of goodness it is written, "And doing mercy for thousands" (Exod. 20:6).
>
> F. You must therefore conclude that the measure of goodness is five hundred times greater than the measure of retribution. (*t. Sotah* 4:1)

Having made that point, we revert to the specifics of cases involving mortals, not God, and here, we wish to show the simple point that reward and punishment meet in the precision of justice.

Justice means that not only does the sinner lose what he or she wanted, but the sinner also is denied what formerly he or she had possessed, a still more mordant and exact penalty indeed. At *t. Sotah* 4:16, the statement of the Mishnah, "Just as she is prohibited to her husband, so she is prohibited to her lover" [*m. Sotah* 5:1], is transformed into a generalization, which is spelled out and then demonstrated by a list lacking all articulation; the items on the list serve to make the point. The illustrative case—the snake and Eve—is given as follows:

> A. Just as she is prohibited to her husband, so she is prohibited to her lover:
>
> B. You turn out to rule in the case of an accused wife who set her eyes on someone who was not available to her:
>
> C. What she wanted is not given to her, and what she had in hand is taken away from her. (*t. Sotah* 4:16)

The poetry of justice is not lost: what the sinner wanted he does not get, and what he had he loses:

> A. And so you find in the case of the snake of olden times, who was smarter than all the cattle and wild beasts of the field, as it is said, "Now the serpent was smarter than any other wild creature that the Lord God had made" (Gen. 3:1).
>
> B. He wanted to slay Adam and to marry Eve.
>
> C. The Omnipresent said to him, "I said that you should be king over all beasts and wild animals. Now that you did not want things that way, 'You are more cursed than all the beasts and wild animals of the field' (Gen. 3:14).
>
> D. "I said that you should walk straight-up like man. Now that you did not want things that way, 'Upon your belly you shall go' (Gen. 3:14).
>
> E. "I said that you should eat human food and drink human drink. Now: 'And dust you shall eat all the days of your life' (Gen. 3:14). (*t. Sotah* 4:17)

> A. "You wanted to kill Adam and marry Eve? 'And I will put enmity between you and the woman' (Gen. 3:15)."
>
> B. You turn out to rule, What he wanted was not given to him, and what he had in hand was taken away from him. (*t. Sotah* 4:18)

The sages' mode of thought through classification and hierarchization to uncover patterns does not require the spelling out of the consequences of the pattern through endless cases. To the sages the archetypal sinners are the generation of the flood, the generation of the dispersion (from the Tower of Babel), the Sodomites, the Egyptians, Samson (in the list from *Leviticus Rabbah* that follows, Amnon and Zimri). The cases turned into a general rule before us prove of special importance, since they clarify, through the very listing, a major issue, the standing of gentiles in world order. Listing these six cases yields a generalization: the same God who exacted punishment from the archetypal sinners will exact punishment from anyone who does as they did, and with Samson, Amnon, and Zimri, we move from the world of gentiles to the world of Israel; justice then is equal for all of humanity, both those within, and those beyond, the limits of the Torah defined by Israel:

> 1.   A. R. Ishmael taught, "'You shall not do as they do in the land of Egypt, where you dwelt, and you shall not do as they do in the land of Canaan . . . I am the LORD your God' [Lev. 18:3-4].
>
> B. "And if not, it is as if I am not the LORD your God."

The key point is now introduced: the case supplies a rule, and here, "I am going to exact punishment from anyone who does as they did:"

2.   A. R. Hiyya taught, "[The text states,] 'I am the LORD your God' two times [Lev. 18:4, 5].
      B. "I am the one who exacted punishment from the Generation of the Flood and from the men of Sodom and Gomorrah and from Egypt.
      C. "'I am going to exact punishment from anyone who does as they did.'"

A list of names with little elaboration serves to prove the proposition at hand:

5.   A. "I am the Lord" (Lev. 18:4):
      B. "I am he who exacted punishment from Samson, Amnon, and Zimri, and I am going to exact punishment from whoever does as they did.
      C. "I am he who rewarded Joseph, Jael, and Palti. I am going to reward whoever does as they did." (*Leviticus Rabbah* XXIII:IX)

I see nothing surprising in this list, until we reach Samson, at which point Israel joins the gentiles in the domain of justice. And we cannot then miss the point: justice is universal, the way in which the one and only God governs all of humanity.

The sages not only accept the burden of proving, against all experience, that goodness goes to the good and evil to the wicked. They have also alleged, and here propose to instantiate, that the holy people Israel itself, its history, its destiny, conform to the principle of justice. And if the claim that justice governs in the lives and actions of private persons conflicts with experience, the condition of Israel, conquered and scattered, surely calls into question any allegation that Israel's story embodies that same orderly and reasonable principle. Before us the sages take one step forward in their consideration of that very difficult question, how to explain the prosperity of the idolaters, the gentiles, and the humiliation of those who serve the one true God, Israel. That step consists only in matching what Abraham does with what happens to his family later on.

The sages take a step further, their conviction of the systematic rationality of divine justice carrying them to an extreme view. It is, specifically, that if we know how someone has sinned, we also know not only that but exactly how that person will be penalized. And the same goes for rewards either in this world or in the world to come. Not only individuals, but classes of sinners and of sins, will be penalized in a manner appropriate to the character of the sin. That accounts for the certainty that justice always prevails and that the one who is punished bears full responsibility for his or her fate. All the more urgent, then, is the concept of judgment, resurrection and life after death, and the world to come, which in its way addresses the necessary corollary of the perfection of divine justice: the manifest injustice of the workaday fate of perfectly righteous people. In due course, we shall have much more to say about the same matter.

When Israel ("Those Who Know God") Sins

Within Judaic monotheism, Israel—those who know God the way God wishes to be known, which is through the Torah—sins and is punished, but then atones and is forbidden and reconciled with God. When it comes to Israel, the principle of commensurate response to each action extends, also, to God's response to Israel's atonement. Israel is punished for its sin. But when Israel repents and God forgives Israel and restores the holy people's fortunes, then that same principle that all things match takes over. Hence we should not find surprising the logical extension, to the character of God's forgiveness and comfort of Israel, of the principle of measure for measure. When Israel sins, it is punished through that with which it sins, but it also is comforted through that with which it has been punished.

What is important to us is not only the logical necessity of the sages' reaching such a position. It also is the character of their demonstration of that fact. Here is a remarkably successful exposition of the way in which the sages assemble out of Scripture facts that, all together, demonstrate the moral order of reward and punishment, along with the merciful character of God and God's justice. Here is a fine case in which a single pervasive logic coordinates a mass of data into a cogent statement of a position that prevails throughout. A passage such as the following from *Pesiqta de Rab Kahana* can be understood only in light of the insistence at the outset that the sages conduct their inquiries in the manner of natural philosophy, the raw data—the cited verses of Scripture—being recast into a coherent demonstration of the desired proposition:

1.   A. "[Comfort, comfort my people, says your God.] Speak tenderly to the heart of Jerusalem and declare to her [that her warfare is ended, that her iniquity is pardoned, that she has received from the LORD's hand double for all her sins]" (Isa. 40:1-2).
      B. When they sinned with the head, they were smitten at the head, but they were comforted through the head.

C. When they sinned with the head: "Let us make a head and let us return to Egypt" (Num. 14:4).

D. . . . they were smitten at the head: "The whole head is sick" (Isa. 1:5).

E. . . . but they were comforted through the head: "Their king has passed before them and the Lord is at the head of them" (Mic. 2:13). (*Pesiq. R. Kah.* XVI:XI.1)

The construction is pellucid, the triplet of sin, punishment, and comfort, applied first to the head, and, predictably, to the other principal parts. Why predictably? Because the sages wish to match nature with supernature, the components of the natural world with the parts of the body, as we saw in chapter 1, the components of the body with the paradigmatic actions of Israel through time. All things match in exact balance: the natural world and the body of humanity, the body of humanity and the actions of Israel. From the head we now proceed to the eye, the ear, the nose, mouth, tongue, heart, hand, foot—the agencies of the expression of humanity's will. Once more what is important is not the end product, which is a tedious and repetitious demonstration, but the way in which the facts of Scripture (proof-texts) are coordinated, selected, and organized to form a pattern that, left on their own, they do not establish at all. The entire passage follows without interruption, because at every point the exposition is pellucid:

2.   A. When they sinned with the eye, they were smitten at the eye, but they were comforted through the eye.

B. When they sinned with the eye: "[The daughters of Zion . . . walk] . . . with wanton eyes" (Isa. 3:16).

C. . . . they were smitten at the eye: "My eye, my eye runs down with water" (Lam. 1:16).

D. . . . but they were comforted through the eye: "For every eye shall see the Lord returning to Zion" (Isa. 52:8).

3.   A. When they sinned with the ear, they were smitten at the ear, but they were comforted through the ear.

B. When they sinned with the ear: "They stopped up their ears so as not to hear" (Zech. 7:11).

C. . . . they were smitten at the ear: "Their ears shall be deaf" (Mic. 7:16).

D. . . . but they were comforted through the ear: "Your ears shall hear a word saying, [This is the way]" (Isa. 30:21).

4.   A. When they sinned with the nose [spelled *af,* which can also mean, "yet" or "also"], they were smitten at the nose, but they were comforted through the nose.

B. When they sinned with the nose: "And lo, they put the branch to their noses" (Ezek. 8:17).

C. . . . they were smitten at the word *af* [also]: "I also will do this to you" (Lev. 26:16).

D. . . . but they were comforted through the word *af* [now meaning yet]: "And yet for all that, when they are in the land of their enemies, I will not reject them" (Lev. 26:44).

5. A. When they sinned with the mouth, they were smitten at the mouth, but they were comforted through the mouth.

B. When they sinned with the mouth: "Every mouth speaks wantonness" (Isa. 9:16).

C. . . . they were smitten at the mouth: "[The Aramaeans and the Philistines] devour Israel with open mouth" (Isa. 9:11).

D. . . . but they were comforted through the mouth: "Then was our mouth filled with laughter" (Ps. 126:2).

6. A. When they sinned with the tongue, they were smitten at the tongue, but they were comforted through the tongue.

B. When they sinned with the tongue: "They bend their tongue, [their bow of falsehood]" (Jer. 9:2).

C. . . . they were smitten at the tongue: "The tongue of the sucking [child cleaves to the roof of his mouth for thirst] (Lam. 4:4).

D. . . . but they were comforted through the tongue: "And our tongue with singing" (Ps. 126:2).

7. A. When they sinned with the heart, they were smitten at the heart, but they were comforted through the heart.

B. When they sinned with the heart: "Yes, they made their hearts as a stubborn stone" (Zech. 7:12).

C. . . . they were smitten at the heart: "And the whole heart faints" (Isa. 1:5).

D. . . . but they were comforted through the heart: "Speak to the heart of Jerusalem" (Isa. 40:2).

8. A. When they sinned with the hand, they were smitten at the hand, but they were comforted through the hand.

B. When they sinned with the hand: "Your hands are full of blood" (Isa. 1:15).

C. . . . they were smitten at the hand: "The hands of women full of compassion have boiled their own children" (Lam. 4:10).

D. . . . but they were comforted through the hand: "The LORD will set his hand again the second time [to recover the remnant of his people]" (Isa. 11:11).

9. A. When they sinned with the foot, they were smitten at the foot, but they were comforted through the foot.

B. When they sinned with the foot: "The daughters of Zion . . . walk . . . making a tinkling with their feet" (Isa. 3:16).

     C. . . . they were smitten at the foot: "Your feet will stumble upon the dark mountains" (Jer. 13:16).

     D. . . . but they were comforted through the foot: "How beautiful upon the mountains are the feet of the messenger of good tidings" (Isa. 52:7).

10.   A. When they sinned with "this," they were smitten at "this," but they were comforted through "this."

     B. When they sinned with "this:" [The people said, . . . "Go, make us a god], for as for this man Moses . . . , [we do not know what has become of him]" (Exod. 32:1).

     C. . . . they were smitten at "this:" "For this our heart is faint" (Lam. 5:17).

     D. . . . but they were comforted through "this:" "It shall be said in that day, 'Lo, this is our God'" (Isa. 25:9).

11.   A. When they sinned with "he," they were smitten at "he," but they were comforted through "he."

     B. When they sinned with "he:" "They have denied the LORD and said, 'It is not he'" (Jer. 5:12).

     C. . . . they were smitten at "he:" "Therefore he has turned to be their enemy, and he himself fought against them" (Isa. 63:10).

     D. . . . but they were comforted through "he:" "I even I am he who comforts you" (Isa. 51:12).

12.   A. When they sinned with fire, they were smitten at fire, but they were comforted through fire.

     B. When they sinned with fire: "The children gather wood and the fathers kindle fire" (Jer. 7:18).

     C. . . . they were smitten at fire: "For from on high he has sent fire into my bones" (Lam. 1:13).

     D. . . . but they were comforted through fire: "'For I', says the Lord, 'will be for her a wall of fire round about'" (Zech. 2:9).

13.   A. When they sinned in double measure, they were smitten in double measure, but they were comforted in double measure.

     B. When they sinned in double measure: "Jerusalem has sinned a sin" (Lam. 1:8).

     C. . . . they were smitten in double measure: "that she has received from the LORD's hand double for all her sins" (Isa. 40:2).

     D. . . . but they were comforted in double measure: "Comfort, comfort my people, says your God. [Speak tenderly to the heart of Jerusalem and cry to her that her warfare is ended, that her iniquity is pardoned, that she has received from the Lord's hand double for all her sins]" (Isa. 40:1-2). (*Pesiq.R. Kah.* XVI:XI.2ff.)

Here is the kind of exegesis that fully realized paradigmatic thinking produces. The basic proposition—when they sinned with this, they were smitten at this, but they were comforted through this—maintains that an exact match unites sin and punishment; through that with which one sins, one is punished. But then, that same match links the modes of consolation as well, that is, through that trait through which one sinned, one also will be comforted. So the conviction of an orderly and appropriate set of correspondences setting forth a world in balance and proportion generates the details. The proofs for the proposition involve an extensive survey of both the media of sin and the character of punishment therefor. But in the restorationist theology—last things recapitulating first things—a passage such as this plays a typical role. It shows how at stake in world order is not a cataclysmic disruption at the end, but rather a serene restoration of the perfection that prevailed at the outset.

Measure for Measure

The principle of measure for measure accounts for the course of a human life, there too perfect justice prevails. And that is the point of insistence even in the implacable position taken in the following passage from Bavli tractate *Shabbat,* with the pertinent factual foundations carefully delineated:

> A. Said R. Ammi, "Death comes about only through sin, and suffering only through transgression.
>
> B. "Death comes about only through sin: 'The soul that sins, it shall die; the son shall not bear the iniquity of the father, neither shall the father bear the iniquity of the son; the righteousness of the righteous shall be upon him and the wickedness of the wicked shall be upon him' (Ezek. 18:20).
>
> C. "And suffering only through transgression: 'Then will I visit their transgression with the rod and their iniquity with stripes' (Ps. 89:33)."

Now comes the challenge:

> D. [55B] An objection was raised: Said the ministering angels before the Holy One blessed be he, "LORD of the universe, how come you have imposed the penalty of death on the first Adam?"
>
> E. He said to them, "I commanded him one easy commandment, but he violated it."

Surely saints die too. What is to be said of them?

F. They said to him, "But isn't it the fact that Moses and Aaron, who kept the entire Torah, also died?"

G. He said to them, "There is one fate to the righteous and to the wicked, to the good . . . " (Qoh. 9:2).

Saints sin, and that is why they too die:

H. [Ammi] concurs with [the view of matters expressed by] the following Tannaite authority, as has been taught on Tannaite authority:

I. R. Simeon b. Eleazar says, "So, too, Moses and Aaron died on account of their sin: 'Because you didn't believe in me . . . therefore you shall not bring this assembly into the land that I have given them' (Num. 20:12)—lo, if you had believed in me, your time would not yet have come to take leave of the world."

J. An objection was raised: Four died on account of the snake's machinations [and not on account of their own sin]: Benjamin the son of Jacob, Amram the father of Moses, Jesse the father of David, and Caleb the son of David. But all of them are known by tradition except for Jesse, the father of David, in which case Scripture makes it clear, as it is written, "And Absalom set Amasa over the host instead of Joab. Now Amasa was the son of a man whose name was Itra the Israelite, who went in to Abigail the daughter of Nahash, sister of Zeruiah Joab's mother" (2 Sam. 17:25). Now was she the daughter of Nahash? Surely she was the daughter of Jesse: "And their sisters were Zeruiah and Abigail" (1 Chron. 2:16). But she was the daughter of him who died on account of the machinations of the snake [Nahash]. Now who is the authority here? Shouldn't we say, the Tannaite authority who stands behind the story of the ministering angels?

K. But there were Moses and Aaron, too. So it must be R. Simeon b. Eleazar, and that proves that there can be death without sin, and suffering without transgression. Isn't that a refutation of the position of R. Ammi?

L. It is a solid refutation. (b. Shab. 5:3 XII.12/55a-b)

That penalties for not carrying out vows prove extreme, which we have already noted, is shown by appeal to the exemplary precedent set by Jacob or by Abraham.

If therefore the sages had to state the logic that imposes order and proportion upon all relationships—the social counterpart to the laws of gravity—they would point to justice: what accords with commonsense justice is logical, and what does not is irrational. Ample evidence derives from Scripture's enormous corpus of facts to sustain the sages' view that the moral order, based on justice, governs the affairs of persons and nations.

In the sages' discourse justice never requires explanation, but violations of justice always do. When what happens does not conform to the systemic givens but violates the expectations precipitated by them, then the sages pay close attention and ask why. When what happens does conform, they do not have to: their unarticulated conviction of self-evidence is embodied, therefore, in the character of their discourse: not only the speech but the silence. Justice therefore defines the rational, and injustice, the irrational. And that judgment extends to all humanity.

But to address all humanity and not only Israel, Judaic monotheism had to address the actualities of everyday life. That is where, in humble matters of home and family, humanity is differentiated not in the large aggregates of idolaters or worshipers of one God, but in small ways. And there justice prevails only now and then. Humanity's fate rarely accords with the fundamental principle of a just order but mostly discredits it. But if the human condition embodied in Israelites' lives one by one defies the smooth explanations that serve for justifying the condition of Israel in the abstract, then the entire logic of the oral Torah fails.

How, then, do we reveal God's justice in the chaotic, scarcely manageable detritus of private lives? It is, as chapter 4 has already shown, through articulation of the doctrine of reward and punishment, the insistence on the justice of God in whatever happens. Within the logic at hand, reward and punishment not only precipitates but defines the teleology of all thought. In terms of the alternatives set forth in the Preface, God is always God, but by no means good to all. This is stated in so many words in this passage from *Lamentations Rabbah,* as is every critical proposition of the entire theological system animating the oral Torah:

1.   A. "The LORD is good to those who wait for him, to the soul that seeks him:"
     B. Might one suppose that God is good to all?
     C. Scripture says, "to the soul that seeks him."

May we distinguish Israel from the gentiles? Not at all:

2.   A. Along these same lines: "Surely God is good to Israel" (Ps. 73:1).
     B. Might one suppose that God is good to all?
     C. Scripture says, "Even to those who are pure in heart" (Ps. 73:1).
     D. That is, those whose heart is pure and in whose hand is no wickedness.

Then to whom is God good? To those who keep the Torah:

3.   A. Along these same lines: "Happy is the one whose strength is in you" (Ps. 84:6).

        B. Might one suppose that God is good to all?

        C. Scripture says, "In whose heart are the highways" (Ps. 84:6)—
those in whose heart the paths of the Torah are kept."

God is good to those who are sincerely upright:

4.   A. Along these same lines: "Do good, O LORD, to the good"
(Ps. 125:4).

        B. Might one suppose that God is good to all?

        C. Scripture says, "And to those who are upright in their hearts"
(Ps. 125:5).

God is good to those who sincerely seek him:

5.   A. Along these same lines: "The LORD is near to all those who call
upon him" (Ps. 145:18).

        B. Might one suppose that God is good to all?

        C. Scripture says, "To all who call upon him in truth" (Ps. 145:18).

God is good to the remnant of Israel, those who are forgiven their sin:

6.   A. Along these same lines: "Who is a God like you, who pardons
iniquity and passes by transgression?" (Mic. 8:18).

        B. Might one suppose that God is good to all?

        C. Scripture says, "Of the remnant of his heritage" (Mic. 8:18).
(*Lamentations Rabbah* LXXXVII.i.1ff.)

God is selective and elects those that ought to be selected, punishes
and rewards those that deserve the one or the other. So God's justice is
what is explained. God is good to those who deserve it and punishes
those who deserve it.

Scripture explains the matter through the qualifying language that it
uses in context; it is Scripture's cases that are ordered into the governing principle of the whole: Torah is the key. When Paul invokes faith in
Christ as the medium of salvation, he says no less, and no more, than
the sages do in promising God's goodness to the upright of heart and
sincere of soul. The criterion, the requirement, is the same. And the
Torah is no more, if no less, particularistic than Christ, as the medium
of salvation. God's goodness is accessible to all who sincerely seek to
know him. Then Christianity differs from Judaism on the place where
God is to be known, but not on the access accorded to all humanity for
knowing God. I see here none of that arrogant exclusivism that James
D. G. Dunn imputes to Judaism: "[an] attempt to mark off some of
God's people as more holy than others, as exclusive channels of divine
grace."[1] God is good "to all who call upon him in truth." That suffices.

Predestination and Free Will

If the nations are responsible for their condition, according to the sages, so is Israel. So too is the rule of justice, and justification, for private lives. Everything begins with the insistence that people are responsible for what they do, therefore for what happens to them, as much as Israel dictates its destiny by its own deeds. Justice reigns, whatever happens. The reason that humanity singly and jointly in groups is responsible for its own actions is that humanity enjoys free will. Humanity is constantly subject to divine judgment; having free choice, humanity may sin. God judges the world in a generous way; but judgment does take place:

> A. R. Aqiba says, "Everything is foreseen, and free choice is given. In goodness the world is judged. And all is in accord with the abundance of deeds."
> B. He would say, "(1) All is handed over as a pledge, (2) And a net is cast over all the living. (3) The store is open, (4) the store-keeper gives credit, (5) the account book is open, and (6) the hand is writing.
> C. "(1) Whoever wants to borrow may come and borrow. (2) The charity collectors go around every day and collect from man whether he knows it or not. (3) And they have grounds for what they do. (4) And the judgment is a true judgment. (5) And everything is ready for the meal." (*m. 'Abot* 3:15)

God may foresee what is to happen, but humanity still exercises free will. It is humanity's attitude and intentionality that make all the difference. Because humanity is not coerced to sin, nor can humanity be forced to love God or even obey the Torah, an element of uncertainty affects every life. That is the point at which humanity's will competes with God's. It follows that, where humanity gives to God what God wants but cannot coerce, or what God wants but cannot command—love, generosity, for instance—there, the theology of the oral Torah alleges, God responds with an act of uncoerced grace. But in all, one thing is reliable, and that is the working of just recompense for individual action. Expectations of a just reward or punishment, contrasting with actualities, therefore precipitate all thought on the rationality of private life: what happens is supposed to make sense within the governing theology of a just order.

But that expectation rarely is met. How then do the sages justify— how do they show the justice of—what happens in private lives? Let us first consider how sages explained private fate as a consequence of individual behavior. Their first principle, predictably, is that, as Israel defines its own fate, so individuals bear responsibility for their own condition. A person is responsible for his or her own character. Even one surrounded by wicked people may still remain righteous, and vice versa. A measure of righteousness is not to conduct oneself in the manner of one's wicked neighbors. Not only so, but the righteous son of a wicked father enjoys much admiration but bears no burden of responsibility for his ancestry, and so for the contrary circumstance:

A. "[Then drew near the daughters of Zelophehad] the son of Hepher son of Gilead son of Machir son of Manasseh:"
B. Scripture thus informs [us] that just as Zelophehad was a first-born, so all of them were first-born [daughters to their mothers]; that all of them were upright women, daughters of an upright man.
C. For in the case of whoever keeps his [worthy] deeds concealed, and his father's deeds are concealed, Scripture portrays a worthy genealogy, lo, this was a righteous man, son of a righteous man.
D. And in the case of whoever keeps his [unworthy] deeds concealed, and his father's deeds concealed, Scripture portrays a disreputable genealogy, lo, this is a wicked man son of a wicked man.

The matter is now subject to amplification, with concrete cases of Scripture linked to the governing generalization:

E. R. Nathan says, "Scripture comes to teach you [about] every righteous man who grew up in the bosom of a wicked man and did not act like him, to tell you how great is his righteousness. For he grew up in the bosom of a wicked man but did not act like him.
F. "And every wicked man who grew up in the bosom of a righteous man but did not act like him—that tells you how great is the wickedness of such a one, who grew up in the bosom of a righteous man but did not act like him.

Now come the cases:

G. "Esau grew up between two righteous persons, Isaac and Rebecca, but he did not act like them. Obadiah grew up between two wicked persons, Ahab and Jezebel, but did not act like them. And he prophesied concerning the wicked Esau, who grew up between two righteous persons, Isaac and Rebecca, but did not act like them, as it is said, 'The vision of Obadiah: thus says the Lord GOD concerning Edom: we have heard tidings from the LORD and a messenger has been sent among the nations' (Obad. 1:1)." (*Sifré to Numbers* CXXXIII:II.1)

As usual, Scripture provides ample facts to be organized into the proposition that each person is responsible for him- or herself. The corollary must follow that what happens to the private person in the end cannot produce an anomaly for the governance of justice but, in some way or other, must accord with the rules of world order.

Not only so, but the principle that humanity is responsible for what it does is established in the very creation of the first human. Just as individuation is explained by appeal to the figure of Adam, so now, humanity's responsibility for its own deeds is adumbrated and exemplified by Adam. Adam acknowledged that he bore full responsibility for his own fate; and built into the human condition, therefore, is that same recognition, according to *Pesiqta de Rab Kahana:*

> A. It is written, "Thus said the LORD, 'What wrong did your fathers find in me that they went far from me and went after worthlessness and became worthless?'" (Jer. 2:5)
>
> B. Said R. Isaac, "This refers to one who leaves the scroll of the Torah and departs. Concerning him, Scripture says, 'What wrong did your fathers find in me that they went far from me?'
>
> C. "Said the Holy One, blessed be he, to the Israelites, 'My children, your fathers found no wrong with me, but you have found wrong with me.'"

Now a case—the archetypal one, Adam himself—will illustrate the generalization contained within the statement of Rabbi Isaac. People who violate the Torah do so on their own volition, not by reason of a tradition of rebellion. They therefore bear responsibility for their own sins.

> D. "'The first Man found no wrong with me, but you have found wrong with me.'
>
> E. "To what may the first Man be compared?
>
> F. "To a sick man, to whom the physician came. The physician said to him, 'Eat this, don't eat that.'
>
> G. "When the man violated the instructions of the physician, he brought about his own death.
>
> H. "[As he lay dying,] his relatives came to him and said to him, 'Is it possible that the physician is imposing on you the divine attribute of justice?'
>
> I. "He said to them, 'God forbid. I am the one who brought about my own death. This is what he instructed me, saying to me, 'Eat this, don't eat that,' but when I violated his instructions, I brought about my own death."

Adam is the archetype; he brings upon himself his own death:

J. "So too all the generations came to the first Man, saying to him, 'Is it possible that the Holy One, blessed be he, is imposing the attribute of justice on you?'

L. "He said to them, 'God forbid. I am the one who has brought about my own death. Thus did he command me, saying to me, 'Of all the trees of the garden you may eat, but of the tree of the knowledge of good and evil you may not eat' (Gen. 2:17). When I violated his instructions, I brought about my own death, for it is written, 'On the day on which you eat it, you will surely die' (Gen. 2:17)." (*Pesiq. R. Kah.* XIV:V.1)

God is not at fault for Adam's fall; Adam brought about his own death. So justice governs, and people may appeal to that sense for the fitting penalty for the sin to explain what happens in ordinary, everyday affairs.

Suffering Is Reasonable Too

Suffering represents not an anomaly in, but the confirmation of, the monotheist theological logic that begins all thought with the principle of God's justice and benevolence. Suffering helps humanity to help itself, returns humanity to God, precipitates humanity's repentance. What more can one ask of a just God than the opportunity to shape one's own will to conciliate God? No wonder, then, that the oral Torah's framers, focused as they are on the patriarchs as themselves paradigms for their children, Israel, and enduring sources for a heritage of virtue, go so far as to invoke the fathers as the founders of suffering. Here, the patriarchs themselves asked God to bestow old age, suffering, and sickness, because the world needed them. These components of the human condition not only do not form challenges to the logic of God's just governance of the world, but express that very benevolence that infuses justice. So the patriarchs themselves initially beseeched God to bestow on humanity the blessings of old age, suffering, and sickness, each for its rational purpose. Here in this passage from *Genesis Rabbah* the theology transcends itself:

A. "When Isaac was old, and his eyes were dim, so that he could not see, he called Esau his older son, and said to him, 'My son,' and he answered, 'Here I am'" (Gen. 27:1).

B. Said R. Judah bar Simon, "Abraham sought [the physical traits of] old age [so that from one's appearance, people would know that he was old]. He said before him, 'Lord of all ages, when a man and his son come in somewhere, no one knows whom to

> honor. If you crown a man with the traits of old age, people will know whom to honor.'
>
> C. "Said to him the Holy One, blessed be he, 'By your life, this is a good thing that you have asked for, and it will begin with you.'
>
> D. "From the beginning of the book of Genesis to this passage, there is no reference to old age. But when Abraham our father came along, the traits of old age were given to him, as it is said, 'And Abraham was old' (Gen. 24:1)."

So much for old age, but what about what goes with it, the suffering of infirmities? Here Isaac makes his contribution, now being credited with that very conception that, as we have seen, explains the justice of human suffering:

> E. "Isaac asked God for suffering. He said before him, 'Lord of the age, if someone dies without suffering, the measure of strict justice is stretched out against him. But if you bring suffering on him, the measure of strict justice will not be stretched out against him. [Suffering will help counter the man's sins, and the measure of strict justice will be mitigated through suffering by the measure of mercy.]'
>
> F. "Said to him the Holy One, blessed be he, 'By your life, this is a good thing that you have asked for, and it will begin with you.'
>
> G. "From the beginning of the book of Genesis to this passage, there is no reference to suffering. But when Isaac came along, suffering was given to him: his eyes were dim.'"

Finally, what of sickness, the third in the components of humanity's fate? That is Jacob's contribution, and the wisdom and goodwill of God come once more to full articulation in suffering:

> H. "Jacob asked for sickness. He said before him, 'Lord of all ages, if a person dies without illness, he will not settle his affairs for his children. If he is sick for two or three days, he will settle his affairs with his children.'
>
> I. "Said to him the Holy One, blessed be he, 'By your life, this is a good thing that you have asked for, and it will begin with you.'
>
> J. "That is in line with this verse: 'And someone said to Joseph, "Behold, your father is sick"' (Gen. 48:1)."
>
> K. Said R. Levi, "Abraham introduced the innovation of old age, Isaac introduced the innovation of suffering, Jacob introduced the innovation of sickness.

We proceed now to a further case of the same classification, now chronic illness and its origin in the wisdom of the saints, now Hezekiah:

L. "Hezekiah introduced the innovation of chronic illness. He said to him, 'You have kept a man in good condition until the day he dies. But if someone is sick and gets better, he will carry out a complete and sincere act of repentance for his sins.'

M. "Said to him the Holy One, blessed be he, 'By your life, this is a good thing that you have asked for, and it will begin with you.'

N. "'The writing of Hezekiah, king of Judah, when he had been sick and recovered of his sickness' (Isa. 38:9)."

O. Said R. Samuel b. Nahman, "On the basis of that verse we know that between one illness and another there was an illness more serious than either one." (*Genesis Rabbah* LXV:IX.1)

Old age, suffering, and sickness do not represent flaws in creation but things to be desired. Each serves a good purpose. All form acts of divine mercy. The mode of explanation appeals to reason and practical considerations attached thereto. Another version from Bavli tractate *Baba Mesia* has it that Abraham, Jacob, and Elisha brought about old age, illness, and healing:

A. Until the time of Abraham there was no such thing as old age. One who wanted to speak with Abraham might well speak with Isaac and one who wanted to speak with Isaac might well speak with Abraham. Abraham came along and begged for mercy, and old age came about, as it is said, "And Abraham was old, getting along in years" (Gen. 24:1).

B. Until Jacob, there was no such thing as illness, but Jacob came along and begged for mercy, and illness came about, as it is said, "And someone told Joseph, behold your father is sick" (Gen. 48:1).

C. Until Elisha came along, there was no one who ever got sick and then got well again, but when Elisha came along, [Elisha] begged for mercy and he was healed, as it is written, "Now Elisha had fallen sick of the illness of which he died" (2 Kings 13:14), which proves that he had been sick earlier but had recovered. (*b. B. Mes.* 7:1.IV.19/87a)

What is fresh is the initiation of recovery from illness, an extension of the initial tale of how the patriarchs asked for suffering.

Still, matters do not come out even; all die, but not everyone suffers premature death or sickness. Much more galling: sometimes wicked people live long, healthy, and prosperous lives, happily making everyone around them miserable, then die peacefully in their sleep at a ripe old age. And—then or now—one need not visit a cancer ward to find misery afflicting genuinely good and pious people. So while the doctrine of the benevolence expressed by sickness, suffering, and old age, serves, it hardly constitutes a universal and sufficient justification. And, however reasonable suffering may be shown to be, in the end reason hardly suffices in the face of the raw agony of incurable illness. That is why, in the sages' view, further responses to Job, Jeremiah, and Qoheleth are called for. One further effort to bring suffering within the framework of the rational, to show the justice of the matter, is called forth.

Anomalies in the Just Order

Specifically, the same anomalies in the just order encompassing private life may come about for yet another reason, God's own plan. Specifically, when the righteous suffer, according to *Genesis Rabbah,* it is God who is testing them.

> LV:II.1.A."The Lord tries the righteous, but the wicked and him who loves violence his soul hates" (Ps. 11:5):

This is now embodied in metaphors drawn from the potter, the flax maker, and the farmer:

> B. Said R. Jonathan, "A potter does not test a weak utensil, for if he hits it just once, he will break it. What does the potter test? He tests the strong ones, for even if he strikes them repeatedly, they will not break. So the Holy One, blessed be he, does not try the wicked but the righteous: 'The LORD tries the righteous' (Ps. 11:5)."
> C. Said R. Yosé bar Haninah, "When a flax maker knows that the flax is in good shape, then the more he beats it, the more it will improve and glisten. When it is not of good quality, if he beats it just once, he will split it. So the Holy One, blessed be he, does not try the wicked but the righteous: 'The LORD tries the righteous' (Ps. 11:5)."
> D. Said R. Eleazar, "The matter may be compared to a farmer [Hebrew: householder] who has two heifers, one strong, one weak. On whom does he place the yoke? It is on the one that is strong. So the Holy One, blessed be he, does not try the wicked but the righteous: 'The LORD tries the righteous' (Ps. 11:5)."

We conclude the exercise with the juxtaposition of the base verse, Gen. 22:1, and the intersecting verse, Ps. 11:5, at the meeting of which the point just now stated was triggered:

> LV:III.1.A.Another interpretation: "The LORD tries the righteous, but the wicked and him who loves violence his soul hates" (Ps. 11:5):
> B. The cited verse speaks of Abraham: "And it came to pass after these things God tested Abraham" (Gen. 22:1). (*Genesis Rabbah* LV:II.1f.)

The suffering of the righteous pays tribute to their strength and is a mark of their virtue. That is shown by appeal to both analogies (potter, flax maker, householder) and Scripture. Suffering then shows God's favor for the one who suffers, indicating that such a one is worthy of God's attention and special interest. That suffering is a valued gift explains the critical importance of the theological principle that one should accept whatever God metes out, even suffering. In a context defined by the conviction that suffering forms a gift from a benevolent, just God, we cannot find surprising that a loving God should involve accepting punishment as much as benefit. This is stated in so many words: one is obligated to bless over evil as one blesses over good, as it is said, "And you shall love the LORD your God with all your heart, with all your soul, and with all your might" (Deut. 6:5). "With all your heart"—with both of your inclinations, with the good inclination and with the evil inclination. "And with all your soul"—even if he takes your soul. "And with all your might"—with all of your money (*m. Ber.* 9:4A-E). Accordingly, the correct attitude toward suffering entails grateful acknowledgment that what God metes out is just and merciful. The same matter is amplified in the following exegesis from *Sifré to Deuteronomy* of the same verses of Scripture:

1. A. R. Aqiba says, "Since it is said, 'with all your soul,' it is an argument a fortiori that we should encompass, 'with all your might.'
   B. "Why then does Scripture say, 'with all your might'?
   C. "It is to encompass every single measure that God metes out to you, whether the measure of good or the measure of punishment."

Now further verses are shown to deliver the same message:

2. A. So does David say, "[How can I repay the LORD for all his bountiful dealings toward me?] I will lift up the cup of salvation and call upon the name of the LORD" (Ps. 116:12-13).
   B. "I found trouble and sorrow but I called upon the name of the LORD" (Ps. 116:3-4).

Job, who formulated the problem of evil in its most dramatic statement, takes the same position, so far as the sages are concerned:

3. A. So does Job say, "The LORD gave and the LORD has taken away. Blessed be the name of the LORD" (Job 1:21).
   B. If that is the case for the measure of goodness, all the more so for the measure of punishment.
   C. What does his wife say to him? "Do you still hold fast your integrity? Blaspheme God and die" (Job 2:9).

D. And what does he say to her? "You speak as one of the impious women speaks. Shall we receive good at the hand of God and shall we not receive evil?" (Job 2:10).

Now we show the contrasting attitude, one that substitutes for gratitude churlishness, and for acceptance of punishment, which the sages admire, dignity in dumb submission:

4.   A. The men of the generation of the flood were churlish as to the good, and when punishment came upon them, they took it willy-nilly.

B. And is it not an argument a fortiori: if one who was churlish as to the good behaved with dignity in a time of punishment, we who behave with dignity in response to good should surely behave with dignity in a time of trouble.

C. And so he say to her, "You speak as one of the impious women speaks. Shall we receive good at the hand of God and shall we not receive evil?" (Job 2:10).

Now we turn to the familiar position that since suffering is a medium of atonement and repentance, people should accept it thankfully:

5.   A. And, furthermore, a person should rejoice in suffering more than in good times. For if someone lives in good times his entire life, he will not be forgiven for such sin as may be in his hand.

B. And how shall he attain forgiveness? Through suffering.

6.   A. R. Eliezer b. Jacob says, "Lo, Scripture says, 'For whom the LORD loves he corrects, even as a father corrects the son in whom he delights' (Prov. 3:12).

B. "What made the son be pleasing to the father? You must say it was suffering [on account of correction]." (*Sifré to Deuteronomy* XXXII:V.1-12)

So the sages mounted argument after argument. They framed and found scriptural bases for doctrine after doctrine.

All this was to try to persuade themselves that somehow the world conformed to a universally regnant rationality defined by justice. True, the claim that anguish and illness, premature death and everyday suffering fit under the rules of reasonable world order; that insistence that when the wicked prosper, justice still may be done—these propositions, necessary to the system, may well have transcended the here and now and conformed to a higher reality. But still, when all is said and the day is done, the doctrine of suffering could not encompass all cases, let alone persuade everybody who raised the questions, why me? why now? Nor did the sages so frame matters as to suggest they found theology's Panglossian solutions, if necessary, wholly sufficient let alone compelling.

True, suffering is to be accepted as a mark of God's grace, a gift, an occasion, a mode of atonement and reconciliation with God. True, the patriarchs found much good in humanity's fate and asked God to arrange matters as they are. And yet the fact remains that some folk suffer more than others, and not uncommonly, the wicked prosper and the righteous do not. So the doctrine of suffering on its own could not, and did not, complete the oral Torah's account of the confrontation with the key dilemma of the sages' theology of world order, the anomalies that manifestly flaw private lives, viewed in comparison and contrast with one another. Say what they would, the sages in the end had to complete the circle: some do not get what they deserve, whether for good or for ill, and, if their time is replicated in our own, those some were very many. To that protean problem the sages found in their larger theology a commensurate and predictable response.

The sages identified with the Torah the promise of life eternal, with idolatry the extinction of being. This would come about, to correspond with and complete the first days of creation. Justice will be done only when the world is perfected. With that conviction's forming the foundation of their very definition of world order, divided between those who will overcome the grave, Israel with the Torah, and those who will not, the gentiles with idolatry, the sages found in hand a simple solution. The righteous suffer in this world and get their just reward in the world to come, but the wicked enjoy this world and suffer in the world to come. Since the theology of the oral Torah to begin with distinguished the Torah and life from idolatry and death, what happens in this world and in this life does not tell the whole story. And when that entire story is told, the received formulation of the problem of evil no longer pertains, and the final anomalies are smoothed out.

Beyond Reason, the Human Condition

But the sages were no fools, and hope for the at-present-intangible future did not obscure the dark vision of the ordinary experience of life, its nonsense, its anomalies. And if it had, Job and Jeremiah would have reminded them that the wicked prosper, the righteous suffer, and (in contemporary terms), where was God when Germany constructed Auschwitz? While pursuing philosophical modes of thought, in the end the sages valued sagacity beyond reason, however compelling. For all their insistence upon the rule of God through a just order, the sages accepted that beyond the known and reasonable lay the unknowable, the realm of God beyond the part set forth in the revealed Torah. They affirmed, in the end, their own failure, which makes them plausible and human in their claims to account for much, if not all, of the anguish of which private lives even of the most holy of humanity are comprised. In the end we all die, and who knows how long the interval until the resurrection? So the sages' last word on the reasonable rule of the just order consists of a single imperative: humility, the gift of wisdom, not of wit.

Here is a passage from Bavli tractate *Menahot* that generations of Talmud students have found sublime, the statement of all things, all in all, where any account of normative Judaism concludes, with the affirmation that, beyond all reason, God is always God:

5.   A. Said R. Judah said Rab, "At the time that Moses went up on high, he found the Holy One in session, affixing crowns to the letters [of the words of the Torah]. He said to him, 'Lord of the universe, who is stopping you [from regarding the document as perfect without these additional crowns on the letters]?'

B. "He said to him, 'There is a man who is going to arrive at the end of many generations, and Aqiba b. Joseph is his name, who is going to interpret on the basis of each point of the crowns heaps and heaps of laws.'

C. "He said to him, 'Lord of the Universe, show him to me.'

D. "He said to him, 'Turn around.'

E. "He went and took a seat at the end of eight rows, but he could not grasp what the people were saying. He felt faint. But when the discourse reached a certain matter, and the disciples said, 'My lord, how do you know this?' and he answered, 'It is a law given to Moses from Sinai,' he regained his composure.

F. "He went and came before the Holy One. He said before him, 'Lord of the Universe, How come you have someone like that and yet you give the Torah through me?'

G. "He said to him, 'Silence! That is how the thought came to me.'

H. "He said to him, 'Lord of the Universe, you have shown me his Torah, now show me his reward.'

I. "He said to him, 'Turn around.'

J. "He turned around and saw his flesh being weighed out at the butcher-stalls in the market.

K. "He said to him, 'Lord of the Universe, such is Torah, such is the reward?'

L. "He said to him, 'Silence! That is how the thought came to me.'"
      (*b. Menah.* 3:7 II.5/29b)

God rules, and humanity in the end cannot explain, account for the rationality of, everything God decrees. The sages offer more than reasonable explanations for the perceived violation of justice. They offer also the gift of humility in the form of silence. That forms the barrier before the ultimate terror—not understanding, not making sense of things.

Accordingly, the sages placed humility before God above even the entire theological enterprise with its promise of the explanation, understanding, and justification. But the last word must register: that God decrees, however inexplicable those decrees to the mind of humanity, bears the comforting message that God cares. And since the premise of the mystery of suffering is formed by the conviction of God's justice (otherwise why take note of the case at hand as an anomaly?), that God cares also means God loves. And it is a love for humanity, taken care of one by one, a love so deep as not to leave anybody ever unattended— even Aqiba in his martyrdom, but especially ordinary folk, when they suffer, when they bleed, when they die, as all do. And therein is the ultimate demonstration of the systemic universality of Judaic monotheism: the command of silence—awe, fear, reverence—before the creator of all humanity.

Epilogue: Recovering Judaism

A great many Jews, and a large part of Christian theological opinion past and present, concur that the Jews form an ethnic group, to which the religion of Judaism is an ethnic appendage. The generality of Christian opinion is represented not only by James Dunn,[1] whom we met at the outset, but by the contemporary fabrication, *Messianic Judaism,* which offers Christianity as Judaism and insists that, rejecting the Torah of Moses our rabbi in favor of Christianity, Jews continue to constitute that "Israel" of which Scripture spoke. The apostle Paul framed matters more elegantly but not much differently.

But the contemporary character of the Jewish community, in its fully realized secularity, adds to the world's burden of intense ethnicities yet another, depriving humanity of the vision of that second chance for Adam and Eve in Eden represented by Israel in the embodiment of God's kingdom on earth. That is a vision of the unity of humanity, standing under judgment before God, that competes with the Christian one, but, Judaism would claim, realizes the Israelite Scripture's own promise. That is to say, Judaism reads from Scripture forward, while Christianity reads from the Gospels backward. Surely that is an argument between Scripture's joint heirs worth joining in the age in which Judaism and Christianity renew their long-interrupted discourse about what it means to seek God's kingdom. But how is Christianity to engage in argument with an absent partner, with a religion unable to express itself in the here and now of contemporary social discourse? So Christianity has a stake in the recovery of Judaism as a religion that shapes an ethnicity, transforming and transcending the secular facts.

But, it is self-evident, the Jews have still more at stake in addressing the claim upon them that they constitute that holy Israel of which the Torah speaks. So let us focus on the Jews and their reworking of Judaism into Jewishness. In Jewry today Judaism, the religion, today competes with Jewishness, the ethnicity, however defined, that characterizes the Jews as a social entity. Within the Jewish community flourishes a secular bias, which defines the Jews as an ethnic group of political near-unanimity and sets forth "being Jewish" as a matter of taste and individual predilection, beginning with birth to a Jewish parent. That ethnicity may involve loyalties to a social group, an allegation of common memory, shared response to reconstructions of what is represented as a single, unitary, linear history. It may involve less exalted matters as well. But ethnic Jewishness always rests upon individual taste and predilection, not on a sense of obligation, of being part of that holy Israel of which the Torah, written and oral, speaks.

That yields not only the construction, *"my* Judaism," as though Judaism stood for a set of quite individual choices. That same bias emphasizes the material, political condition of the Jews as a social group, dismissing as marginal all questions of conviction and conscience of the holy people to whom the Torah speaks. In concrete terms, Jews who convert to another religion, in North America to Christianity in particular, deem themselves not Christians but *Messianic Jews,* retaining the ethnic identification, giving up the religious one. And the organized Jewish community celebrates the Jewishness, an ethnic category, that is expressed in customs and ceremonies, not the Judaism, a religious structure and system, that is embodied in the response to God's commandments that is entailed in acceptance of the yoke of God's kingdom of heaven, of which the liturgy of the synagogue speaks.

The secularization into "the Jewish People" of the "Israel" of which the Torah speaks on the part of both Christianity and a massive sector of the Jewish community has denied the religion, Judaism, a hearing among Jews, Christians, Muslims, and the secular world beyond. That ancient religion, the first of the three monotheisms, framed a message for its Israel that addressed all humanity. That religion successfully competed with its monotheist rivals, Christianity and Islam. The story that it tells and the life that it shapes defined the life of faithful communities for millennia. Alas, these marks of a vital religious tradition are today obscured! Not only so, but Judaism sets forth propositions of a universally accessible character and argues in their behalf in a manner that should compel assent on the part of any reasonable person—just as do all universalistic and philosophical or theological constructions of religious belief and behavior.

If I had to explain in this-worldly terms the principal concern that animates the ethnicization of Judaism by the Jewish community, I should appeal to a single consideration. The Jewish people find themselves so concerned with their continuity as a distinct community that they fear the mainstream and would (if they could) isolate themselves from the commonalities of culture, including—perhaps especially—religion. To state the matter simply, presenting Judaism as a universalistic religion, addressing all humanity, contradicts the policy of self-isolation that Jews think alone guarantees a long future: continuity. For religious discourse involves the threat of ideas alien to one's own, and Jews outside of limited circles of Judaic faithful have no confidence in their own relationship to Judaism. Presented as the embodiment of ethnic culture, speaking particularly to them, Judaism is afforded a privileged refuge from the competition with other religions that the classification "religion" entails. Then it is safer, from the perspective of continuity, not to say even the unity of the Jewish community, to stress what Jews have in common with one another—the ethnic dimension. Ethnicity, "Jewishness," takes the place of what Jews have in common with all humanity: confronting the challenge of Sinai set forth by the Torah of Moses our rabbi that the world calls Judaism.

In my own career, I have tried to speak the languages of Jews in representing the universal discourse of the Torah. That involved a lot of work, studying two or three years with tutors to give one or two addresses in a language not my own. It entailed speaking in Stockholm and Lund in the Swedish language, or to the Jews of São Paulo in Portuguese, or to those in Paris in French, and so on through Genoa, Rome, Naples, and Bari in Italian; Frankfurt and Vienna in German; Madrid and Montevideo in Spanish; not to mention Hebrew in Tel Aviv and Connecticut-Yankee-American throughout my own country. In my person, with a great deal of effort, I have meant to make a statement not through what I say but through what I do. That statement is that it is right and proper for us Jews to swim in the mainstream of world civilization. And it is through Judaism the religion that we address all of humanity—for the reasons spelled out in chapters 2–6 in behalf of the sages of normative Judaism.

The facts speak for themselves. We Jews swim in the mainstream of those sectors of our common humanity where we are located. We form a principal part of the cultural lives of the many countries where we live. We take part in the politics of those countries. I do not mean merely that we vote, but that we take a very active role in politics; for instance, 10 percent of the United States senators are Jewish, and 7 percent of the members of the House of Representatives, though we are scarcely 2 percent of the population. No ethnic group does better, is more accepted in the norm of politics. In higher education, though excluded a generation ago, Jews now take on the presidencies of the ancient universities of America. And the pattern repeats itself—in politics, literature, culture, education—the components of the mainstream of national life, throughout the West. The state of Israel was meant to normalize the Jews, turn them into a political, empowered entity like other nations or peoples of the world, and so it did. But so did the United States and Canada, Australia and France, Britain and Mexico, and most of the other countries of the diaspora. Even Russia, of all places, now has its Jewish martyr to Russian democracy, buried with national honors by a rabbi in Moscow.

A hundred years ago, if I wanted to identify with Jews I might meet throughout the world, I should not have had to know eight or ten languages, but only one, Yiddish. And I should not have traveled to every continent, as I have, from Latin America to Scandinavia, São Paulo to Stockholm. One trip would have sufficed, because approximately 90 percent of the Jews of the world spoke Yiddish and lived in Poland, Ukraine, White Russia, and the other lands of eastern Europe. And if we now can use English as the international Jewish language, with Hebrew the language of education and culture, then, at that time, with Hebrew yet to accomplish its renaissance, I should have used German as the medium of culture. A hundred years ago, the Jews did not form part of the mainstream of life and culture. Our grandparents' grandparents spoke a Jewish language, Yiddish. They dressed in clothing that was regarded as distinctively Jewish. They ate food that they deemed Jewish, and they would not eat the food that gentiles ate. They lived in large Jewish settlements, towns that were a third or half or three-quarters Jewish in population. They practiced Jewish trades. They read Jewish books, sang Jewish music, danced Jewish dances, fought among themselves about the issues of Jewish existence. They were Jews and only Jews. The politics of the democracies excluded Jews or treated them as exotic, defining them as a problem. Cultural life received Jews on condition that they relinquished all marks of difference: English but not Jewish.

But their religion embodied a message for all humanity. True, in the ages in which Judaism defined the Jews—rather than the Jews, Judaism—the religious community concentrated on realizing the imperatives of the Torah, not necessarily engaging others to accept those same imperatives. The religion, Judaism, defined the Jews in a way that entirely fit the cultural and social and political circumstances of Judaic existence. That is to say, just as the Jews were only Jewish, were always Jewish, and never conceived of themselves in any other framework but the Jewish and Judaic one, so the religion, Judaism, answered the question, who is this Israel, the people that dwells apart? And what is the meaning of the life of this unique people, absolutely separate and distinct from all the nations of the world? These are issues that, I have shown in these pages, encompass the existence of all of humanity, for by "Israel" the Torah means those who accept the Torah of Sinai and God's kingdom in the here and now and at the end of days.

The Jews have entered the mainstream but emphasize how they differ from the rest of humanity, thus, once more, ethnicity in place of religiosity. Most Jews speak English, the international language of humanity. If we have common clothing, no one can tell from what we wear that we are Jews; our clothes are those of the world at large. Not many of us walk around with covered heads. If we read the same books, they are the international best-sellers, and if we talk about the same subjects, they concern pretty much the same subjects we should talk about with gentiles of the same age group or class in society or educational and professional level. Jews play a major role in the formation of education and culture, leading the universities and staffing them, even in the humanities, whence values flow. Not only so, but our rabbis are comparable to the clergy of other religions. Our worship services include the use of the languages of the countries where we live; I have sung Adon Olam in Portuguese and at my Seder have had Jews from Mexico read their parts in Spanish, from Brazil in Portuguese, and from Paris in French.

The contrast between the way we were and the way we are may be summed up in a simple way. Jews now swim in the mainstream. So we emphasize about ourselves the very opposite traits. We have made the decision to be like everybody else, except in the ways in which we are not like everybody else. That swimming in the mainstream represents a decision that should not be taken for granted. Many Jews object, and the present social policy of Jews throughout the world, including the state of Israel, provokes considerable debate. There is much self-segregation within the religious communities of Orthodox Judaism, the best realizations of the Torah of Moses our rabbi. In North America, Western Europe, and the state of Israel tens of thousands of Jews do not want to swim in the mainstream. In the state of Israel they distinguish themselves by their clothing, their schooling, their way of life, and their profession. In North America they speak Yiddish. In Western Europe they form tight little communities, apart from the rest of Jewry, rejecting the mainstream orthodoxy that predominates. In fact, a great debate rages through Jewry between integrationists and segregationists. The integrationist position is clear.

The self-segregationist position takes the view that the Jews cannot and should not swim in the mainstream. Yet that same position prays in a language of universality and embodies the Torah that addresses all humanity in the name of a God who is bound by the rationality of justice. Some argue that the Jews in the mainstream will assimilate not only in the ways that they want, in language and culture, but in the ways that they do not want, in religion and in family, so that in the end, the powerful currents of the mainstream will sweep the Jews away into that vast ocean of undifferentiated humanity that in all languages listens to the same loud music, in all cuisines eats the same fast food, in all cultures lives and dies for pretty much the same worldly goods. Others in the segregationist camp take the view that even if the Jews can sustain themselves in the mainstream, they should not do so. We Jews are holy Israel, the people whom God has called into being at Sinai, and our task is not to be like the gentiles but to be *not* like the gentiles; to live a holy way of life; to study the Torah; to pray; to live out the eternal rhythms of the week with its climax at the Sabbath; of the year with its holy seasons of sanctification; of nature, with its new moons; and of eternity in the here and now. And, the segregationists hold, we live in God's dominion, we have no place and should want none in the nations of the world. That position is taken not only in the diaspora, but in the state of Israel by the non-Zionist political parties, and they represent more than a negligible proportion of the population of the country.

Now we err if we imagine that segregationist Judaism speaks out of some dim past to people who do not know the world that we know. And we are wrong if we suppose that, if those people knew what we know, they would do what we do. Segregationist Jews read the same newspapers, watch the same television if they wish, read the same history, know the same science, that we do. They know what we call "the modern world" because they live in the same time and place that we do. They choose segregation, they do not merely inherit it, and they do so because they want to. They have seen the world into which we have flowed, and they want no part of it. They actively seek sanctification, they define their lives around the Torah, and they regard Torah study and not natural science as the highest form of knowledge, culture, and science. This is not by default but by choice, and the choice for many, the generation of return, is one of rejection of the one in favor of acceptance of the other. When we go among the Lubavitcher Judaic groups in the United States, while we hear Yiddish, their chosen language, it is spoken by people with an American accent, who speak good old American English just the same way the rest of the Jews do.

The debate in Jewry between integration and segregation forms the counterpart to equally vivid struggles in Islam and Christianity. What we stupidly call "Islamic fundamentalism" represents a movement to build the theological abode of Islam in the here and now. The people we call the "Muslim moderates" (who are equally religious but in a different way) turn out to form a cultural and political ideal in the context of Islam that is remarkably similar in its outlines and structure to the cultural and political ideal of the Zionist religious parties in the state of Israel, or of integrationist orthodoxy in Western Europe and of Reform, Conservative, and so-called Modern Orthodoxy in the United States. So too the battle between Muslim fundamentalism and moderation or between integrationist and segregationist Judaisms forms the counterpart to the struggle between Christian fundamentalism and what we call in the United States the mainstream denominations. The Christian fundamentalists hear God's word in Scripture, define their lives and their children's education around direct encounter with God or the Holy Spirit, and form their own judgments in light of the Bible about the claims of science and even technology. They too read the same newspapers as the mainstream Christians, vote in the same elections, work in the same economy. Indeed, they are in the aggregate better educated than the American population in general, and they certainly are more articulate about the things that they profess.

What is at stake, therefore, vastly transcends the Jewish condition. The issue of swimming in the mainstream as we Jews have chosen to formulate matters—Jewish survival on terms other than complete segregation—turns out to confront Islam and Christianity, and the formulation of the issue in Islam and in Christianity differs in detail but not in character. For in fact, what divides Islam, Christianity, and Judaism is not segregation versus integration, as I put matters for Judaism, or fundamentalism versus modernism, as Christianity will have it (whether Protestant or Roman Catholic), or Muslim fundamentalism versus democratic secular states, as we in the West wrongly formulate matters. The issue is not particular to the various religious groups; it addresses all of them. And in this international debate within the great transnational religious communities—Judaism as I have defined matters out of the normative sources, also Islam and Christianity—the stakes are high, the outcome still in doubt. Right now it seems that the fundamentalists in Christianity, the Muslims out to build the Nation of

Islam, and the Judaic self-segregationists, hold all the high cards. They exhibit the enthusiasm that the integrationists call fanaticism, they fill the media with their violence, whether demonstrations against archaeology in Jerusalem, or against abortion in the United States, or against tourism in Egypt. Their numbers appear to grow, those of the integrationists to diminish. So people suppose that the wave of the future flows toward the past. But that is because they wrongly imagine that, in the case of Judaism, the more Orthodox, the more antiquated but authentic; in the case of Christianity, the more fundamentalist, the more devoted to Jesus Christ; in the case of Islam, the more devoted to Islam, the closer to the message of the prophet.

I leave it to the theologians (including myself in a different guise, and I do my theology in American English) to evaluate claims of authenticity, devotion, true faith. I leave to sociologists and political scientists the estimation of whether, in deed, the future will see Christian, Muslim, and Judaic segregationism take over the world. Social science may tell us what is going to happen, and theology, what ought to happen. I want to say only what I hope happens and why I hope so.

Viewing Judaism in its authentic message, a statement to all of humanity, forms a vision to replace the cramped conception of the Jews as an ethnic group only or mainly. And despite all that has happened in this dreadful century of ours, I hope that the path of integration shows the way forward for us all. I understand, I think, the aspirations of the Christian, Judaic, and Muslim segregationists, those who reject what they regard as the modern world while in fact forming an indicator of modernity. They read books that bear clear and present messages and want to realize those messages: the sanctification of holy Israel, for example, leaves no space for negotiation between integration and segregation. The segregationists have taken the measure of modern science and seen the triumph of the industrialization of murder in the death camps of Germany in World War II. They have taken the measure of modern values and have seen the triumph of the devaluation of human life in abortion upon demand. They have witnessed the disruption of the social order, of established patterns of human relationships and modes of raising children, and they have seen the result in the destruction of the family, so that more than half of all children in the United States and elsewhere now are raised without fathers, or even without parents at all, with catastrophic results for the psychological strength of the coming generation. Talk with the Muslim fundamentalists, the Christian evangelicals, the Judaic segregationists in yeshivas, and one will hear not ignorance of the world as it is but a reasoned, vigorous rejection of it. And that is not irrational but well-reasoned and rigorously argued. For the segregationists, that complex of values and ideals, political attitudes and public policy for the family, education, culture, even sexuality, that we call "modernity" represents a world that they reject. They do not seek integration with that world but exclusion of it, isolation from it.

What have we integrationists to say in response? It is to rely on God's promises in the Torah. Our answer cannot take the path of a disingenuous response: modernity may be bad enough, but the age of faith was worse. The segregationists, after all, do accept the outcomes of modernity, contemporary medicine, for example; most of them fly in airplanes, drive cars, use computers, communicate by fax. So it is not modernity that the segregationists reject, but the condition of humanity in modernity. They choose segregation because they have had enough of the human condition of integration. To take the Judaic case once more, the Judaic segregationists find the study of the Torah more sanctifying, more ennobling, more fitting to the human condition of holy Israel, than any other study. Then the integrationists' task, in the Judaic setting, is to respond to that ideal. Again, the Judaic segregationists see nothing of value in gentile life, nothing of consequence in shared cultural or social or political enterprise with gentiles. Let them have theirs, and we keep ours. Then the integrationists' task in the Judaic setting is to explain what good there is in working with, and living among, gentiles. And if the matters of cultural and social policy be resolved, there still is the segregationist insistence that their vision of the human condition, and not the integrationists', matches the vision of God: this is how God wants things, our way, not your way. At stake, after all, is the language of faith, because the issues in the end take shape around the deepest concerns and commitments of human beings concerning what it means to be "in our image, after our likeness." If we cannot respond to Judaic segregationism in religious terms, then there is no response to be set forth. For Judaic segregationism does not represent merely a continuation of a dead past, as I have argued, nor a response to a problem of sociology or demography. At stake is what it means to be human in God's image: the language of segregationist and the language of integrationist Judaism comes from the same Torah and appeals to the same God. Here we conduct a religious debate about issues of religion.

But can we make the case for the integration of humanity that this is how God wants things, when the Qu'ran, the Torah, and the Bible, all are set forth by obviously knowledgeable people who maintain otherwise? Does the human condition demand that we live not only among, but with, other people, different from ourselves? And is it the highest value that sanctification mean, holier than thou, or can God have in mind something other when we contemplate the diversity of created humanity, all in God's image and after God's likeness? The issues of integration and segregation burn hot, not because anyone wishes to push blacks back into their corner anymore, but because many people, of various races, religious, and ethnic origin, seek preference and privilege by reason of ethnic or racial origin. But Europeans face precisely the same issue of integration versus segregation, Germans with Turkish Germans, French with African French, Italians with Somali Italians, to name three examples among many. The theological issues of integration versus segregation turn out to frame, in the language of revelation, God and God's will for humanity, the very crisis of public policy in culture and politics that all of the Western nations face in the matter of immigration, nationalism, and the determination of language, culture, and citizenship.

So what do we really conceive to nurture the human condition at its most authentic? It is to aspire to be "in our image, after our likeness": like God. Since I introduced the problem by reference to the discipline I have imposed upon myself of trying to speak to Jews in the natural sounds of the Jewish condition, whether Swedish or Spanish or Hebrew or English, let me turn once more to language. Here the issue is not one language or many, but whether we speak more than one language; we do not have the choice, the segregationists do not have the choice, of imposing one language upon all, any more than they can impose one religion upon all. Segregationism takes the view that connections to the other yield nothing of value, and that the outsider has nothing to say to us. Integrationism takes the view that the other has something to say, and that we have to learn to hear; we have to overcome the barriers of language and thought because something on the other side of the wall is of value. Phrasing matters in these terms, of course, we are led directly to a discussion of this very matter in the Torah, where, in the tale of the Tower of Babel, we find an explicit and profound reflection on the unity of humanity. When everybody spoke one language, then humanity formed the ambition to build a tower to reach heaven. But God laughed at the plan, thinking it arrogant, and confused their languages, so people spread out to all the ends of the world and no longer spoke the same words at all.

Speaking in the language of the Torah, then, we may say that God has not so formed us as to speak only one language, that is, our own. It is not good for humanity to want to be all alike—and to keep the outsider outside—because, the Torah says, that leads to arrogance, to building towers to heaven. In our framework, that means, the arrogance to think we can make a holy nation of Islam, making all things into one thing; a holy people of Israel, dismissing the rest of humanity as faceless and lacking differentiation; or a single, uniform Christianity, in the name of that Christ that other Christians have found it possible to portray in all the colors, shapes, and sizes, of humanity.

Speaking in the language of ordinary affairs, we may say yet one more thing. It is that we are many things, not only Jews or Christians or Muslims, but fathers and sons, or mothers and daughters, athletes and artists, young and old and much else, including, I think above all, neighbors and friends. There is more to life than being Jewish or Christian or Muslim, and when we are only among Jews or Christians or Muslims, then we are conscious of many other things and no longer define ourselves by the Jewish or the Christian or the Muslim point of difference. And that is the human condition as we know it, and I should think, as much of humanity through much of history has known it. The fantasy of uniformity that makes possible segregationist Christianity, Judaism, or Islam defies the everyday and the here and now of difference. And the difference is not by reason of religion exclusively or even mainly, because we differ from other people in a vast range of possible points of difference.

That is because we are many things, besides Jews or Christians or Muslims: we are human in all the ways in which life calls upon our humanity. The world calls upon us for many things, and if we respond in only one way, solely by reference to the Torah, Qu'ran, or the Bible, we turn out to deny that humanity of ours that has given us hearts and minds and souls of our own, defined in our personhood. We are not only Jews, we are ourselves. Not only so, but learning comes to us not only in revelation but also in the use of our own reason, which the Torah frames as what we have in common with God, how in particular we are in God's image, after God's likeness. And, moreover, we experience the social world in diverse and complex settings, and the segregationist setting proves the least determinative. We do see the other as a person; we do live out a life of politics that defines the other not in terms of religion but of interest or right action. We do sustain a life of culture that defines what is interesting or puzzling or engaging not in terms of us and them, but of the here and now of a fragile civilization and an impermanent social order. So my argument for integration appeals not to what is inevitable or merely serviceable, but to what is natural to the human condition. And I appeal not to secular but to religious, revealed truth: this is how God has made us, and it is how, in the Torah, God has told us we have been made. If God had wanted us to segregate ourselves from the rest of humanity, God would not have formed within us that natural sympathy for the other that overcomes our sense of self. And if God had thought it best that in the workaday world of the present age we live wholly by ourselves, God would not have endowed us with the gift of grace to see ourselves in the other, and the other in ourselves. Swimming in the mainstream requires greater effort than paddling in the shallows. But it is natural to the human condition to make that effort. For God has made us what we are: alike and different, down to the last and least individual among us.

God in the Torah defined what he wanted of Israel, the Israel God called into being at Sinai. And it was not the commandment to continue a distinct group in humanity. It was the commandment of Lev. 19:2, 18, the one addressed to Israel as Israel: "You shall be holy, for I the LORD your God am holy . . . . you shall love your neighbor as yourself: I am the LORD."

Notes

Preface

1. By rational, rationalistic, reasonable, and kindred words, I mean what is accessible to a common logic, what can be analyzed and demonstrated in terms accessible to anybody. This is a public truth, subject to the criticism and argument of anyone possessed of intelligence. This is the intellectual counterpart to that theological universalism that I impute to the Judaism of Scripture as portrayed by the Rabbinic documents of ancient times.

2. Bethesda, Md.: CDL Press, 1996.

3. Kingston and Montreal: McGill-Queens University Press, 1998. See also *The Theology of the Halakhah* (in press).

4. Leiden, 2000: E. J. Brill. I-V.

Chapter 1

1. Philadelphia: Trinity Press International, 1991. This is a commonplace position among liberal Protestant theologians. Dunn merely states it with special clarity, by reason of the invidious distinction that he draws.

2. Dunn, *The Partings of the Ways,* 230. Not surprisingly, in a blurb in *Religious Studies News* (February 1998, 19), Dunn (fatuously) endorses the racial theory of Judaism set forth by Daniel Boyarin in his *A Radical Jew: Paul and the Politics of Identity* (Berkeley: University of California Press, 1994). He likes Boyarin's concurrence that Paul criticizes "the ethnocentrism, the practice of works of the law to mark off Jew from gentile." This has been the judgment of generations of Christian theologians from Paul onward, not to mention of modern and contemporary secular anti-Semites and anti-Judaists.

3. Dunn, *The Partings of the Ways,* 258–59.

4. I have represented "Israel" as Judaism's social metaphor in my analysis, *Judaism and its Social Metaphors: Israel in the History of Jewish Thought* (New York: Cambridge University Press, 1988).

5. *Biblical Theology of the Old and New Testaments: Theological Reflection on the Christian Bible* (Minneapolis: Fortress Press, 1993), 720.

6. See for one example Boyarin, *A Radical Jew.*

7. Dunn, *The Partings of the Ways,* 230. And see my systematic reply, focusing upon Rabbinic conceptions of "Israel" as supernatural, not ethnic, in my *Children of the Flesh, Children of the Promise: An Argument with Paul about Judaism as an Ethnic Religion* (Cleveland: Pilgrim Press, 1995).

Chapter 2

1. James D. G. Dunn's *The Partings of the Ways between Christianity and Judaism and Their Significance for the Character of Christianity* (Philadelphia: Trinity Press International, 1991), 258–59.

2. This I demonstrate in detail in my *Judaism as Philosophy: The Method and Message of the Mishnah* (Columbia: University of South Carolina Press, 1991).

3. In work for my *The Halakhah: An Encyclopaedia of the Law of Judaism* (4 vols.; Leiden: E. J. Brill, 2000), I found to my surprise that nearly the entire corpus of normative statements occurs in the Mishnah and the Tosefta, and to these, in substance, the two Talmuds add remarkably little, even in the stratum of *baraitot,* or formulations of law external to the Mishnah and the Tosefta, that they contain. In sheer volume, I should estimate that 90 percent of the corpus of Halakhah down to the closure of the Talmud of Babylonia comes to expression in the Mishnah and the Tosefta, and, as to innovation beyond what is presented in those documents, not merely analysis and extension thereof, scarcely 10 percent in volume is found in the Talmuds and in the compilations of exegesis of the Halakhic portions of the Pentateuch.

4. Still, the autonomy and originality of the latter are beginning to find recognition even now, as I have shown in my *Encyclopaedia.*

5. I am inclined to think the entire question of the Tosefta, its definition and standing, requires reconsideration. But that will not impede the present task.

6. Were we to read the Tosefta as a freestanding document, not as subordinate to the Mishnah, we should come to the same conclusion for that document as well.

7. Murray, Gilbert, *Five Stages of Greek Religion: Studies Based on a Course of Lectures Delivered in April 1912 at Columbia University* (2d ed.; New York: Columbia Univ. Press, 1930, 75.

8. Much as that of Christianity may be classified as eschatological.

9. My *Judaism as Philosophy* provides a systematic account of the matter in rich detail. In my *Jerusalem and Athens: The Congruity of Talmudic and Classical Philosophy* (Supplements to the *Journal for the Study of Judaism.* Leiden: E. J. Brill, 1997), I deal with the comparison of dialectical argument in Greek philosophy with the same in the Rabbinic literature, particularly in the Talmud of Babylonia.

10. But here I restrict my presentation to the issue of the method of hierarchical classification. In chapter 3 I turn to the message that through the halakah the Judaic monotheism sets forth. It has to do with the principles of Eden and its restoration, as I shall show in detail.

11. That proposition, on the essential unity of the hierarchical nature of all being, falls into the classification of philosophy, since it forms one important, generative premise of neo-Platonism. But here I concentrate on the issue of method and the theological implications of the choices made by the Mishnah's philosophers.

12. I leave for philonic scholarship the comparison of the Mishnah's neo-Platonism with that of Philo. Philo's mode of writing, his presentation of his ideas, seems to me so different from the mode and method of the Mishnah that I am not sure how we can classify as Aristotelian (in the taxonomic framework of natural philosophy, which seems to me the correct framework for the Mishnah's philosophical method) the prin-

cipal methodological traits of Philo's thought. But others are most welcome to correct what is only a superficial impression. I think the selection for comparison and contrast of Aristotle and neo-Platonism, first method, then proposition, is a preferable strategy of analysis (and exposition, as a matter of fact), and I willingly accept the onus of criticism for not comparing and contrasting the method and message of Philo with those of the Mishnah. I mean only to suggest that the questions Wolfson's Philo raised may well be reopened, but within an entirely fresh set of premises and in accord with what I conceive to be a more properly differentiated and therefore critical reading of the data. What about direct connections between sages and philosophers? No one conjures the fantasy and anachronism of the Mishnah authorship's tramping down a Galilean hill from their yeshiva to the academy in a nearby Greek-speaking town, Caesarea or Sepphoris, for example, there studying elementary Aristotle and listening to the earliest discourses of neo-Platonism, then climbing back up the hill and writing it all up in their crabbed backcountry idiom made up of the cases and examples of the Mishnah.

13. And I need hardly add that the very eclecticism of the philosophy of Judaism places it squarely within the philosophical mode of its time. See J. M. Dillon and A. A. Long, eds., *The Question of "Eclecticism." Studies in Later Greek Philosophy* (Berkeley and Los Angeles: University of California Press, 1988).

14. So the Mishnah's fundamental intellectual structure in its method and message falls into the classification, defined by circumstance and context, of philosophy addressing undifferentiated humanity through uniform logic and reason. The method, I shall show, is standard for natural philosophy, exemplified by Aristotle, and the proposition proves entirely congruent to one principal conception of Middle Platonism, exemplified by Plotinus.

15. I consulted Jonathan Barnes, *Aristotle's Posterior Analytics* (Oxford: Clarendon Press, 1975).

16. And, as to proposition about the hierarchical ordering of all things in a single way, the unity of all being in right order, while we cannot show and surely do not know that the Mishnah's philosophers knew anything about Plato, let alone Plotinus's neo-Platonism (which came to expression only in the century after the closure of the Mishnah!), we can compare our philosophers' proposition with that of neo-Platonism. For that philosophy, as we shall see, did seek to give full and rich expression to the proposition that all things emerge from one thing, and one thing encompasses all things, and that constitutes the single proposition that animates the system as a whole.

17. For this section I consulted the following: A. W. H.Adkins, *From the Many to the One: A Study of Personality and Views of Human Nature in the Context of Ancient Greek Society, Values, and Beliefs* (Ithaca, N.Y.: Cornell University Press, 1970; D. J. Allan *The Philosophy of Aristotle* (London, New York, Toronto: Oxford University Press/Geoffrey Cumberlege, 1952); A. H. Armstrong, "Platonism and Neoplatonism," *Encyclopaedia Britannica* (Chicago, 1975), 14:539–45; A. H. Armstrong, "Plotinus," *Encyclopaedia Britannica* (Chicago, 1975), 14:573–74; Émile Bréhier, *The History of Philosophy: The Hellenistic and Roman Age,* trans. Wade Baskin (Chicago and London: University of Chicago, 1965); Harold Cherniss, *Selected Papers,* ed. Leonardo Tarán (Leiden: E. J. Brill, 1977); Louis H. Feldman, "Philo," *Encyclopaedia Britannica* (Chicago, 1975), 14:245–47; Goodenough, Erwin R., *An Introduction to Philo Judaeus,* 2d ed. (Lanham: University Press of America/Brown Classics in Judaica, 1986); P. Merlan, "Greek Philosophy from Plato to Plotinus," in *The Cambridge History of Later Greek and Early Medieval Philosophy,* ed. A. H. Armstrong, 14–136 (Cambridge: Cambridge University Press, 1967); Lorenzo Minio-Paluello,

"Aristotelianism," *Encyclopaedia Britannica* 1:1155–1161; Joseph Owens, *A History of Ancient Western Philosophy* (New York: Appleton, Century, Crofts Inc., 1959); G. F. Parker, *A Short History of Greek Philosophy from Thales to Epicurus* (London: Edward Arnold Publishers Ltd., 1967); and Giovanni Reale, *A History of Ancient Philosophy. III. The Systems of the Hellenistic Age*, ed. and trans. John R. Catan (Albany: State University of New York Press, 1985).

18. Adkins, *From the Many to the One*, 170–71.

19. But only Aristotle and the Mishnah carry into the material details of economics that conviction about the true character or essence of definition of things. The economics of the Mishnah and the economics of Aristotle begin in the conception of "true value," and the distributive economics proposed by each philosophy then develops that fundamental notion. The principle is so fundamental to each system that comparison of one system to the other in those terms alone is justified.

20. Minio-Paluello, "Aristotelianism," *Encyclopaedia Britannica*, 1155.

21. Allan, *The Philosophy of Aristotle*, 60.

22. Ibid., 126ff.

23. Owens, *A History of Ancient Western Philosophy*, 309ff.

24. And for that decision they are criticized by all their successors, chief among them, the authorship of *Sifra*. See my *Uniting the Dual Torah: Sifra and the Problem of the Mishnah* (Cambridge: Cambridge University Press, 1990).

25. A. H. Armstrong, "Man in the Cosmos," *Plotinian and Christian Studies*, Variorum Reprints, No. XVII (London, 1979), 11.

26. Which is Plato's and Plotinus's.

27. That judgment does not contradict the argument of my *Uniting the Dual Torah* concerning the *Sifra* authorship's critique of the Mishnah philosophers' stress upon classification through intrinsic traits of things as against through classes set forth solely by the Torah. Here I mean only to stress the contrast between appeal to Scripture and to nature, which I find in the philosophy of Judaism, and appeal to the ecclesial cosmos.

Chapter 3

1. But not a messianic one.

2. In *The Theology of the Oral Torah* (Kingston: McGill-Queens University Press, 1998), chapters 13–14, I characterize the theology of the oral Torah as restorationist, and there I show that the messiah-theme does not form a principal category, but plays a role in the exposition of principal categories; the figure of the messiah is instrumental, he announces a phase in the restorationist teleology, but he plays only a subordinate role in the restoration itself. To characterize the halakah, or the mishnaic statement of the halakah, as messianic vastly distorts matters; indeed, the Mishnah, for its part, defines a teleology that to begin with scarcely exhibits the indicators of eschatology! While, as we shall see even in this opening part of matters, restorationism governs critical category-formations within the halakah, the messiah-theme contributes to none. In its classical statement in the formative age, Rabbinic Judaism certainly encompasses the messiah-theme, but so far as its teleology finds it possible to frame a vision of last things to which the messiah merely contributes, indeed, a vision that encompasses the death of the messiah, we may not characterize formative Rabbinic Judaism as a messianic system. How things worked out in later stages in the unfolding of that same Judaism is for others to say.

3. Alan J. Avery-Peck, *The Talmud of the Land of Israel: Shebi'it* (Chicago: University of Chicago, 1987) 2.

4. Ibid., 6.

5. Ibid., 3.

6. Ibid., 4.

7. Louis Newman, *The Sanctity of the Seventh Year: A Study of the Mishnah Tractate Shebi'it* (Atlanta: Scholars Press for Brown Judaic Studies, 1986), 15.

8. Neither the haggadah nor the halakah makes articulate categorical provision for the radically isolated individual, that is, the Israelite not within the household or not as part of "all Israel." But the reading of Paul as the founder of the introspective conscience of the radically isolated individual has long since lost all purchase. The halakah for its part sets forth a monotheism addressed to the social order. That accounts for my reference to "the Israelite household," where the Hebrew counterpart would prefer to speak of *"ben adam le 'asmo,"* that is, "between a man and himself." I cannot identify a tractate of the Mishnah that could yield a theory of the life of the private person, in abstraction from the household, hence my resort to "household" rather than "individual Israelite."

9. That is not to suggest that the sages have imposed upon Scripture meanings that will have surprised the framers of the system of the written Torah. On the contrary, one may make a solid case that the sages have penetrated into the depths of the logic of the pentateuchal narrative itself (or of the Priestly component thereof). In *The Four Stages of Rabbinic Judaism* (London: Routledge, 1999), I turn to that question.

Chapter 4

1. James D. G. Dunn, *The Partings of the Ways between Christianity and Judaism and Their Significance for the Character of Christianity* (Philadelphia: Trinity Press International, 1991), 258–59.

Chapter 5

1. When we consider the longer list of paradigms that we have examined in these pages, we notice a number of paradigms that do not serve in the teleological context, not to mention exemplary figures that are given no assignment in that setting. In manipulating the persons and events of Scripture as components of a paradigm, the sages clearly choose those appropriate for a given purpose; symbolic speech, then, goes forward as much through choices of paradigmatic media as through the formulation of propositions illustrated or embodied in those paradigms; that is to say, through silences as much as through statements.

Chapter 6

1. James D. G. Dunn, *The Partings of the Ways between Christianity and Judaism and Their Significance for the Character of Christianity* (Philadelphia: Trinity Press International, 1991), 258–59.

Epilogue

1. James D. G. Dunn, *The Partings of the Ways between Christianity and Judaism and Their Significance for the Character of Christianity* (Philadelphia: Trinity Press International, 1991).

Glossary

'Abodah Zarah—The laws governing Israelite relationships with idolaters on occasions of idolatrous worship

'Abot—The fathers', or founders' sayings, from Moses and Joshua through the authorities of the third century C.E.

b.—Abbreviation for Bavli tractates; see Bavli

Baba Mesia—"The Middle Gate," the second of the three systematic expositions of the civil law of Judaism; abbreviated *B. Mes.*

Bavli—The Talmud of Babylonia, which reached closure at ca. 600 C.E., a commentary to the Mishnah; abbreviated as *b.* with tractate names
   b. 'Abod. Zar.—tractate *'Abodah Zarah*
   b. Pesah.—tractate *Pesahim*
   b. Sanh.—tractate *Sanhedrin*
   b. Shab.—tractate *Shabbat*

B.C.E.—Before the Common Era, equivalent to B.C.

Berakhot—Blessings, the tractate of the law that sets forth the regulations for reciting the Shema ("Hear O Israel, the Lord our God, the Lord is one"), the prayer, grace after meals, and other expressions of faith and gratitude

C.E.—Common Era, equivalent to A.D.

'Erubin—Fictive markings of boundaries that indicate shared ownership of an area, so forming diverse properties into a single domain for purposes of Sabbath observance; or a fictive meal that signals that same commingling of ownership of private domains in a common property

Genesis Rabbah—A compilation of interpretations of the book of Genesis by the Judaic sages of the fourth and early fifth centuries C.E., worked out in response to the triumph of Christianity in that same period

haggadah—Lore, norms of belief, expressed in narrative, including midrash, the rereading and retelling of scriptural stories; a type of writing in Rabbinic literature

halakah—Law, norms of behavior, expressed in legal formulations of rules of correct conduct. The halakah derives from Scripture, the Mishnah, the Tosefta, the two Talmuds (Babylonian and Yerushalmi or Jerusalem), and some exegetical studies of the legal passages of Exodus, Leviticus, Numbers, and Deuteronomy, called Tannaite Midrashim

Hullin—The laws covering the preparation of meat for secular purposes, outside of the temple

Israel—Those who worship God and not idols; those who form the heritage of Abraham and Sarah; Isaac and Rebecca; Jacob, Leah, and Rachel

Keritot—The sins that are penalized by the penalty of extirpation, that is, death before one's allotted years, and those who are subject to it

Lamentations Rabbati—The Rabbinic commentary to the book of Lamentations

Leviticus Rabbah—The Rabbinic commentary to the book of Leviticus, some time after the closure of *Genesis Rabbah.* Lays heavy emphasis on sanctification of the here and now aiming at sanctification in time to come

Listenwissenschaft—The science of making lists; organizing knowledge in a systematic way in accord with shared traits that classify data in common

m.—Abbreviation for Mishnah tractates; see Mishnah

Makkot—Flogging, a form of legal sanction

Megillah—The Scroll of Esther

Mekhilta Attributed to R. Ishmael—Rabbinic commentary to the book of Exodus

Menahot—Meal offerings, comparable to animal sacrifices but much cheaper

midrash—Exegesis of Scripture in accord with the rules of Rabbinic interpretation of Scripture

Midrash Haggadah—Exegesis of narrative and hortative passages of Scripture

Midrash Halakah—Exegesis of legal passages of Scripture

Mishnah—A law code, organized along philosophical principles of topical category-formations, produced at the end of the second century, that forms the first document of the oral Torah. Tractates use the abbreviation *m.*

    m. Ber.—tractate *Berakhot*
    m. Ker.—tractate *Keritot*
    m. Sanh.—tractate *Sanhedrin*
    m. Shabu.—tractate *Shebu'ot*
    m. Sotah—tractate *Sotah*
    m. Ta'an.—tractate *Ta'anit*
    m. Zebah.—tractate *Zebahim*

oral Torah—Traditions revealed by God to Moses at Sinai and handed on in memory, through orally formulated and orally transmitted sayings, until written down in the Mishnah or recorded in other compilations of Rabbinic teachings

Pe'a—The laws covering leaving for the poor gleaners the crop at the corner of the field; not cropping the field too closely

Pesahim—The laws governing the celebration of the Passover festival, with special reference to the offering of the paschal lamb, the removal of leaven from the Israelite household, and the conduct of the Passover banquet, or Passover Seder.

Pesiqta de Rab. Kahana—A compilation of Rabbinic expositions of the themes of various liturgical occasions in synagogue life

Ruth Rabbah—Rabbinic commentary to the book of Ruth

Sanhedrin—The governing body projected by the sages' system of government for holy Israel

Shabbat—The Sabbath

Shabuot—Oaths, taken in the name of God

Shebi'it—The seventh year of the seven-year cycle of agriculture in the land of Israel, during which it is forbidden to cultivate the fields or exercise rights of ownership over the crops; everything is left for anybody to take at will

Sifra—Commentary to Leviticus

Sifré to Deuteronomy—Rabbinic commentary to the book of Deuteronomy.

Sifré to Numbers—Rabbinic commentary to the book of Numbers.

Sotah—The wife accused of unfaithfulness, subjected to the ordeal described at Numbers 5

t.—Abbreviation for Tosefta tractates; see Tosefta

Ta'anit—Fasting

Talmud—A commentary to the Mishnah

Torah—God's revelation to Moses at Mount Sinai, in two media, writing and memory

Tosefta—A compilation of traditions attributed to the same authorities who produced the Mishnah, supplementary to the Mishnah; abbreviated as *t.*
    t. Hul.—tractate *Hullin*
    t. Menah.—tractate *Menahot*
    t. Sotah—tractate *Sotah*

written Torah—The written part of God's instruction to Moses at Mount Sinai, consisting of the Five Books of Moses (Genesis, Exodus, Leviticus, Numbers, Deuteronomy), extending to the whole of the Hebrew Scriptures (= Tanakh, standing for the first letters of the Hebrew words for Torah, Prophets, Writings, Torah, Nebiim, Ketubim).

y.—Abbreviation for Yerushalmi tractates; see Yerushalmi

Yerushalmi—The Talmud of the land of Israel ("Yerushalmi = of Jerusalem), which reached closure at circa 400 C.E., a commentary to the Mishnah; abbreviated *y*
    y. Ber.—tractate *Berakhot*
    y. Pe'a—tractate *Pe'a*
    y. Pesah.—tractate *Pesahim*

Zebahim—Animal offerings

Index of Ancient Sources

Babylonian Talmud
b. 'Abod Zara
1:1 I.2/2a-b   133

b. Megillah
4:4/I.10/29a   119

b. Menah.
3:7 II.5/29b   170

b. Pesah.
10:5-6 II.6/116A   122

b. Sanh.
11:1   102
11:1/I.2-14/90b-91b
        106
11:1-2 I.22ff/91b   101,
        124
4:5 VI.1/39b   49
5:3 XII.12/55a-b   157

Mishna
m. 'Abot
3:15   160
m. Ber.
9:4A-E   167

m. Hul.
12:5A   128

m. Ker.
1:1   21
1:2   21
1:7   21
3:2   21
3:4   21
3:9   19

m. Sanh.
6:2   44, 46
6:5   47
10:1   44, 102
10:2   102
10:3   103
10:4   104
10:5   104
11:1   5

m. Shab.
1:1   22
1:1-7   24
1:1-2   24
2:1-5   24

m. Sotah
1:7   145
1:7a   149
1:8   146
1:9a   149
5:1   149

m. Ta'an.
4:6   69
4:7   70

m. Zebah.
14:4-9   82
14:4-8   68

Bible
Genesis
1:1—2:3   51
1:1   92
2:4   47
2:15   8
2:16   9
2:17   163
3:1   150
3:11   9
3:14   150
3:15   150
3:2   90
3:4   107
3:9   9
3:24   110
3:24   9
6:3   102
7:23   148
11:8   103
12:1   87
13:13   103
14:9   92

195

16:12	135	5:17	20	34:6	147
18:23	142	6	23	34:15	148
18:24	136	9:1	71	7:19	46
18:25	142	13	23	7:25	46
19:11	148	14	128		
19:36	135	17:13	83	*Judges*	
22:1	166	18:3-4	150	16:21	146
22:2	87	18:4-5	151		
24:1	164f.	18:4	151	*1 Samuel*	
24:2	87	19:2	184	2:6	104
24:7	87	19:18	184	2:27	119
25:23	132	19:19	19		
27:1	163	21:1	19	*2 Samuel*	
27:15	91	23:7	19	14:25-26	146
27:22	134	24:2	9	15:6	146
27:40	134	25:8-10	38	17:25	157
40:11	117	26:3	107	18:14	146
40:13	117	26:16	154	18:15	146
40:14	117	26.44	154		
48:1	164f.			*2 Kings*	
50:7	146	*Numbers*		13:14	165
50:9	146	1:51	89	19:37	91
		3:12-13	67		
Exodus		5:20-22	145	*1 Chronicles*	
2:4	146	5:23-28	147	2:16	157
6:4	105	6:6	19		
6:6-7	117	8:16-18	67	*2 Chronicles*	
8:12	115	12:15	146	33:13	102
13:19	146	14:35	103		
14:4	148	14:37	103	*Job*	
14:20	49	14:4	153	1:21	167
15:26	102	15:29	20	2:9	167
16:29	51	18:28	105	2:10	168
19:12	87	20:12	157	3:3	115
19:17	133				
20:5	149	*Deuteronomy*		*Psalms*	
20:6	149	4:4	106	1:5	103
20:13	134f.	4:44	133	6:2	79
27:20	9	6:5	167	11:5	166
32:1	155	8:15	88	11:6	118
		11:21	106	16:5	118
Leviticus		22:6-7	129	20:7	79
5	23	28:63	49	22:21	87
5:1-6	23	29:28	104	23:5	118
5:6-7	20	30:3	119	48:8-9	130
5:11	20	31:16	106	50:2	126
5:17-19	20	32:39	101, 124	50:4	104

50:5	103	9:16	154	13:16	155
56:13	128	11:4	80	15:1	9
73:1	158	11:11	154	16:19-20	131
75:9	118	15:19-20	108	20:18	131
84:6	158f.	20:18	131	23:7-8	112
89:33	156	23:5	115	25:15	118
114	74	24:23	100	26:18	89
114:1	121	25:9	100, 155	31:8	100
114:3	121	26:19	106	33:11	128
114:4	121	30:21	153	51:6-7	118
115:1	74, 120–21	30:26	100		
116	74	34:5	127	*Lamentations*	
116:3-4	167	34:9	117	1:13	155
116:4	121	34:11	115f.	1:16	153
116:9	121	35:6	100	1:8	155
116:12-13	167	36:20	91	4:4	154
116:13	118	37:3	80	4:10	154
118:27	125	38:9	165	5:17-18	89
118:27	74	38:21	80		
118:28	74	40:1-2	152, 155	*Ezekiel*	
125:4	159	40:2	154f.	2:1	71
125:5	159	43:3-4	130	8:17	154
126:2	154	43:4	130	17:2	71
138:4	135	43:9	132	18:20	156
145:18	159	43:14	119	24:7	83
		44:9	132	24:8	83
Proverbs		48:11	120	37:9	104
3:12	168	51:12	155	38:16	127
11:10	48	51:16	92	38:22	115f.
		52:7	155	39:17-19	116
Qoheleth		52:8	153		
1:12	72	53:5	80	*Hosea*	
9:2	157	54:9	111	2:16	88
		60:21	5, 102	4:2	84
Song of Solomon		61:5	100	6:7	8
7:9	106	63:11	111	9:10	87
		65:20	100	9:15	9
Isaiah		66:6	115		
1:5	153f.			*Obadiah*	
1:15	154	*Jeremiah*		1:18	91
2:2	127	2:2	71		
3:16	153f.	2:7	9	*Micah*	
4:3	107	4:23	92	2:13	153
5:1	80	5:12	155	5:14	135
8:2	89	7:18	155	7:16	153
9:11	154	9:2	154	8:18	159

Habakkuk
1:7   90f.

Haggai
2:8   133

Zechariah
2:12   88
7:12   154
8:4   89
14:2   80
14:12   116

Malaki
3:4   111
3:7   110

Jerusalem Talmud
y. Berakhot
1:6 I:7   113

y. Meg.
2:1 I:2   74, 125

y. Pe'a
1:1 XXXII.1 109

y. Pesah.
10:1 II:3   118

Index of Subjects and Authors

Adkins, A. W. H., 27, 187n. 17
Allan, D. J., 29, 187n. 17, 188n. 21
Aristotle, 27–31
Armstrong, A. H., 31ff., 187n. 17, 188n. 25
Avery-Peck, Alan J., 37–38, 188n. 3

Barnes, Jonathan, 187n. 15
Baskin, Wade, 187n. 17
being,
 nature of, 18
 unity of, 20ff., 31
Boyarin, Daniel, 185n. 2n. 5,
Bréhier, Émile, 187n. 17

Catan, John R., 188n. 17
Cherniss, Harold, 187n. 17
Childs, Brevard, 4
Christianity
 difference from Judaism, 159
 insufficiency of its explanation, 32
creation, 9ff., 51
 as model of redemption, 119

death, 165
death penalty, 43ff., 47
dialectic, in Aristotle and Judaism, 30
Dillon, J. M., 187n. 13
divine punishment, 44, 145–46, 148, 150
divine reward, 149

Dunn, James D. G., 2f., 5, 16, 159, 173, 185nn. 1, 2, 3, 7, 189n. 1

Eden, 55, 97
 as an ideal of the land, 39, 41
 as perfect time, 37
 restoration, 100
eschatology, 98, 110–14, 118, 131
eternal life, 9, 43, 47–48, 169
exemplary figures, 86
exile and return, 111–14

fall, 7f., 48
Feldman, Louis, 187n. 17
final judgment, 99, 106
free will, 160ff.

Gehenna, 109, 130
gentiles,
 idolaters vs. non-idolaters, 122
 place in world to come, 118, 123, 129, 131–35
God
 fatherly emotions, 49
 goes into exile with Israel, 119
 inscrutability, 171
 justice, 43–44, 46–47, 140ff., 144ff., 149, 151, 158–59
 mercy, 43–44, 46–47, 165
 ontology of., in paganism and

Christianity, 31
  relation to Israel through the land, 43
  as the summation of rational process,
  25
Goodenough, Edwin R., 187n. 17

halakah, 15–18, 35, 51, 60
  as an Aristotelian, 26
  universalization
  of the particular, 60–61
hierarchical classification, 16–19, 23,
  26ff., 32
historical thinking, Judaism rejects,
  64–65, 67, 69, 71, 75, 93
history, theology of, 10
hope, for Israel's future, 113
human will, 10

identity, paradigm as essential element,
  77
idolaters, 100
idolatry, 45–46, 129
integrationists, Jewish, 181
Israel
  "after flesh"
  vs. "after Spirit", 123
  as a political entity, 124
  as microcosm of humanity, 7, 12
  as paradigm, 76
  identity, 99
  inclusion in, criminals and sinners,
  44
  its capacity to perfect the world, 42
  sinfulness, 152
  transcends time, 88–89

Jews, in mainstream, 177
Judaism
  as a philosophy of monotheism, 33
  as a rational system, 16
  as a universal vs. ethnic religion,
  2–3, 5, 75, 122–23, 173ff.
  relation to mercy, 46

Land of Israel, 36, 41
Listenwissenschaft, 26
logic, 12, 32
  in Aristotle and Judaism, 29
Long, A. A., 187n. 13

memory, 86
Merlan, P., 187n. 17
messianic Judaism, 173–74
Minio-Paluello, Lorenzo, 28, 187n. 17,
  188n. 20
monotheism, x, xi
  as a rational system, 18
  categorical vs. intellectual, 11
  Christian, 3, 5ff.
  Islamic, 6–7
  Jewish, 3, 5, 7, 11, 13, 16
  universally understandable, 138

nations, possibility of redemption, 130ff.
natural history, 24
nature, 17, 94–95
nature, understanding in Christianity,
  Judaism and paganism, 33
neo-platonism, 26
Newman, Louis, 37, 41, 189n. 7

old age, 163ff.
oral Torah, 3–4, 11–12, 38
  timelessness, 66
Owens, Joseph, 187n. 17, 188n. 23

paradigmatic thinking, 63–95, 97, 99,
  109, 116, 120, 123–26, 156
Parker, G.F., 188n. 17
political economy, theology of, 10
political power, Jewish, 176
predestination, 160
private property, 53–54, 56,
public vs. private domain, 55, 57

rationality, xii, 11ff., 15
Reale, Giovanni, 188n. 17
redemption, from Egypt, 114–17, 119,
  121
remission of debt, 42
restoration, 11–12, 109–10, 156
restoration, of creation, 42
resurrection, 7, 45, 101, 124
  necessary adjunct to monotheism,
  98–99
retribution, against the nations, 119

sabbath, 38, 50, 56
  celebration of creation, 43
  eternal state of the world, 67
  laboring on, 50, 57ff.
  of the land, 53
  relation to creation, 51ff.
  relation to Eden, 50–51, 54
sabbatical year, 36–39, 54
sages, as social philosophers, 64, 66–67
salvation, 120–22, 126
sanctification, 182
self-evident truth, 15–16
self-segregation, Jewish, 178
sickness, 164f
suffering, 163ff., 167ff.
supplication, and divine response, 120

tabernacle, 59
taxonomic indicator, 24–25
Temple, restoration of, 127
Thanksgiving prayers, 127

time, 70, 73ff., 82, 93
  no meaning in Judaism, 77, 94
  paradigmatic vs. historical, 81
Torah, 10, 13
  as bearer of universal Torah, 6
  as means of revelation, 33
  paradigms in, 85
  relation to private life, 50

universalism, 1, 9, 16
  Jewish, ix–x, 1, 4–5, 7

World to Come, 45–46, 106–9, 113–14,
  118, 122, 124, 126–57
  those denied entrance, 102
written Torah, 37